WHY DIDN'T I THINK OF THAT?

Think the Unthinkable and Achieve Creative Greatness

Charles W. McCoy, Jr.

Prentice
Hall Press

Library of Congress Cataloging-in-Publication Data

McCoy, Charles W.
    Why didn't I think of that? / Charles W. McCoy.
      p. cm.
    Includes bibliographical references and index.
    ISBN 0-7352-0257-5
    1. Thought and thinking.   2. Problem solving.   3. Decision making.
  I. Title.

  BF441 .M38 2002
  153.4'2—dc21   2001053109

Acquisitions Editor: *Tom Power*
Production Editor: *Eve Mossman*
Page Design/Layout: *Robyn Beckerman*

©2002 by Prentice Hall Press

The illustration on page 10 is printed by permission of the Norman Rockwell Family Trust, Copyright ©1943, the Norman Rockwell Family Trust.

Printed in the United States of America

10 9 8 7 6 5 4 3 2 1

ISBN 0-7352-0257-5

 Paramus, NJ 07652

http://www.phpress.com

To Jan

who taught me how to think with my heart

Acknowledgments

While this book embodies the author's many years of personal thinking experience, it became a tangible work only with the help and patience of many people, beginning with my wife, Jan, and my daughter, Jamie, who respected and protected my solitude for the countless hours of thinking and writing required to create a worthwhile book. My mother, Mary Kay McCoy, read the initial conceptual draft, and, as she has for as long as I can remember, inspired me to pursue my dreams. Dean Richardson Lynn and Associate Deans Charles Nelson and Shelley Saxer of Pepperdine Law School offered me the unique opportunity design and teach a novel course on decision-making, which provided a laboratory for testing key thinking concepts on the bright minds of talented students whose future success as lawyers depends entirely on their ability to think well. Associate Dean Doreen Heyer of Southwestern University School of Law generously funded the work of student research assistant Nuit Robin, who located several key stories used to illustrate main themes of the book. Roy Weinstein, founder of the economic consulting firm Micronomics, painstakingly edited an early draft, which law professor and author F. LaGard Smith reviewed and enthusiastically encouraged me to submit for publication. Literary agent Michael Snell saw promise in the concept and patiently led me through the mentally exhausting process of creating an effective book proposal. Undaunted by setbacks, Mike persistently urged me to think and rethink proposal ideas until together we came up with the winning combination. Prentice Hall's Tom Power expressed interest in the work and, following a much needed conceptual re-orientation, prompted in part by Tom's thoughtful suggestions, Prentice Hall purchased the as yet unfinished work. Over the next year, with Mike Snell's deep editing and creative contributions, and with inspirations from every imaginable source, including answered prayer, *Why Didn't I Think of That?* matured into the finished work now resting in your hands. In reading this book, you honor not only me, but all the talented minds who inspired and contributed to its creation. Authorship is, indeed, a humbling experience when one looks back with gratitude and acknowledges those who helped make a dream come true.

Contents

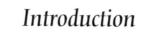

Introduction

Why Didn't I Think of That?

When Motorola introduced its 68000 microprocessor in direct competition with Intel's 8086, customers began switching in droves to Motorola's faster running, cheaper, and technically superior product. Lacking a more competitive new microprocessor it could quickly bring to market, it appeared that Intel might soon lose control of the industry to its powerful rival. How could the company possibly thwart this deadly competitive challenge?

As we will see in a moment, Intel snatched victory from near defeat with a dazzling display of creative problem-solving and decision-making, the sort of thinking that inspired me to write this book.

We may not run an Intel or Motorola, but we do wrestle everyday with perplexing problems and tough decisions where sharp thinking can make all the difference between success and failure. Most of us, however, take our thinking skills for granted, unwittingly allowing flaws to accumulate that only hindsight tells us we should have spotted and corrected. We fail to see opportunities, we reject ideas our competitors later exploit, we miscalculate the significance of events that prove crucial, we fall for deceptions only to marvel later at our naivete. Time and again, like Motorola's executives eventually did, we ask ourselves, "Why didn't I think of that?" Then habitually we just go on "thinking as usual," making the same old mental mistakes over and over again.

This book stops that cycle with proven approaches you can use to sharpen your thinking at work and home. It breaks down the complex process of creative problem-solving and decision-making into simple steps anyone can follow, and it illustrates those steps with the stories of history's best minds at work, from Madame Curie to Albert Einstein and NASA's talented flight controllers to Intel's brilliant marketeers.

With every illustration, every example of both brilliant and shoddy thinking, you will find yourself challenged to apply what you've learned in practical exercises designed to reinforce your best thinking and close the loopholes that can leave you vulnerable to costly errors. In the end, you will grasp the mental keys we all need to unlock the doors to success the way Intel did with its 8086 microprocessor.

Microprocessors, the brains of digital computers, had become increasingly vital to Intel's bottom line as Japanese competition drove down memory chip prices, once the largest segment of Intel's business. Depending more and more on microprocessors for future profitability, and knowing Motorola had started developing a revolutionary and powerful new 16-bit microprocessor it called the 68000, Intel hurriedly designed its competing 16-bit 8086, which it introduced in June 1978, one full year ahead of Motorola. Unfortunately, Intel's product, developed on a crash schedule, fell short, in technical terms, of Motorola's more deliberately developed competitor, the 68000. Intel soon felt the pinch of lost sales as customers began choosing Motorola's 68000 over the 8086, until, ultimately, the daunting task of opposing Motorola's challenge fell on the shoulders of division manager Bill Davidow.

Davidow, deliberating for three full days with the company's best marketing minds, considered every imaginable strategy. Intel could not afford to overlook any competitive option, only to look back later in defeat wondering, "Why didn't I think of that?" Under enormous pressure, Davidow and his team crafted a bold strategy. They would try to broaden the competition beyond a single microprocessor to include a full range of related products and services, where Intel enjoyed many competitive advantages. Intel would try to lure Motorola into concentrating its efforts on defending against

Intel's existing strengths and away from taking full advantage of its own great strength, the technical superiority of the 68000.

Naming Davidow's strategy "Operation Crush," after the Denver Bronco football team's formidable "Orange Crush" defensive unit, Intel launched its plan with a baited hook, hoping Motorola would bite. Fashioned in the form of a "Futures Catalog," the hook touted a host of Intel products not yet on the drawing boards. The catalog caught Motorola entirely by surprise because, in the past, Intel had never announced new products before they actually existed.

Swallowing the bait—hook, line, and sinker—Motorola immediately produced its own futures catalog that fell short of Intel's presentation. By attempting to compete against Intel's as-yet undeveloped devices, Motorola inadvertently reminded customers of its own comparative lack of depth in microprocessor-related products. Losing focus as it tried to match Intel's every claim, Motorola strayed from the core issue Intel feared most, the technical superiority of the 68000.

Intel ultimately emerged victorious when IBM selected the 8086 for its new Personal Computer, a machine that forever changed the landscape of the computer business worldwide. IBM's choice of Intel's 8086 microprocessor and Microsoft's MS-DOS operating system software made these products industry standards in their fields, and, in time, both Intel and Microsoft profited tremendously as most of IBM's competitors, such as Compaq, followed suit, installing 8086s and MS-DOS in their machines.

Intel today ranks at the top of its industry. To its chagrin, Motorola did, indeed, find itself "crushed," not by physical force as in football, but rather by the brilliant thinking of a sharp-minded competitor. In the end, realizing they had fallen prey to a misdirection play, Motorola's executives could only look back asking themselves the eight crucial questions that form the chapters of this book.

Like Motorola, we sometimes swallow bait dangled before our eyes, without noticing the hook embedded within, and end up asking Chapter 1's painful question: "Why didn't I *see* that?" How we see problems is often our worst problem, as we will learn in our study of

George Vincent, one of Ford Motor Company's shrewdest plant managers, who went head-to-head with the automobile unions. Needing to increase assembly-line speed to meet impossible production schedules set by upper management in Detroit, Vincent secretly cut 3 inches off the 48-inch wooden sticks separating cars as they moved along the assembly line. Sensing the increased workload, the unions complained but never spotted the ploy. Had they thought about it more perceptively, they could easily have discovered Vincent's artifice, but instead they only learned his secret years later.

Like Motorola, we occasionally allow ourselves to become distracted and, only after serious errors occur, do we ask ourselves the disturbing question: "Why didn't I *concentrate* on that?" I made that mistake myself during a deadly fight in Vietnam, as you will see in Chapter 2. There you will also explore the inspiring story of NASA Flight Director Gene Kranz, who remained focused under unimaginable pressure while leading the rescue of three brave astronauts from the precipice of certain death in the Apollo 13 drama.

When circumstances reach crisis proportion, as they did for Intel, and even in calmer times, we sometimes overlook elegant solutions and, after suffering the consequences, must ask ourselves the unsettling question: "Why didn't I *catch* that?" Only by controlling the quality of our thinking can we achieve the consistency that characterizes sharp minds. Without standards such as clarity and accuracy, sloppy thinking can end in disaster, as we'll see in Chapter 3, where we explore how Avianca Flight 52 ran out of fuel and crashed on Long Island.

Circling New York's Kennedy Airport in a holding pattern for more than one hour and running dangerously low on fuel, Flight 52's captain instructed his co-pilot to declare an "emergency." The co-pilot radioed ground controllers, "We're running out of fuel," but he did not clearly and accurately declare an "emergency" as ordered. An unambiguous transmission of the words "fuel emergency" would have prompted ground controllers to clear the aircraft for immediate landing. When the captain followed up with "Advise him [air traffic control] we are *emergency* . . . Did you tell him?" the co-pilot answered, "Yes, Sir . . . I already advised him."

Moments later all four jet engines flamed out and Flight 52 plunged to Earth.

By not touching all the mental bases, as Motorola failed to do, we sometimes take ill-conceived actions that leave us asking the troubling question: "Why didn't I *realize* that?" Systematic thinking of the sort that leaves no important stone unturned begins with a definite plan in mind. For Intel, that plan was to divert Motorola from fully exploiting its significant technical advantage. As we'll see in Chapter 4, my grade school art teacher designed a plan to fascinate me with the thinking behind great works of art.

Holding up an attractive portrait she had recently completed, my crafty teacher asked what lay underneath the surface of her fresh paint. "Canvas," the class answered in chorus. "Yes," she responded, "but there's something much more valuable than canvas under there, something *between* the canvas and the paint." Clueless, I sat mystified as she passed around a photograph of a charcoal sketch she had drawn on the canvas before applying paint to her portrait in oils. In the coming weeks she showed us many techniques great artists used to create their masterpieces. Some began with sketches on separate slips of paper, others sketched directly on canvas, but, in all cases, the artists formulated plans, even if only in their minds, before dipping brush into paint. Sharp minds never wander aimlessly into important thinking projects.

When others, like Intel, come up with highly creative solutions to tough problems, while we, like Motorola, do not, we end up asking ourselves the somewhat embarrassing question: "Why didn't I *come up* with that?" As Bill Davidow knew well, imaginative thinking illuminates the pathway to success especially in the face of dire adversity. In Chapter 5 we'll witness how Father Edward Sorin, Notre Dame University's founder, did just that when his life's work suddenly burned to the ground.

Having built the institution from its humble beginnings during pre-Civil War days, Father Sorin watched helplessly one night as the efforts of nearly forty years went up in the smoke and flames that wiped out all the university's major buildings, save its stone church. In the aftermath, Sorin gathered his despondent colleagues and students in the church for mass. "The fire is really my fault," he said. "I came here as a young man and dreamed of building a great university in honor of Our Lady. But I built it too small, and she had to burn it to the ground to make that point. So, tomorrow, as soon as the bricks cool, we will rebuild it, bigger and better than ever." They did, brick by glorious brick. Sorin, like Intel, used his imagination to convert potential defeat into consummate triumph.

Outmaneuvered, like Motorola, and wishing we could have peeked into another's mind, we must occasionally ask ourselves the haunting question raised in Chapter 6: "Why didn't I *sense* that?" Sharp thinkers warmly welcome intuition, the inner voice that alerts us to dangers we might not otherwise detect, as a dear friend. To appreciate that approach, we will examine police trainees taking classes on deadly force.

Many large metropolitan police departments use computers and laser simulators to train officers how to handle armed suspects. Trainees confront computer-simulated situations requiring them to make lightning-quick decisions whether to draw and fire their weapons. Imagine you're a police officer standing ten feet from a floor-to-ceiling screen where life-sized people act out a convenience store robbery. You see a masked man pointing a revolver at the sales clerk. If you draw your pistol and command the robber to "drop it," as I did the first time I stood in front of a training screen, the robber freezes. Then he slowly turns his back to you, still holding his weapon, but blocking your view of his revolver. What does the robber intend to do: Give up or shoot you? Will you fire or wait to see if the robber drops his gun? If you choose to wait and see, your reaction will inevitably lag behind his action. Actions always beat reactions. He might fire the first shot and kill you before you can pull the trigger. Only intuition supplies the answer in the split-second available. You don't need to be a police officer to know you must often rely on intuition to make the best decisions in perilous situations.

Sometimes people catch us by surprise, despite the fact that we should have sensed trouble brewing, leaving us with Chapter 7's disquieting question: "Why didn't I *appreciate* that?" By thinking empathetically, we can discover what really motivates others, as Intel's executives understood when they figured out how to bait the hook for Motorola, a technique as old as the California hills.

One example in Chapter 7 involves two unknowns named Arnold and Slack, who in 1872 took full advantage of the principle when they handed a bag full of diamonds to a San Francisco bank clerk who worked for William Ralston, a man notorious for his greed. Determined to discover where they obtained the diamonds, Ralston wheedled the two into revealing they had mined the gems in Wyoming. When Ralston's mining engineer examined the site and reported diamond dust and loose gems scattered on the ground, Ralston pressured Arnold and Slack into allowing him to invest $700,000 in their enterprise. Soon Ralston brought Charles Tiffany, Horace Greeley, and Baron de Rothschild into the venture. When news of the strike made national headlines, a curious engineer visited the site and discovered that Arnold and Slack had salted the mine with diamonds purchased in England. The two instantly disappeared with their ill-gotten gain, and Ralston went to his grave embarrassed that his notorious avarice had made him such an easy mark. Of course, no honest person would condone the behavior of Arnold and Slack, but they correctly predicted how Ralston would react when presented with an apparent opportunity to make an easy fortune.

When our ill-conceived words and deeds create unexpected consequences, we invariably ask Chapter 8's distressing question: "Why didn't I *anticipate* that?" By thinking consequentially, sharp minds ferret out hidden risks, something a group of highly trained engineers failed to do when they conducted the unauthorized "safety experiment" that led to history's worst nuclear catastrophe.

While theoretically possible, an explosion of Chernobyl's nuclear reactor was so unthinkable the plant's engineers felt comfortable proceeding with a risky procedure that literally blew the lid off the huge reactor. As highly radioactive black graphite particles spewed out of the reactor's inner core onto surrounding grounds, Chernobyl's engineers peered outside wondering what had happened. Certain the reactor had remained intact, they simply could not believe their eyes, even with obvious evidence falling from the sky.

In just a few hours, from Intel to Chernobyl and many points in between, this book will greatly strengthen your creative decision-making and problem-solving skills by replacing old habits with new methods that transform workable decisions into brilliant ones, acceptable solutions into spectacular ones. Rather than taking your thinking for granted, you will break the cycle of "thinking as usual," and open your mind to possibilities that before only came to you through hindsight. You will emerge a far better thinker who, more often than not, comes up with innovative solutions and wise decisions that leave *others,* rather than you, asking, *"Why didn't I think of that?"*

Charles W. McCoy Jr.

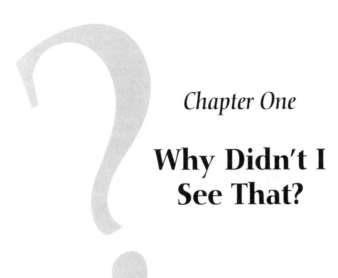

Chapter One

Why Didn't I
See That?

Think Perceptively

I watched from my seat on the bench as Tucker, leaning heavily on his crutches, hobbled awkwardly across the courtroom floor and allowed the bailiff to help him safely up to the witness stand. He swore to tell the truth, sank down in the witness chair, and began recounting his story.

Years earlier, Tucker had built a successful $600,000-a-year career as an investment banker in downtown Los Angeles. In his free time he ran marathons, consistently finishing high in amateur races throughout the United States and abroad.

On one of his typically hectic workdays, Tucker had stepped out for a quick sandwich. Along the way he passed a subway construction site where steel workers were unloading heavy beams from a flatbed truck blocking the street and parked halfway across the sidewalk. With traffic snarled and car horns blaring, the workers hurried to unload beams and move the truck, but, in their haste, they failed to attach a required safety harness to the shifting cargo. Suddenly a beam snapped loose, striking Tucker on the back of the head, then crushing the hood of a nearby car. Tucker fell unconscious onto the pavement and woke up hours later in a local hospital with a brain concussion and a fractured back. On the plus side, however, doctors found no spinal cord damage.

In my courtroom now I heard Tucker's words slow as he described his lingering injuries. Merely lifting an arm would cause him hours of excruciating back pain, and the concussion had permanently impaired his ability to think quickly and accurately, indispensable skills in the investment banking business. When he had returned to work six months after the accident, he could not think straight, and eventually lost his job. He would never, of course, compete in another marathon.

Tucker's doctors and an expert on brain injuries followed as witnesses. The doctors all agreed he had suffered permanent, debilitating mental and physical damage. Tucker endured constant, intense, and real physical pain. His only relief came from powerful, addictive, prescription drugs. The brain specialist used X-rays to show how the heavy blow slammed the frontal lobes of Tucker's brain against his inner skull. The resulting injury irreversibly diminished his capacity to perform even simple thinking tasks. None of the doctors offered the slightest hope that Tucker could return to anything remotely approaching a normal lifestyle, let alone resume his mentally challenging career.

When Tucker's lawyer rested his case late on Friday afternoon, I recessed until Monday morning. The defense would then call its first witness. I felt such deep sympathy for Tucker, I wrestled over the weekend with just how much to award him in damages. In the end, $600,000 a year for 15 years, or $9 million seemed fair.

As I entered the courtroom on Monday, I was surprised to find a large television screen positioned directly in front of my bench. As it turned out, the defense would call as its first witness, not an expert on brain trauma, but a small black videocassette. The scenes it revealed had been taped by a private investigator starting about a year after the accident and ending only two weeks before trial. Neither Tucker nor his lawyer had suspected such a tape existed before viewing it in court. Both sat stonefaced as the tape rolled.

That video wouldn't win any Academy Awards: It just showed Tucker doing everything competitive runners do—stretching, bending, twisting, sprinting like a gazelle, running effortlessly for miles with an ease only champions achieve—all without the slightest hesitation or grimace, and all at night when the star apparently assumed no one could see him. He had not counted on the investigator's night-vision lens. No, the real Oscar-winning performance had occurred the week before, when Tucker testified about his ruined life. He didn't stick around to accept any award, though; he just stomped out of the courtroom, leaving behind his crutches and his thunderstruck lawyer.

The defense continued with a string of medical and psychological experts who described how Tucker had manipulated his doctors into overprescribing powerful medications, not because he needed relief, but because he wanted to fake a brain injury. Tucker's pharmacist girlfriend apparently taught him that the side effects of certain pain medications mimic brain damage. None of his several doctors knew what the others had prescribed. The charade not only fooled me, but it completely pulled the wool over the eyes of his own physicians and a renowned brain specialist as well.

Later, I stood alone in my chambers embarrassed that I had allowed shallow perceptions to blur my thinking. "Why didn't I see that?" I wondered. Judging much too soon, I had fallen for Tucker's ruse, letting my heart overrule my head. I had forgotten an essential rule: Look beneath the surface before jumping in head first. What must I do, I wondered, to make sure this never happens again in my judicial career?

Having taken a long, hard look at the role perceptions play in my thinking, I realized that despite all my specialized legal training and experience I can be deceived just as easily as anyone else. My decisions, however well reasoned, are never better than the perceptions on which I base them. My mind, however quick and logical, remains subject to the same ruinous error as the most sophisticated computer—*garbage in, garbage out!*

After a long hour brooding in chambers over the Tucker incident, I reached for a blank pad, penned the words "Think Perceptively" at the top, and, in the ensuing days, conceived a set of principles I now use whenever dealing with the Tuckers of this world and the problems they present.

NOW YOU SEE IT, NOW YOU DON'T

The human brain and the senses that feed it data, while true wonders of biology, have their limitations. Observe the shadowy gray spots at the intersections in the following figure.

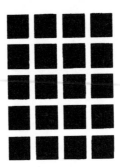

Those spots don't exist; they're *constructs of your mind.* You can make a few disappear by focusing on a single intersection, but you cannot mentally eliminate all the spots for any sustained length of time. Your mind and eye will *not* allow it, no matter how hard you try.

Consider this figure.

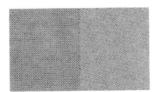

How much would you bet that the shading on the left is darker than the right? Would you wager $1,000 if I offered $100,000 in return? If so, you would lose your money. Cover the intersection between the two areas with a pen, and you'll see *identical* shading on both sides. Lift your pen—*viola!* Your mind and eye will *not* let you perceive the truth.

Here's another one.

This tile-like figure consists of perfectly shaped black squares aligned in precisely parallel rows. Place a straight-edged piece of paper along each horizontal row to prove it. Your mind *insists* on seeing wedge-shaped figures, even though they do not exist. No amount of willpower overcomes your mind's stubbornness.

Try one more.

Place your nose about 6 inches directly over the woman. Cover your right eye with your right hand and slowly move your head backward while keeping your nose directly over the woman. Does the man disappear when your nose reaches about 16 inches above the woman? If you move out about one inch more, the man will reappear. We all have this blind spot.

Now you see it, now you don't. Gray spots appear and disappear; one shade of gray appears as two; squares are wedges, wedges are squares; a blind spot hides reality. All these exercises prove one simple truth: You can't trust initial perceptions without further thought. You can't make the best decisions or find the best solutions without *thinking* perceptively, using your mind to penetrate depths your senses alone cannot reach.

The cause of our surprisingly frequent misperceptions is rooted in something we rarely, if ever, consider. How we perceive things depends as much, or more, on what we *think* as what we see or hear. Far more than just a sensory activity, perception is a *thinking* skill. Our brains refuse to think the tiles are squarely aligned, even though our eyes see otherwise. We end up thinking we see things as they really are when, in fact, we may perceive only an unclear, inaccurate, shallow version of the truth. Worse, our minds can actively interfere with our perceptions of reality.

Sharp thinkers fully appreciate the often unconscious mental process by which we perceive events, people, and things. Much remains for scientists to discover about the human brain, but one thing we know for certain: People use patterns to think through every task, sophisticated and mundane. Whether designing a new software program or crossing the street, we all navigate through life's tasks using learned mental patterns. Computer programmers use embedded logic to create complicated software; pedestrians use rules of the road to dodge other people, cross the street, and get where they're going.

The ability to think with patterns is at once the greatest strength and the most pernicious weakness of healthy human brains, regardless of IQ. Thankfully, we do not need to reinvent the wheel time and again, but occasionally we find ourselves using wheels when we need to invent new forms of transportation. Entrenched patterns, right or wrong, become extremely difficult to change, as Galileo discovered when he suggested, counter to Church dogma, that the Earth does not occupy the center of the Universe. We may chuckle today at the Church's opposition to Galileo, but we have our own share of favorite preconceptions embedded in our consciousness. Sharp minds like Galileo's resist the temptation, indeed compulsion, to rely on old mental patterns when only new ones will do.

Unafraid of truth, Galileo sought a clear view of reality. Concentrating on a few key facts observed with his primitive telescope, Galileo asked penetrating questions challenging dogmatic views; imagined our solar system from a new, wider perspective; and correctly concluded that the ground beneath his feet moved around the Sun, even though he could not feel it. While others clung emotionally to an old pattern that seemed to make sense, Galileo realized that the ages-old view people had in mind did not match reality. Prosecuted by the Church for heresy, he narrowly escaped with his life. Still, in the years that followed, thoughtful people realized the heavenly bodies moved as Galileo had said, and could only ask in awe, "Why didn't I see that?" The answer: They lacked Galileo's perceptiveness.

Thinking perceptively begins with a clear, accurate view of reality that allows us to identify and concentrate on the crucial facts. By asking penetrating questions, studying both the forest and trees, and leading with our minds before our hearts, we sift the wheat from the chaff and acquire crucial information needed to make wise decisions and correctly solve difficult problems.

Warm up your perceptive mind with this pattern exercise.

Mental Warm–Up
Something Made of Nothing

Describe everything you see in this lattice work.

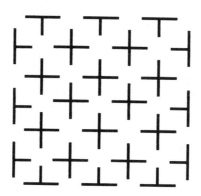

Do you see a criss-crossed pattern of white strips? Can you see white squares or circles at the intersections of the white strips? If you concentrate on white squares, they can change to circles and vice versa. Do you see that the black lines do *not* actually form any of the white shapes you see?

False perceptions occur more often than we ever realize. With this in mind, recall *specific* instances when you made unwise decisions based on false perceptions that, at the time, seemed true beyond doubt. Have some of those decisions caused harmful consequences that continue even today?

OBTAIN A CLEAR VIEW OF REALITY

Like Galileo, perceptive thinkers strive to see clearly all that reality offers, helpful and harmful, reassuring and provoking, pleasant and offensive, significant and seemingly insignificant. I learned this lesson best when, as an attorney, I represented Massey Business Systems, one of the first computer integration companies. Massey had made a fortune packaging computer hardware and software into complete systems, an enterprise that relied on a patented computer chip Massey obtained from Quantum Technics under an exclusive, long-term contract. Massey couldn't turn out systems fast enough to meet demand.

The company's future seemed secure until one day, out of the blue, Quantum, citing production snags overseas, cut its chip deliveries to Massey by two-thirds. Unable to produce promised systems, Massey watched helplessly as customers switched to other integrators. The company soon ran short of cash, defaulted on its loans, and wound up in bankruptcy.

In the wake of Massey's failure, Quantum stepped forward to offer "technical support" to Massey's stranded customers, a precursor to Quantum offering its own integrated system. As customers flocked to the new product, Quantum quickly took over a large slice of the market originally pioneered by the now-defunct Massey.

One year later, a disgruntled Quantum employee approached Massey's former owners, claiming that Quantum had faked the chip shortage in order to destroy Massey and steal its profitable business. Massey hired me as its lawyer, and, on the strength of the whistleblower's sworn affidavit, I filed suit against Quantum. When the court ordered Quantum to produce every document in its files relating to the chip shortage, Quantum responded with more than thirty file boxes crammed with loose papers.

Despite many late hours scanning letters, memos, marketing plans, notes, and complicated technical documents, I found nothing that even remotely confirmed the whistleblower's story. On the contrary, I saw clear evidence of an authentic chip shortage. Quantum had repeatedly written its Taiwanese chip-maker begging for product, and it had continually expressed deep sympathy for Massey's predicament.

It didn't take long for Quantum's lawyers to file a motion seeking to dismiss Massey's case and hinting they might sue both Massey and *me* for malicious prosecution. My fledgling legal career hanging in the balance, I frantically searched through the mound of Quantum documents looking for some shred of evidence to support Massey's suit, but the effort failed, with me slumped at my desk, exhausted and disheartened.

You can imagine the relief when my eagle-eyed secretary saved the day. She noticed a faint half-inch mark midway down the left margin of one page while photocopying Quantum documents. Walking into my office, she laid the page down on my desk with a knowing smile. "See this?" she said. "It's a tape mark. Somebody's doctored this memo." Sure enough, the paragraphs above and below the mark appeared slightly out of line. "Why didn't I see that?" I wondered. Before long, we had collected more than fifty similarly altered documents.

The truth came clear: Quantum had faked many key documents, using a photocopying machine to replace incriminating paragraphs with fabrications. The deletions and insertions all occurred at points where I had initially expected to find incriminating entries. I had missed them all, even though I conscientiously studied the documents time and again. How could I have been so blind?

In the end, Quantum agreed to pay Massey an enormous cash settlement, but I won much more than a lawsuit. I gained a deeper understanding of the crucial role perception plays in sharp thinking.

Perceptive thinkers try at every turn to see the world as it *really* is, opening wide the mind's eye to gather every relevant scrap of information. Searching for truth, rather than inventing substitutes for it, and making every effort to obtain a clear view of reality, perceptive thinkers pay close attention to details others might miss or ignore.

Mental Aerobics
April Fools

Seek a clear view of reality and all its fascinating details as you examine this illustration created by Norman Rockwell for the *Saturday Evening Post* in April 1943. Open your mind and find every possible incongruity. How many do you count?

NORMAN ROCKWELL'S
APRIL-FOOL COVER
SEE PAGE 4

Norman Rockwell, April 1943 by permission of Thomas Rockwell

You must look beyond the ordinary to see the extraordinary. There's nothing unusual about a portrait of a man, for example, but the ordinary becomes extraordinary when you see the man's hands hanging over the edge of the picture frame. The Notes at the end of this chapter contain the magazine's solution, but don't peek at it until you exhaust all your perceptive talents.

─────────────────────────────── Practice Makes Perfect

See Things as They Really Are

This exercise will sharpen your perception skills. Select an object within reach. Pick something fairly simple you can hold in your hand. Describe every detail of the object you can identify. Use this list as an aid:

Shape	Function
Color	Weight
Texture	Size
Substance	

Notice how much you can discover when you think at your perceptive best.

Now apply your perception skills to a much more complicated object, such as an artwork in your office or a plant or tree outside. Notice how your perception of the object clarifies as you observe its details.

If you want to stretch your perceptive skills to their limits, apply them on the most complicated of all organisms, a human being. Pick someone you know well, and search for traits you have not noticed before.

You possess enormous, often untapped, resources for seeing things as they really are. Now that you more fully appreciate your perception skills, put them to work in your private and professional lives. Hold yourself to higher standards of clarity in all your perceptions of people, things, and events.

DOUBLE-CHECK PERCEPTIONS

What we see clearly does not always match reality, and, in these instances, we may miss the truth unless we double-check our perceptions, particularly when people try to manipulate our senses, as advocates sometimes do with judges and juries. After listening to oral argument one morning in a hotly contested civil case, I ruled in favor of the plaintiff and instructed my court clerk to prepare an order reflecting that decision. To my surprise, the losing defense lawyer interrupted, asking rather bluntly if I had taken into account a very recent case that she said required a different result. No, I had not read that case, an admission I sheepishly made to a packed courtroom. Judges, like most people, do not enjoy confessing to flaws in their thinking. Vacating my initial decision, I promised to read the new case later, then decide.

That afternoon, examining the case in chambers, I had to agree with the losing lawyer: It did require a result opposite from the one I had announced earlier. Dismayed that I had somehow missed the case, I changed my mind, wrote out a new decision, and handed it to my clerk for publication. Still, an uneasy feeling remained in the back of my mind. "Why didn't I see that?" I asked.

By law, attorneys must only cite valid cases, and I assumed the losing defense lawyer had honored the rule in this instance. But could it be otherwise? Had I missed the case because it was not among the body of binding case law?

Switching on my computer, I ran a "cite check." Sure enough, the case in question had been "depublished," rendering it utterly invalid. My near-complete acceptance of the losing defense lawyer's case without double-checking its validity nearly caused a gross miscarriage of justice. Later I sanctioned the losing defense lawyer for misconduct, but the most important disciplinary action occurred in the privacy of my own mind, where I gained renewed appreciation for not accepting things at face value.

Perceptive thinkers take time to verify their perceptions, because one tiny false premise can produce massive error. Suppose, for example, that you must solve a problem using three items of information: x, y, and z. Each produces a different solution, fifteen combinations: x, y, z, xy, yx, xz, zx, yz, zy, xyz, xzy, yxz, yzx, zyx, and zxy. If x is wrong and will always cause a false answer, then *eleven* of fifteen solutions that rely on x fail. If both x and y are incorrect, then only *one* answer produces a correct result. The chances of error caused by only one or two misperceptions are astonishing. As the following table shows, if one of two items is wrong, three out of four combinations produce error; if two of four items are wrong, then sixty out of sixty-four possible combinations fail.

Items of Information	Combinations	Erroneous Combinations Caused by One Inaccuracy	Erroneous Combinations Caused by Two Inaccuracies
1	1	1	—
2	4	3 in 4	4
3	15	11 in 15	14 in 15
4	64	49 in 64	60 in 64
5	325	261 in 325	310 in 325

Knowing that the odds of success diminish dramatically when even slight error creeps into the process, perceptive thinkers pay excruciating attention to details. It's not so easy as it sounds, however. Quickly count the f's in this sentence:

Looking back at the fall of Rome, we see how unimaginable excesses of every kind created a nearly universal feeling among people living in the city that moderation, even for an instant, made life unsatisfying, dull, and far from the kind of existence the people of Rome felt they deserved.

Did you accurately count all *twelve* the first time? If not, try again. Many people can't easily come up with the right number even *after* they know the correct answer. Keep working at it until you get it right.

If accuracy requires effort in this simple example, imagine how difficult it becomes in the more complex situations we encounter day-to-day. Yet, we often do not double-check our observations and risk making huge mistakes caused by relatively small misperceptions.

Sharpen your double-checking skills with this magical challenge.

Sleight of Mind

One evening you go out for entertainment at the Magic Castle in Hollywood. A magician wanders over to your dinner table and lays the following string of cards in front of you. He says, "Pick a card mentally and don't tell a soul which you have in mind. I'm going to read your thoughts."

Go ahead. Choose a card. Do you have one in mind?

The magician reaches for the cards, takes one out of the group, places it in his pocket, and spreads the remaining cards back on the table as shown here.

Now he announces triumphantly, "See! The card in your mind has disappeared. I read your thoughts, didn't I?"

Are you willing to admit the magician read your mind? If not, double-check your perceptions to disprove his claim. The Notes to this chapter contain the answer, but don't turn too quickly for a solution you can produce on your own.

———————————————————————————— Practice Makes Perfect
Make Sure You Have It Right

This exercise helps you appreciate the importance of double-checking perceptions. Think of things you habitually double-check to make sure you've gotten them right. Add your own items to the following list. *I habitually double-check:*

- ✔ Directions given to me over the phone.
- ✔ Dates and times on wedding invitations.
- ✔ Whether I turned off the stove before leaving home.
- ✔ Where I parked my car as I walk toward the airport terminal.
- ✔ What I put into an envelope before sealing it.
- ✔ The time I set on my alarm clock the night before an early morning meeting.

Think of specific instances where your failure to double-check caused real difficulties for you or others.

Now, make a list of items you should double-check more carefully. Add your own items to the following suggestions. *I need to double-check more thoroughly:*

- ✔ What I think people say to me.
- ✔ Information I rely on when making decisions.
- ✔ The contents of documents I write.
- ✔ The figures on my tax returns, even if a professional prepares them.
- ✔ The terms and conditions of agreements I sign.

Finally, consider what you will do to develop habits of double-checking the items you listed above.

Concentrate on Crucial Facts

Double-checking helps insure you do not misperceive crucial facts needed to make sound decisions and correctly solve problems. In most situations, a relatively few crucial facts lead to the best decisions and solutions. Perceptive thinkers concentrate their attention where it counts most, something auto union leaders failed to do in the mid-1950s when they locked horns with one of Ford Motor Company's shrewdest plant managers, George Vincent.

Vincent, like Henry Ford, believed that manufacturing, not finance, drove the company's business. Naturally, then, he disdained the corporate "whiz kids" in Detroit almost more than he did union organizers. The whiz kids tried to manage Vincent by the numbers; but people, not numbers, assemble cars. Still, Vincent knew how to play the game, giving corporate headquarters the numbers demanded with a vengeance. When Detroit insisted that no leftover parts remain at the end of production runs, Vincent surreptitiously dumped tons of spare parts into the Delaware River and came out squarely "on the numbers."

The whiz kids talked "quality," but to Vincent's ears that mostly sounded like the latest management buzzword. All the time demanding more production, the home office nonetheless entered into contracts with the unions setting limits on the speed at which production lines could move. To Vincent it felt like trying to cram five pounds of Jell-O into a one-pound container, an impossible dilemma for a man unwilling to accept sloppy results. So, the ever-ingenious Vincent came up with a resourceful solution, secretly building a "kitty" of extra cars as protection against absurd production quotas.

This is how he did it. Cars coming down the assembly line were normally separated by wooden sticks 48 inches long. Vincent surreptitiously chopped 3 inches off each stick, effectively increasing production by 6 percent. Only a handful of his closest associates were in on the scheme.

The unions and their members working the assembly line sensed the added workload and jumped to the obvious conclusion that Vincent had violated the union contract by increasing line speed. The unions had learned from past experience that plant managers had access to controls that they could slowly adjust upward to increase line speed in small, virtually imperceptible increments. But on this occasion, timing the line day after day with stopwatches revealed nothing. The unions' preoccupation with "line speed" created a flaw in their thinking that Vincent exploited to his advantage.

By measuring line speed rather than output, the unions had failed to spot the one crucial fact: More cars were indeed rolling off the assembly line because Vincent had increased the number of cars in production at any given time. Without that crucial fact, the unions could neither see nor infer the ultimate source of their problem. They exhausted all their energy attempting to prove an assumed but false "fact," and their single-minded measurements of speed, while entirely accurate, led them astray. Or, rather, a 45-inch stick did. Years later, on learning of Vincent's deception, the union leaders had to ask themselves, "Why didn't we see that?"

Perceptive thinkers sift all the facts at hand, constantly on the lookout for those few facts that really matter. The following exercise sharpens your ability to focus on crucial facts.

Mental Aerobics
A New Kind of Horse Race

You and your best friend each own a race horse. Both horses placed dead last in their most recent outings. "I bet I own the slowest horse in the country!" you grumble in frustration. "Not hardly," your friend retorts, "I do." Both you and your friend enjoy a good bet, so you agree on a hefty wager to determine who owns the slower horse. As the jockeys take the horses to the starting gates, you realize you have a problem. When the race starts, the jockeys will slow their horses to a dead stop as they try to finish last. You must somehow design a new kind of race that will accurately and honestly determine the slower horse. How will you run the race?

Ignore Distractions Intended to Throw You Off Track

In your quest for the crucial facts, you must remain wary of distractions that can throw you off track. This exercise shows how you can guard your perceptions from active attempts by others to distract your attention away from what really counts. Those who want to prevent us from obtaining a clear view of reality often use diversions to avoid or hide the real issues. What the talking heads do nightly to Chris Matthews on MSNBC's *Hard Ball* happens daily in our own lives as well. People change the subject on us, dodge our questions, reply with empty answers, and, unless we follow up tenaciously, the truth never comes out.

Dad wants to know why his daughter stayed out too late last night. Daughter responds, "You don't trust me." Dad only wants facts. Daughter does not want to discuss facts, so she tries to switch the topic to trust.

An employee misses a crucial deadline. The boss asks, "Why?" The employee responds, "Did Frank snitch on me again? He's causing real morale problems in the department these days." *Switch.*

A grown son asks his elderly mother whether she's taking her medicine on schedule. She launches into a discussion of her unhappiness with the doctor who wrote the prescription. *Switch.*

When people actively try to derail our inquiries, we must *actively* put the discussion back on track. Identify persons in your life who use distractions to throw you off course. Recall specific situations.

Now, think of ways you can quickly move the discussion back on track with each person. The following two methods usually work. Can you come up with others?

- *Never-the-less* and *Regardless.* You ask a question. The person tosses out a distraction. You respond "never-the-less" or "regardless," and immediately ask the question again, continuing until the person realizes you refuse to take the bait.

- *We'll get to that later.* You ask questions. People respond, but not to the exact questions you ask. They cleverly answer different questions which they, in effect, ask themselves. You respond "we'll get to that later," and instantly ask your original questions again, continuing until the people understand you expect direct answers.

Ask Penetrating Questions

Concentrating on crucial facts does not guarantee you will find them. That requires asking the right questions, looking in the right places. When perceptive thinkers say "I'll look *into* it," they mean it. They develop *insight* by probing beneath the surface of situations, asking penetrating questions that expose reality and uncover truth.

Max Steuer, one of America's most talented trial attorneys, possessed what lawyers call an "ear for witnesses." Steuer practiced in New York City during the early 1900s when many immigrants found work in the city's sweatshops. The Triangle Shirt Waist Company operated one such sweatshop in a lower Manhattan loft, where 500 to 600 young women, mostly under 20, worked in a multistoried structure.

When Triangle's owners learned that some of the young women were taking unauthorized smoking breaks outside on the building's fire escapes, they nailed shut the fire doors, not to stop smoking, but to prevent workers from slacking off for even a few minutes.

Tragically, a fire broke out in the building and killed almost 400 women. Indicted by the district attorney for manslaughter, the owners hired Max Steuer to defend them in a trial no one thought he could win. The late Professor Irving Younger of Cornell Law School described the turning point of the trial as follows:

The prosecution called the first witness, a girl about seventeen years old. She speaks in heavily accented English:

Q: What is your name?

A: Sophie Shapiro.

Q: How old are you?

A: Seventeen.

Q: How long have you been in this country?

A: One year.

Q: Where did you come from?

A: Poland.

Q: Do you live with your parents?

A: Yes.

Q: Where?

A: Lansing Street.

Q: Do you work?

A: Yes.

Q: Where?

A: Triangle Shirt Waist Company.

Q: Were you working on the day of the fire?

A: Yes.

Q: Tell us what happened.

A: Well, we were working, and it was about nine in the morning. I was on the fourth floor with about fifty girls. One of the girls said that she was going to have a cigarette. We used to go out on the fire escape, but we couldn't because the doors were nailed shut. So this girl went out in the stairway, and she smoked a cigarette. She came back, and she said, "You know, it is funny, I smell smoke." And we all said, "You are smelling your own cigarette, there's no smoke." We went back to work. In about five minutes we all smelled the smoke, and then the girl who was nearest the door to the stairway went out, and she came back in and she said, "There's fire coming up the stairs." Now the girls who were nearest the fire exit went to open the door, but of course they couldn't. It was nailed shut. And they began to try to pull the door open, but they couldn't; the nails were so strong, and now the fire had reached the top of the stairs and was coming into the room.

Well, the girls at the far end of the room came piling up on top of the girls who were near the fire door, screaming, "Let us out, let us out," but they couldn't get out. And the girls who were near the door were screaming, "You're crushing me, you're crushing me," and they were underneath the pile of fifty girls, and the girls were crying and trying with their fingernails to pull the fire door open, and they couldn't and the flames came into the room, their hair started to burn, and the screaming was awful, and I didn't know what to do.

There was a broom closet. I stepped into the broom closet and I closed the door. After that I couldn't see what happened, but I could hear it, and I could smell it, and the girls screamed, "I'm burnt," and I could smell it, the burning flesh.

And then I fainted, and when I woke up, a fireman was carrying me out.

The prosecutor finished his questioning, turned confidently toward Max Steuer, and said, "You may inquire." Where could Steuer begin? The defendants were guilty, and the witness was unimpeachable.

"Sophie, tell it again," Steuer said. Sophie told her story again, in exactly the same words.

"Tell it again, Sophie," Steuer said. She repeated her story in exactly the same words—exactly.

"Tell it again," Steuer commanded. This time Sophie changed one word. A "that" became a "which."

"Sophie, didn't you make a mistake?" Steuer asked. "Didn't you say 'which' instead of 'that?'"

"Oh yes, I'm sorry," she replied. "I did make a mistake," and she corrected herself.

Max Steuer returned to his seat, his cross-examination complete. He had carefully listened to Sophie's story on its first telling and spotted a crucial error. The testimony sounded too eloquent, too well-rehearsed for a young woman who spoke only a halting, heavily accented English. The jury thought so too. Offended by the district attorney's manipulative tactics, it acquitted the defendants.

While the outcome of the trial remains controversial, a clear lesson emerges. Max Steuer's careful listening and penetrating questions won the case. The district attorney scripted the witness, turning an otherwise honest person into a trained parrot, not the kind of witness juries warm to in criminal cases. Most lawyers, if standing in Steuer's shoes, would miss the opportunity he saw and, only as an afterthought, ask themselves, "Why didn't I see that?"

Recent studies show high correlations between sensory perception skills and mental insight. An ability to quickly identify the subject of out-of-focus pictures, for example, more accurately predicts insightfulness than the Scholastic Aptitude Test. Obviously, then, if you wish to improve your insightfulness, you should enhance perception skills. You can dramatically do that by learning to ask penetrating questions and to listen with your ears wide open.

Sharp thinkers such as Max Steuer do both. They apply the fundamental rule of journalism, asking six questions about every circumstance: Who? When? Where? What? How? Why?

Perceptive people use the technique to probe deep into reality. I often urge law students to carry a card in their wallets as an ever-present reminder that the simplest questions frequently lead to the deepest insights. The card reads:

Who?	*Who is involved: who might be involved?*
When?	*When did it happen: when might it happen?*
Where?	*Where did it occur: where might it occur?*
What?	*What happened: what might happen?*
How?	*How did it occur: how might it occur?*
Why?	*Why did it happen: why might it happen?*

Make a card like this for yourself, and apply it *from top to bottom in the exact sequence.* The questions build on each other, starting with basic facts and moving deeper and deeper to the heart of matters. Try it out on the following exercise, probing the facts of the problem to develop a final penetrating question that leads to success.

Mental Aerobics

Truth vs. Lies

You're camping in Virginia's Shenandoah Mountains and decide to take a solo afternoon hike into the surrounding woods. After several hours, the setting sun reminds you to return to camp before darkness envelops the wilderness. You follow an apparently familiar trail. A cold, hard rain starts falling. You hear wolves yapping in the distance. The trail leads back to your camp, but you realize you don't know which of the two possible directions to take. Suddenly you encounter two men. They both know the correct direction to your campground. One carries an axe; the other, a pitchfork. One man always tells the truth, the other always lies, and you don't know who tells what. You may ask one question of only one man.

What one penetrating question will you ask and of whom?

The Notes to this chapter contain a suggested question, but try to think of one on your own. Remember, wolves are yapping in the distance.

Practice Makes Perfect

Master the Art of "Why?"

Of all the questions you can ask, "Why?" often penetrates most. This exercise shows how you can quickly find the bottom line by relentlessly pursuing the question "Why?"

Write a statement relating to some aspect of your work that you want to do particularly well. If you're a salesperson, your statement might read: "I want to sell as many units as possible."

Write and answer as many relevant "Why?" questions as you can come up with in five minutes. Build your questions on your answers until you reach the bottom of each line of questioning. As an example, if you're a salesperson, your questions and answers might read:

    I.   Why do I want to sell as many units as possible?

        A. Because I want to make more money

        B. Because I want a promotion to sales manager

    II. Why do I want to make more money?

        A. Because I want to do a better job of providing for my family

1. Why do I think I need to do a better job of providing for my family?
   a. Because our house is too small for our needs
   b. Because my spouse wants to move to a more rural setting
III. Why do I want a promotion to sales manager?
   A. Because I'm more talented at leading people than selling product day-to-day

Master the art of "Why?" in real life by trying the technique on a wide variety of problems you encounter in the coming days. Asking "Why?" will help you avoid asking yourself in hindsight "Why didn't I see that?"

STUDY BOTH THE FOREST AND THE TREES

Even if you look in the right place, you can still misperceive reality if you do not view it from the proper perspective, as Coke's executives discovered when challenged by a better-tasting Pepsi. In the mid-1980s, the Pepsi-Cola Company launched the tremendously successful "Pepsi Challenge" commercials in which people always picked Pepsi over Coca-Cola in blind taste tests. As Pepsi increasingly captured market share from its rival, Coke's executives set out to develop a better-tasting cola formula that could beat Pepsi at its own game.

Coke's scientists worked around the clock, concocting new formulas and conducting super-secret taste tests, until finally they hit upon one that people definitely preferred over Pepsi. Once the scientists declared victory, Coke's executives swiftly withdrew traditional Coke from the marketplace and replaced it with "New Coke."

Coca-Cola's loyal customers revolted, swamping Coke's headquarters in Atlanta with thousands of protest letters and even lawsuits. One consumer said, "I don't think I would be more upset if you were to burn the flag on the front yard."

Coke's dumfounded executives resisted the onslaught far too long before they reluctantly returned traditional Coke to the shelves as "Coke Classic." In that time, Coke's sales plummeted to a new low market share of 2.3 percent, despite the undeniable fact that studies proved New Coke tasted better in blind tests than *both* traditional Coke and Pepsi.

The fiasco occurred because Coke's executives allowed a flaw to form in their thinking. They failed to account for personal preferences that Coke had itself spent decades ingraining into the minds of its loyal customers.

The same system of mental patterns that influences what we see affects our tastes. To prove the point, *The Wall Street Journal* sponsored a test in which consumers tasted three unidentified colas, including Pepsi and Coke. Most Coke consumers initially believed they could easily identify their favorite brand. After taking the test, the 70 percent who failed became defensive. Preferences built up in their minds over the years so influenced their perceptions that once they knew which was which, Coke consumers said Coke tasted better than Pepsi, even after being told they had picked Pepsi over Coke in the blind test. Their minds suddenly rejected what their taste buds had told them moments before.

The "New Coke" debacle would not have occurred if Coke's executives had more broadly explored the perceptions of cola consumers. Instead of just focusing on finding a formula that could beat Pepsi in blind tests, they should have looked at the big picture, the open market where consumers choose among *known* brands. They should also have checked how loyal consumers of traditional Coke might react to losing their favorite product entirely.

Perceptive minds adopt a wide view of reality. Like the best quarterbacks, they see more of the playing field than others. Like Mozart, who envisioned whole musical scores in his mind before writing individual notes on paper, they see the whole, not just the parts.

Most conventional education and job training teaches us to break down problems into manageable parts, as we must to accomplish many analytical tasks. In fact, the word "analysis" means to "break down." But the narrowing process can cause us to lose sight of the larger context surrounding a decision or problem. Perceptive thinkers strive to see *both* the parts and the sum of the parts. They look for patterns, engaging in what Einstein called "combinatory play." Perceptive minds look for details and then use them as aids for perceiving whole systems of which the details form but small parts. Once you see the whole system, you can delve back into the details with a better understanding of the significance of each part. The trees enlighten perception of the forest, and the forest enhances perception of the trees. Here's two exercises that will sharpen your ability to keep both the forest and trees in proper perspective.

————————————————————————————————— Mental Aerobics
Hearts and Stars

Draw three straight lines through this figure to divide it into areas containing only hearts or stars, but not both in each area. To solve the problem you must pay more attention to the forest than the trees. Take your time, and do not consult the Notes until you find the solution.

Now try another problem that challenges you to find the proper perspective leading to an elegant solution.

Mental Aerobics

Medical Breakthrough

You're a nationally known cancer surgeon who recently discovered a new form of narrow X-ray beam that kills malignant cells better than any known treatment. The FDA approved your technology for clinical trials on human subjects. Your first patient suffers with an inoperable tumor at the center of his brain. Your beam will eradicate the tumor if used at high intensity. But, at that level the beam will destroy all healthy tissue on its way to the tumor and likely kill your patient. If you reduce intensity, the ray will not kill healthy tissue on its way to the tumor, but neither will it destroy the tumor, even if left on for very long periods of time. Effective treatment requires that a full concentration of energy arrive at the tumor at one instant in time.

How will you eradicate the tumor without harming healthy tissue in the process? Take a broad rather than narrow view of the situation to solve the problem and save your patient's life. See the Notes for an answer.

Practice Makes Perfect

Take Charge of Your Health

This exercise reveals how approaching complex problems from many perspectives often provides the elusive key to lasting solutions. We cannot effectively solve problems with many contributing causes if we allow any significant contributor to sneak through a loophole in our thinking and sabotage the whole effort.

Think of a personal health issue that you can, but do not always, control effectively. Perhaps you're overweight. Maybe you're not overweight, but you're seriously out of shape and don't exercise. Possibly you smoke cigarettes or drink more alcohol than you should.

Health issues like these often result from multiple simultaneous causes, all of which must be addressed to solve the problem. Consider excess weight as an example. Concentrating all our willpower on avoiding food only starves us into failure. In order to achieve long-lasting success, we must approach the problem from many directions, changing not only what we eat, but when and how we eat. We must adjust our daily routines, altering activities that do not directly involve food. We may even need to change friends. The number of habits we must alter can be extensive, down to things such as what TV programs we watch. The Food Channel might soon lose an ardent fan.

Consider the origins of, and solutions for, the personal health issue you've identified.

- How many personal choices and behaviors can I identify as contributors to the problem?
- Why have my past efforts to control the problem failed?
- What must I do to take lasting and effective control of the problem?

LEAD WITH YOUR MIND, FOLLOW WITH YOUR HEART

Approaching problems from many perspectives, trying to see both the forest and trees, becomes all the more difficult when strong emotions obscure clear perception. Sentiments intensify the human tendency to focus on what we *want* to see rather than what we *need* to see, as British Prime Minister Neville Chamberlain's catastrophically poor thinking in the months leading up to World War Two made clear for the world to see.

A stubborn man with strong prejudices, Chamberlain ardently hoped to avoid armed conflict with Germany and another world war such as the one he had fought as a young man earlier in the century. Unfortunately, these hopes and fears profoundly distorted Chamberlain's perceptions of reality, creating deadly flaws in his thinking at a time when Great Britain, and the world, desperately needed realistic thinking about events in Europe and the intentions of Adolf Hitler.

When Hitler marched his troops into Austria, Chamberlain, hoping for peace, dismissed the incident as only an isolated event. Hitler next positioned his divisions along the Czechoslovakian border, demanding that Britain and France turn a blind eye to Germany's impending assault on that helpless country. Hitler, knowing his army might suffer a crushing defeat if Britain and France combined forces to resist the attack, and understanding Chamberlain's state of mind better than Chamberlain himself, called for a meeting in Munich, Germany. There, he bullied and cajoled, setting off frightful emotions in Chamberlain. When Hitler called Czechoslovakia his "last territorial demand," Chamberlain deceived himself into believing it, even though reality belied everything Hitler said. Chamberlain even said of the meeting, "I got the impression that here was a man who could be relied upon when he had given his word."

Following a second meeting in Munich, Chamberlain returned to Britain with a piece of paper signed by Hitler, which he waived at reporters saying, "I believe it is peace in our time." By permitting Hitler to take Czechoslovakia without British military opposition, Chamberlain actually *cooperated* in his own deception, allowing his overwhelming desire for peace to prevent any rational consideration of the many clear indications that Hitler intended to plunder all of Europe, including Great Britain. Looking back, history has repeatedly asked, "Why didn't Chamberlain see that?" Time and again Hitler marched his armies through loopholes in Chamberlain's thinking, and only when Hitler later attacked Poland did Britain and France belatedly declare war.

Chamberlain's emotion-driven misperceptions of Hitler left his nation wholly unprepared to defend itself, let alone wage offensive war against Nazi Germany. Britain had done precious little to build up its military strength during the months when Chamberlain hoped to avoid war. Indeed, he refused to strengthen Britain's army because he feared the precaution might "provoke" the German tyrant.

Hitler's blitzkrieg crushed Poland in a few days, Chamberlain later resigned, and Winston Churchill, a man with no illusions about Hitler or the Führer's intentions, took his place. Tragically, Neville Chamberlain died grief-stricken at a point during the war when Britain appeared doomed to certain defeat.

While we may not want to admit it, we all possess a bit of Neville Chamberlain's weakness. Powerful feelings, when ignited, can distort our perceptions of people and events and blind us to even the most obvious realities. When circumstances kindle these feelings, perceptive thinkers force themselves to "get real." While we cannot entirely avoid the effects of our emotions, we can and must try hard to lead with our minds and follow with our hearts. The following exercise gives you an opportunity to sharpen your ability to place emotions in their proper perspective.

Last Game of the Season

Your teenage son Josh runs onto the field to play the last high school football game of the season as you stand proudly in the bleachers. He will letter for the first time if Coach Dixon puts him into the game for even one play. The score remains close until late in the fourth quarter when your team scores two quick touchdowns. With victory now certain, Coach Dixon rotates his graduating seniors off the field to standing ovations between plays. Josh moves next to the coach, hoping to run in for one of the seniors. You see Dixon turn and say something to Josh. Instead of running onto the field as hoped, your son walks slowly back to the bench, drops his helmet, and plops down onto the team bench, head in hands. The gun sounds, and the game ends.

You walk onto the field and put your hand on your son's shoulder. "What happened Josh?" you ask. "Coach said I don't deserve to play, that I'm not good enough to carry the water bucket," Josh replies. As a promising player, Josh worked hard all year, and the coach saying Josh did not deserve to play is *outrageous!* Spotting Coach Dixon on the sidelines, you walk over for a chat.

"Did you tell Josh he didn't deserve to play?" you ask.

"Yes, I did!" Dixon responds curtly.

What will you say or do next? Remember to lead with your mind, then follow with your heart. Make your choice before turning to the Notes for a further discussion of the exercise.

See the Hidden Side of People Before They Blindside You

With this exercise you can practice using your mind to obtain correct perceptions when feelings may create flaws in your thinking and expose you to otherwise avoidable harm. Imagine you manage a company department of over thirty employees. Two years ago, when you hired a highly talented person to run a portion of your department, you took an instant liking to your new manager. You and he share many of the same interests, including your favorite leisure activity, golf. You find yourself spending more time with him because you greatly enjoy his companionship. The company President wants you to visit key customers in the field more often, and you need to select someone you can trust to run your organization while you're away. You've decided to promote your new manager to the number-two position in the department. You feel certain he's right for the job. He's never done anything that gives you the slightest cause for concern, and you can't imagine he ever would.

Word of your intentions leaks out to your employees, and one approaches confidentially to say, "You don't see his other side." Another says, "He's too ambitious." You recently overheard your most senior employee say, "He's a brown-noser, and the boss can't see it." When you share all this with a longtime colleague, she advises: "Watch your backside. He may be out for your job."

Think of ways to discover whether your immensely positive feelings about this person match reality. If he's operating with a hidden agenda, don't expect him to show it directly. You must approach the issue indirectly, and that takes real thought. How many of your own ideas can you add to the following list?

- Assign him to manage a highly stressful situation, then observe how he handles it.

- Assign him to oversee someone you trust, then obtain confidential feedback from that person.

- Find ways to ask your employees casually how they like working for this person, then follow up on any hints of dissatisfaction.

- Expose this person socially to people outside work whom you trust, asking later for their reactions.

Avoid blindsiding in real life. Think of a person occupying a position of trust in your life who may be operating with a hidden agenda adverse to your best interests. Set aside your general trust of the person as best you can, and think of ways to uncover any possible hidden agenda.

PUT IT ALL TOGETHER

Now let's apply everything you've learned in this chapter to a practical problem.

Get to the Bottom of Things

You own a successful software development firm. Your lawyer just called to tell you that a former employee has threatened to sue for wrongful termination, claiming he was fired for refusing to use programming code stolen from your biggest competitor. He insists your lead programmer secretly used pilfered code in your latest and most ambitious new product scheduled for release in three weeks. You've invested millions in the project, and pulling the plug now will inevitably throw your firm into bankruptcy.

Use the perceptive thinking skills learned from this chapter to address and add to the questions raised here.

- *Obtain a clear view of reality.* Which key people must know whether we used stolen code?

- *Double-check perceptions.* How can I quickly confirm whether my key people are telling me the truth?

- *Concentrate on crucial facts.* If we used stolen code, is there a way to clean up our software quickly and still release the product on time?

- *Ask penetrating questions.* What questions do I need to ask to make sure we've gotten to the bottom of this problem and found the very best possible solution?

- *Study both the forest and the trees.* What will happen if I release the product without finding out for sure whether we used stolen code?

- *Lead with your mind, follow with your heart.* How will I set aside my anger and fear to direct all my energy at solving the problem?

Think for Yourself

Apply the full range of your perceptive thinking to a real-life problem of personal significance to you.

Restore a Shattered Relationship

Think of an important personal relationship in your life that is falling apart—a close friend, family member, coworker, or colleague. Choose a relationship you sincerely want to restore.

What can you do to put the relationship back together again? Use the perceptive thinking skills learned from this chapter to develop your thoughts about your real-life challenge. Fully answer all the questions you've raised. Settle on a course of action you believe might best repair the damage, and then set about the task of restoring the relationship.

- *Obtain a clear view of reality.*
- *Double-check perceptions.*
- *Concentrate on crucial facts.*
- *Ask penetrating questions.*
- *Study both the forest and the trees.*
- *Lead with your mind, follow with your heart.*

Think About It

Take a few minutes to consider what you've learned about perceptive thinking and how you can apply these lessons to all the problems and decisions confronting you every day. Ask yourself:

- What situations in my life require my most perceptive thinking, and what specific steps will I take in those situations to improve my perceptivity?

- In what circumstances am I most likely not to pay enough attention to details, and what specifically will I begin doing to double-check the accuracy of my perceptions?

- When am I most likely to take a hit-and-miss approach rather than concentrating on crucial facts and using them to develop successful decision-making and problem-solving strategies?

- In what circumstances do I need to ask far more penetrating questions and listen more carefully to the answers I hear?

- When do I most need to study both the forest and the trees, and what will I do to make sure I do both?

- In what situations am I likely to allow powerful emotions to unduly influence my thinking, and what will I do to guard against that happening in the future?

Always Check to Make Sure

Regardless of the nature or size of any problem you must solve or decision you must make, apply your perceptive thinking skills to improve the reliability of your thoughts:

THINK PERCEPTIVELY:

Obtain a clear view of reality

Double-check perceptions

Concentrate on crucial facts

Ask penetrating questions

Study both the forest and the trees

Lead with your mind, follow with your heart

Notes to Chapter 1

April Fools

The magazine's solution: "The trout, the fishhook, and the water on the stairway; the stairway running behind the fireplace, an architectural impossibility; the mailbox; the faucet; wallpaper upside down; wallpaper has two designs; the scissors candlestick; silhouettes upside down; bacon and egg on the decorative plate; the April Fool clock; the portraits; ducks in the living room; zebra looking out of the frame; mouse looking out of the mantlepiece; a tire for the rim of the mantlepiece; medicine bottle and glass floating in the air; fork instead of a spoon on the bottle; the old lady's hip pocket; the newspaper in her pocket; her wedding ring on the wrong hand; buttons on the wrong side of her sweater; crown on her head; Stilson wrench for a nutcracker in her hand; skunk on her lap; she is wearing trousers; she has on ice skates; no checkers on the checkerboard; wrong number of squares on the checkerboard; too many fingers on old man's hand; erasers on both ends of his pencil; he is wearing a skirt; he has a bird in his pocket; he is wearing roller skates; he has a hoe for a cane; billfold on string tied to his finger; milkweed growing in room; milk bottle on milkweed; deer under chair; dog's paw on deer; mushrooms; woodpecker pecking chair; buckle on man's slipper; artist's signature in reverse."

Do you now notice things in Rockwell's picture that cause you to wonder: "Why didn't I see that?" Did your ordinary expectations create loopholes in your perceptions?

Sleight of Mind

If you accurately compare the cards in both sets, you will see the second group does not contain any cards from the first. Every card in the first set is missing from the second, including whatever card you had in mind.

Did you fall for the magician's trick? If so, do you see how the magician took advantage of a loophole in your thinking that created an opportunity for him to switch all the cards without you noticing?

A New Kind of Horse Race

Switch riders. That way, your jockey will run your friend's horse at top speed trying to make your horse finish last, and vice versa. Did you catch the crucial fact that your jockey's motivation to lose hampered his ability to win the bet? Missing this crucial fact creates a mental loophole much like that experienced by the auto workers' unions when they matched wits with George Vincent.

Truth vs. Lies

Ask either man, "If I ask the other man the direction to safety, what will he answer?" The truth-teller will tell you the truth, and lie as if he were the liar. The liar will always lie. Thus, you will walk in the direction opposite from that recommended by either man. If you did not think of the correct question, were you distracted by irrelevant facts such as the axe and pitchfork?

Hearts and Stars

Medical Breakthrough

Use multiple, simultaneous, low-intensity beams aimed at the cancer from many directions, intersecting only at the precise tumor site. This way you can concentrate sufficient energy on the malignancy without harming healthy tissue along the way.

If you did not think of a correct solution, are you wondering "Why didn't I think of that?" Most people fail to perceive all the possibilities because they see only one big tree (one X-ray) rather than stepping back to see the possibility of many smaller trees in the forest (multiple X-rays). Did seeing only one powerful X-ray produce a flaw in your thinking?

Last Game of the Season

Coach Dixon stands firm, looks you straight in the eye, and says, "Didn't Josh tell you?"

"Tell me what?" you ask.

"I let him dress for the game," Dixon continues, "but told him he couldn't play because he cut practice yesterday and went to the beach with his friends."

"Did you tell Josh he isn't good enough to carry the water bucket?" you ask sheepishly.

"Of course not," the coach replies. "Josh will play first string next year *if he learns to play by the rules.*"

If you did not see the possibility that Coach Dixon's behavior might be justified, did you allow emotions to flaw your thinking?

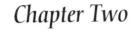

Chapter Two

Why Didn't I Concentrate on That?

Think Deliberately

As Neil Armstrong, Buzz Aldrin, and Mike Collins hurtled through space toward mankind's first small steps on the surface of the Moon in July 1969, I crouched on the other side of the world in an isolated outpost in South Vietnam. I had only recently arrived in-country as an untested, green second lieutenant of artillery. The infantry company to which I was assigned held a strategic hill along an enemy infiltration route leading to the major city of Da Nang. On arrival, I examined the terrain and marked several locations on my map as potential targets on trails the enemy might use to assault our position. That night we sent out several small patrols to guard the pathways and protect the hill from surprise attack. Sometime after midnight my radio operator shook me awake, and together we listened to the muffled whisper of a patrol leader reporting "movement," meaning enemy soldiers might be approaching on the trail guarded by his squad.

Bright pink tracer bullets suddenly streaked rat-a-tat across the night sky. Judging by the huge volume of fire coming our way, the enemy force greatly outnumbered our patrol and might easily overwhelm our main position. I grabbed my map and a flashlight, pinpointed a target close to where I thought the enemy was located, and, without further thought, called for a barrage of heavy mortar shells. Almost immediately a long string of deadly projectiles flew overhead.

While people around the world waited for the far-away words "Eagle has landed," I listened to the thundering boom of high-explosive shells detonating nearby. Immediately after the first rounds struck, I heard the patrol leader yelling over the radio: *"Check fire! Check fire! The rounds are on top of us!"* Instantly halting the ongoing volleys, I could not call back the dozens of rounds already on their way. Having fired unthinkingly in the heat of battle, I could not reverse my hasty decision.

Finally, the last round exploded and, in the wake of its echo, an eerie silence enveloped the scene. My radio operator transmitted the question I dared not ask. "Is everyone okay?" His receiver crackled and hissed unresponsively. "Is everyone okay?" he repeated.

The faint, shaking voice of our patrol leader finally answered, "Affirmative." The bright flashes and loud concussions exploding in the darkness had confused our Marines into thinking the shells were landing on them. Instead, the rounds hit a few meters farther down the trail between the Marines and the approaching enemy. The barrage had panicked the attacking soldiers, who had fled into the night, ending the battle almost as quickly as it had begun.

The next morning I received congratulations for "a job well done," but I knew better. I could just as easily have killed an entire Marine squad in the worst of all battlefield incidents, "friendly fire." As it turned out, when I later examined the battle scene, I discovered the rounds had hit much closer to the Marines than intended. The artillery gunners had apparently made an aiming error and, worse yet, I had mismarked the original target. The combination of both errors, if slightly magnified, could have easily placed the entire barrage on top of our Marines, not only killing them, but blasting open an unobstructed pathway for the enemy to attack our main position.

Looking back on the night before, I could see that I had not properly concentrated on what I might do to protect the Marines short of immediately unleashing a full barrage. The better procedure would have been to fire a couple of test rounds farther down the trail, and open up with full volleys only after adjusting squarely on target, precisely the tactic I had learned in artillery school. I had lost my concentration in the heat of battle, and the lapse nearly proved deadly for the Marines whose lives depended on my good judgment.

Many battles followed in the coming months, some far more frightening than my first encounter that night on the hill. I grew up quickly in Vietnam, more than I realized at the time, and learned to concentrate better in battle, to think before acting. Never again was I forced to look back on a battlefield error and ask, "Why didn't I concentrate on that?"

Mental concentration involves two crucial elements: intensity and focus. Concentration increases thinking intensity and focuses thoughts tightly on the mental task at hand. Sharp thinking requires both. Absent adequate concentration, flaws as dangerous as the one I allowed to occur in Vietnam can form in our thinking, impair our judgment, and ruin our decisions. Accepting full responsibility for our decisions and their results, we must think deliberately in every circumstance, however pressing.

————————————————————————Mental Warm–Ups

The Crystalline Web

Warm up your concentration by finding the five-pointed star in this many faceted shape.

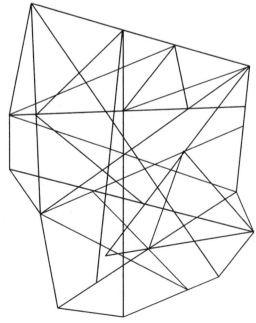

Tangled Hearts

Exercise your concentration by correctly counting the number of white and gray hearts in this tangle.

The Sacrifice

How would you rate your concentration? This life-and-death problem gives you a chance to test it.

You're the engineer on a train out of Chicago bound for St. Louis. The train, filled with more than 150 passengers, averages 80 mph on special high-speed tracks. A railway bridge master checks his pocket watch at noon. "The train from Chicago will be crossing in 15 minutes," he says to his 5-year-old son who is spending the day with his dad in the control shack on top of the massive railway bridge. The center span lifts to allow river barges safe passage underneath. The bridge master keeps the span in the raised position, except when trains cross. An electronic signal from approaching trains prompts him to lower the center span and warn barge traffic not to pass underneath. If he times everything perfectly, high-speed passenger trains cross without ever slowing down.

With 10 minutes remaining, the bridge master lets his boy press the red button that lowers the span. A large electric motor next to the control shack roars into action, and the heavy center span begins slowly lowering into place, as the master peers through the shack window to make sure the operation runs smoothly.

Without warning, the motor loses power and quits just before the span reaches lock-down position. When the motor refuses to restart, the master reaches for his radio handset to warn the approaching train engineer, but the radio will not transmit because all electric power to the bridge has shut down. When the master pushes a button to change track signals to red, the indicator light remains green as he punches the button again and again.

If the master does not quickly lock the span into position, the entire train and its passengers will plunge off the bridge into the river at over 80 mph. Throwing open the control shack door, he scrambles down a rusty steel ladder, grabs the crank of a manually operated winch, and the span responds slowly to his furious cranking. From experience, he realizes that just enough time remains to complete the operation, but when he looks at the point where the upper and lower spans should join, he sees his little boy sitting on top of the heavy steel locking arm. The arm will crush the boy when it snaps into place. The boy had followed his father out of the control shack and now looks away in the direction of the approaching train. When the master yells at his son to climb off the locking mechanism, noise from the creaking bridge span drowns out his voice.

With only seconds remaining to throw the mechanical lever that will drop the locking arm into place, the master starts running to his son, then stops short, realizing he cannot both reach his boy and return to throw the lever and save the train. He can rescue his son, or the train, but not both.

Horrified, he runs back to the manual winch, grabs the lever controlling the locking arm, closes his eyes, and throws the switch. The steel arm drops into position with a heavy thud, and ten seconds later the train roars safely across the bridge. Those on board the train do not know the bridge has malfunctioned and learn only later that their lives have been saved by the tragic sacrifice of a little boy's life.

What would you have done in this situation? Concentrate on all possible options before turning to the Notes for an answer.

DELIBERATE

Concentration of the sort that produces sound judgment, even in emergencies, does not occur by accident. It requires real effort, especially when pressing circumstances seem to demand instant answers. Mahatma Gandhi, the man who led India to independence from Great Britain, showed remarkable determination to concentrate under pressure when his followers had reached their wits' end and it appeared their struggle for freedom might fail.

Gandhi shocked India's pro-independence activists with his belief that nonviolent civil disobedience, more than bullets and bombs, could persuade the British to "walk out of India and go home," and with his insistence on living a simple deliberative life in a mud-brick house among common people. This behavior caused the British to naively dismiss him as weak and indecisive. Britain's Secretary of State for India called Gandhi "pathetic," but the British wholly underestimated their foe.

Political terrorism and labor unrest reached crisis proportions in India during the late 1920s. At first the British appeared willing to negotiate reforms long sought by Indian leaders. Parliament sent a delegation from London to "study" India's political turmoil and make "recommendations." Indians greeted this delegation, the Simon Commission, with open hostility, denouncing it as a transparent ruse. As demonstrators waved black flags in the streets and yelled "Simon, go back," India's leaders defiantly unfurled a new national flag and issued a declaration of independence written by Gandhi. It spoke of "inalienable" rights and powers of the people to "alter or abolish" oppressive governments, phrases echoing those that had earlier stung the British in colonial America. The British had no intention of suffering another Yorktown in Asia or elsewhere. For their part, Indians knew, as did Americans before them, that winning independence from Great Britain would take more than strong words.

Looking back on the situation years later, Jawaharlal Nehru said, "The great question that hung in the air was—how [to make independence a reality]? How were we to begin?" India's leaders discussed many alternatives, some involving violence, but ultimately they looked to Gandhi for a strategy. Offering no quick solutions, Gandhi declared his intention to concentrate on the matter and withdrew to the solitude of his rural home to deliberate.

Calling his deliberation "heart churning," Gandhi focused intensely on the question for many weeks, trying to think of a way to defy British rule without igniting violence. Nothing came to mind. India's activist leaders grew impatient and pleaded with him to come up with something, anything, before the independence movement stalled in its tracks. Advising patience, Gandhi continued deliberating. "I am furiously thinking day and night," he said, "and I do not see any light out of the surrounding darkness."

In early 1930, Gandhi's heart churning eventually produced a breathtakingly simple plan: Stop paying the salt tax. That tax, imposed by the British, who controlled a monopoly on the manufacture and sale of salt, cost a family of four as much as two weeks' wages per year.

How could mere salt topple a government? Neither the nationalist leaders nor the ruling British could comprehend the consequences of such a simple tactic.

On March 12, 1930, at age 61, Mahatma Gandhi set out on a 24-day, 240-mile walk to the sea coast where he intended to gather salt in defiance of British law. Throngs greeted and cheered him everywhere along his route. On arrival at the seaside, Gandhi waited until sunrise, then reached down, removed a pinch of salt from the sand, and lifted it up to signal the start of India's nationwide defiance of British law, which years later resulted in full independence.

It all grew out of one man's deliberation, his intense focus on the problem of independence. Unlike so many activists, who immersed themselves in raucous meetings and demonstrations, Gandhi sought solutions in quiet and solitude. That may seem impossible in today's fast-paced and increasingly noisy world, where rapid-fire thought has become the order of the day. How can you possibly find time for deliberation in a world where fax machines and e-mail make every problem and decision seem so urgent? Then again, given the tremendous potential consequences of even the most simple decision, such as refusing to pay a salt tax, how can you afford *not* to find the time to deliberate important matters?

Effective decision-makers resist pressures to make lightning quick choices because they know that faster does not equal smarter. Habitually "shooting from the hip" may win admiration among gunslingers, but few gunslingers survive the long haul. It's not always easy to slow down the process, however, because other people often misconstrue delay as indecisiveness, as the British did with Gandhi. But concentration, in the form of sustained deliberation, can and does result in sharper thinking. Popular myth holds that Isaac Newton discovered gravity the instant he saw an apple drop from a tree. When asked how he did it, however, Newton replied, "I thought about it all the time." In other words, he deliberated.

In most situations you can find more time for deliberation than you might realize. Pausing to think rarely causes harm, but, given today's "get it to me yesterday" mentality, you must work hard to create that crucial pause. The trick is to make deliberation, and the time it takes to deliberate adequately, a conscious component of every important thinking task. How much deliberation time does the problem or decision require? Does an actual or arbitrary time limit exist? Does that limit allow for sufficient deliberation? If not, what can I do to extend the limit? What risks will I run if I take more time? What might occur if I do not take time to deliberate adequately?

When people pressure you for a snap decision that you believe requires a more deliberate approach:

- Ask them to explain why they need a quick decision.
- Explain to them what might happen if a snap decision proves wrong.
- Ask them to work with you to create adequate deliberation time.

As a judge, I enjoy the luxury of saying to impatient litigants, "I'm going to deliberate for several days before I decide." People accept that because they consider deliberation an important part of my job. Unfortunately, too many people do not consider sustained deliberation a vital part of their own jobs.

After I have heard and seen all the evidence in a case, I take a moment to estimate just how much time I will need to deliberate the matter. Then I reserve that time on my daily calendar in blocks large enough to permit me to make real progress when I turn to the task, and I religiously keep these appointments, just as I do all other appointments.

> ## DELIBERATION
> ### is
> ### an appointment we make with our own minds.

Few of us would embark on an important trip without first making reservations. Sure, we may need to adjust them later, but reservations remain a vital part of the trip. While people rarely fly standby without reservations, many make decisions just that way, expecting to arrive at their mental destinations on a catch-as-catch-can basis. If we permit other priorities to grab the available thinking space, we may end up catching the last thought out of town, the one destined to crash and burn for lack of appropriate deliberation.

Reserving time to think involves more than selecting dates and times. As with most appointments, you need to select the proper location. Some people claim they can think effectively most any place, yet, while "I do my best thinking on the golf course" may hold true for some, most people need a quieter, calmer environment where minds can operate free of distraction. I prefer my judicial chambers. Extraordinary ideas occasionally come to mind when I'm driving my car or strumming my guitar, but my best thoughts emerge most consistently when I'm alone in chambers. My wife, on the other hand, thinks best in our home library surrounded by her favorite books. Some executives maintain a second office where only a select few may intrude. Some think best at their desks. Composer Gustav Mahler built a tiny "composing cottage" on a lakeshore where he worked from early morning until noon. Most people, whatever their roles in life, know which places work best for them. Have you chosen or constructed your equivalent of my judicial chambers or Mahler's cottage, a place that lends itself to sustained deliberation? If not, you should.

The following exercise will likely require you to deliberate for an extended length of time, so you may need to set the problem aside, returning to it from time to time. Most people, however quick-witted, find the exercise enormously challenging. Do *not* allow its difficulty to tempt you into turning to the Notes for the answer rather than finding it on your own. The most lasting and worthwhile thinking lessons occur when we confront and wrestle with problems that at first appear to defy solution.

Mental Aerobics

Chickens and Foxes

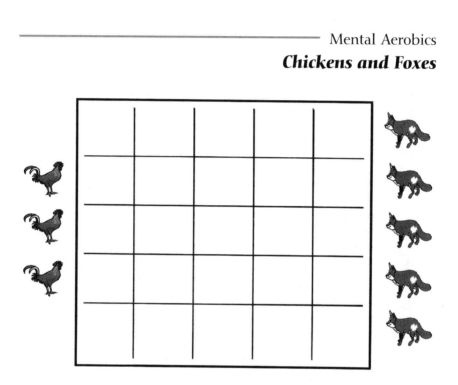

You're a dirt-poor farmer living in the Tennessee hill country. After a ravenous pack of five foxes devours all but three of your small chicken flock, you decide to place all five foxes and your remaining three chickens on a grid so that no fox can reach and eat another chicken. Foxes can move only in straight lines and any number of squares up, down, left, right, and diagonally. Only one animal can occupy a square, and you must place the animals inside squares, not on lines, corners, or outside the grid. Carefully test every solution. Do not compare your answer with the Notes unless you're convinced you have solved the problem. Remember, jumping too quickly to a wrong answer shows a lack of sufficient deliberation.

————————————————————————— Practice Makes Perfect
Deliberately Deliberate

Think of a decision you made in the past that, in retrospect, you wish you had made more deliberately, something you probably would have done differently had you taken more time to think about it. Imagine you now face that same decision without having ever made it and without the benefit of hindsight.

- What will you do to buy more time to deliberate this time around?
- What will you say or do if someone pressures you to speed up the process unnecessarily?
- Where will you do your thinking, and at what times of the day or night?
- How much time will you devote to the process?
- How will you keep your thinking appointments with yourself?

Now, think of an important decision you must make in the near future. Apply the same questions to make sure this decision receives adequate deliberation. Add other questions to the list, such as:

- What might happen if I do not think this through completely?
- What pressures—artificial, real, and imagined—may tempt me to think too quickly?
- How will I prevent these pressures from cutting short my thinking?
- What can I do to make my deliberations an enjoyable experience?

ACCEPT RESPONSIBILITY FOR YOUR THINKING AND ITS RESULTS

As Gandhi proved, responsible people make deliberate choices. Responsibility and deliberation go hand-in-hand. On April 12, 1945, the day President Franklin Roosevelt died, Harry S. Truman raised his right hand and assumed the awesome responsibility of leading the United States in wartime. That same day Secretary of War Henry Stimson met secretly with the new President in the Oval Office to brief him on "S-1," the code name for the atomic bomb, a project hidden from Truman as Vice President. America would soon test what Stimson called "the most terrible weapon ever known in human history" and, if it worked, Truman would need to decide whether to use the weapon in war.

Truman's predecessor, Franklin Roosevelt, had kept the S-1 absolutely secret, even from most top-level military and political advisors. Moreover, scientific and military experts could not guarantee the bomb would even work. Admiral William Leahy, Truman's personal Chief of Staff, called S-1 "the biggest bunk in the world."

Truman quickly appointed a super-secret, all-civilian "Interim Committee on S-1" to help him develop a comprehensive strategy for the new weapon. The Committee's first meeting commenced just two days after Germany surrendered unconditionally to the allies in Europe. Committee members included the presidents of Harvard and M.I.T. For his part, Truman concentrated first on studying conventional, nonnuclear options to end the war with Japan. America and its allies wished for Japan's unconditional surrender, but, since no Japanese fighting unit had ever surrendered on any battlefield for any reason, that seemed unlikely. When the Interim Committee completed its work, it recommended dropping the A-bomb without warning on Japan as soon as possible, shocking the country into surrender.

All this weighed heavily on Truman's mind as he traveled to Potsdam, Germany to meet with Churchill and Stalin to develop strategies for turning the full force of the combined allied armies against Imperial Japan. While at Potsdam, Truman toured nearby Berlin, the world's fourth largest city, which now lay in soot-covered rubble. The smell of open sewers and death hung over the city as Berliners struggled like starving rats to survive among the refuse of war. Truman called it "absolute ruin." At 7:30 P.M. that same evening, Truman received a coded message: "Operated on this morning. Diagnosis not yet complete but results seem satisfactory and already exceed expectations." Earlier that day, while Truman drove through Berlin's rubble, the first atomic bomb had thundered over the desert floor at Alamagordo, New Mexico. America now possessed a weapon that could make the horrors of Berlin pale by comparison, and Truman faced a decision never before or since made by any human being.

Six days after the Alamagordo test, Truman received another encrypted message indicating the military could, if ordered, attempt to drop an atomic weapon on Japan within a few days. The President secretly huddled with his advisors and weighed various options that included detonating a warning explosion offshore or attacking a strategic land target after issuing adequate notice to permit evacuation. However, the Interim Committee's recommendation remained unchanged: Attack without warning. Truman ultimately agreed.

On July 31, 1945, while still at Potsdam, President Truman reached for a simple lead pencil and scratched a cryptic order on the back of a slip of pink message paper. "Suggestions approved. Release when ready. . . ." Seven days later a formation of two lone B-29s flew over Japan and dropped "Little Boy," the first atomic bomb ever used in war. Eighty thousand persons died in seconds as Hiroshima instantly vaporized into a toxic ruin.

Japan's leaders stiffened, resolving to carry on to the bitter end, despite the destruction of one of the country's major cities. Then America dropped its second and *only* remaining A-bomb on Nagasaki. Within 24 hours a thoroughly shaken Emperor Hirohito offered Japan's unconditional surrender, and World War Two came to an abrupt end.

For better or worse, Harry Truman accepted responsibility both for making the decision and for its results. While moral and political controversy still surrounds his choice, few deny Truman's decisiveness. If, as Winston Churchill said, "The price of greatness is responsibility," then Harry Truman stands out as a great American President.

Truman understood a fundamental principle of sharp thinking: Accepting responsibility helps decision-makers and problem-solvers to concentrate fully on making the best possible choices. If you don't feel accountable for the results of your choices, why bother thinking them through at all? When superficial or incomplete thinking produces errors that force us to look back wondering "Why didn't I concentrate on that?" the answer may be "I didn't hold myself fully accountable as I thought it through."

The Navy traditionally removes a ship captain from command if his vessel runs aground, even if the grounding occurs while the captain has temporarily left the bridge and a subordinate officer has assumed command of the helm. At the U.S. Naval Academy, midshipmen learn another version of this rule early in their training. When caught in an error, they must respond with "No excuse, sir!" even though a good excuse might well justify the mistake. At first blush, the "no excuse" rule appears overly harsh. After all, a captain must sleep sometime and novice midshipmen learn by making mistakes. The tradition, however, reaches far beyond a single ship running aground or one midshipman standing tall before an overbearing upperclassman. It reminds all naval officers that they cannot ultimately lay blame on others for the consequences of their decisions, including the choice to delegate responsibilities to others. U.S. Navy officers always remain on the hook.

Many people find it difficult to identify with the strict discipline required of military commanders, but the armed forces must develop leaders who can bring sharp thinking to bear in the most extreme circumstances. The fact that Navy officers cannot point fingers elsewhere provides a potent incentive for them to think matters through completely. Why shouldn't the same hold true in civilian life? Sharp minds do not shun personal responsibility; they welcome it.

As a judge, I may not wrestle with globally significant decisions like the one Harry Truman made, but I'm equally responsible within my own community for the quality and results of my thinking. Fully accepting that responsibility provides the best of all possible incentives for me to concentrate fully on every important thinking task. It will for you as well.

Mature your thinking as you accept full responsibility for the decision required in this exercise.

Mental Aerobics
The German Submarine Fleet

You're the Admiral in command of the German submarine fleet at the beginning of World War Two. You recently lost nearly half your fleet in the period of one month. British warships suddenly appear out of nowhere and attack your submerged U-boats. The British must be operating on more than pure luck, having somehow gained knowledge of the way you position your submarines in the Northern Atlantic for day-to-day operations. From covert sources in London, you learn that British spies have infiltrated German high command, so you launch an intense investigation and soon uncover a high-ranking spy who admits, under interrogation, to passing your super-secret submarine locations to the enemy.

What will you do next, Admiral? The lives of thousands of crewmen and the outcome of a war depend on the quality of your thinking. Accept personal responsibility for your decision and its results to make sure you think through the problem completely.

Practice Makes Perfect

Teach Personal Responsibility to Others

Personal responsibility is a both a skill and a core value, and it can be taught. You're a partner in a management consulting firm specializing in rescuing failing companies. You recently hired an associate straight out of graduate school, easily one of the brightest and most articulate people on your team. Once she gains experience, you're convinced she can someday rise to the very top of the firm. When the associate finishes her first year, you must fill out a written performance evaluation and later meet with her to discuss the results. You complete all but the last block on the form: "Suggested areas for improvement."

Thinking back to your many professional experiences with the associate, you wish that she had more willingly committed herself to definite recommendations and had defended them vigorously. When assigned a consulting issue, the associate generally returns with a list of options, thoroughly analyzed and painstakingly described. At first, her written reports did not contain a "recommended action" section, but you instructed her to add one. The associate's recommendations, however, always hedge. "On the one hand," she might write, "the client could do this. On the other, the client might do that. There are good arguments on either side. The client should carefully evaluate these considerations before making any decision." The associate's advice makes perfect sense, as far as it goes, but she shies away from selecting a particular option and staking her reputation on that. Whenever you instruct her to "make a specific recommendation," she responds as desired, but soon lapses back into the old pattern. When asked why she resists personally taking a stance, the associate says, "I feel I need to defer to your more experienced judgment."

Since you want the associate to do a better job exercising her own judgment, you write a statement to that effect in the "Suggested areas for improvement" block. Tomorrow you will meet personally with her to discuss her performance. You've counseled rookies on issues like this before, and the problem usually boils down to fear of taking personal responsibility. The ladder to success at the firm stands long and high for partners and associates alike. Everyone knows that just one or two serious errors in judgment can cause a person to fall off permanently.

Taking out a sheet of paper, you prepare a list of points you want to make with the associate to help her understand the importance of accepting personal responsibility for recommendations and decisions. Write down at least five points. Arrange them in order of importance from top to bottom. Now, what will you say to the associate during her evaluation session?

Understand Before Judging

While accepting full responsibility upfront opens the doorway to sound decisions, snap judgments can slam it shut prematurely. Never one to blame others for his failures, Henry Ford's original thinking radically altered how Americans lived, worked, produced, and did business. But his thinking gradually narrowed to the point where he judged everything according to his own preconceived notions, however erroneous.

Henry Ford dreamed of making cars available to every American. While competitors remained interested only in building expensive custom cars for the rich, Henry produced affordable standardized cars for working people. His brilliant design, the Model T, was simple, easy to repair, road worthy, light, and highly reliable—the perfect product for its purpose.

In the beginning, teams of craftsmen assembled Model T's one-by-one, one car every twelve and a half hours. Borrowing ideas from other industries such as a Chicago meat factory, where beef moved on overhead trolleys, Ford pioneered moving assembly lines.

He froze the Model T design, refused to allow even minor changes, and concentrated fully on mass-production efficiencies, enthusiastically considering almost any conceivable innovation. As he was fond of saying, "Everything can always be done better than it is being done."

Ford eventually produced one car every ten seconds, with costs dropping dramatically, much like technology products today. Henry passed the savings on to his customers, strategically cutting prices to maximize sales and market penetration. Model T's that originally sold for $780 each ultimately went for a rock-bottom $290. Sales exceeded 15 million cars, all the same color—black—and all with identical features.

Unfortunately, while Henry Ford's manufacturing judgment remained first-rate, his understanding of consumer demand faltered. When the Model T first hit the market, Ford faced no competition, and consumers purchased Henry's cars faster than he could produce them. Then Alfred P. Sloan Jr. entered the market with inexpensive Chevrolets. In contrast to Ford, Sloan concentrated on understanding consumer demand, which inspired him to replace hand cranks with electric starters, add smoother transmissions, and produce cars in a variety of colors and styles. All the while, Henry clung unflinchingly to his outdated judgment that price alone drives consumer demand. Even when consumers abandoned Ford in droves, Henry refused to redesign the Model T. Rather than seeking a better understanding of the marketplace, he stuck to his guns, considering himself a better judge of consumer needs than consumers themselves.

Ford's car dealers pleaded with Henry to upgrade the Model T. He refused. When they asked for just one or two color variations, Henry answered, "You can have them in any color you want, boys, as long as they're black." Once, when Ford's engineers secretly built a modestly changed version of the Model T and presented it to Henry on his return from a European vacation, he circled the car several times, ripped one door off its hinges, then the other, kicked in the windshield, and used his shoe to beat large dents into the roof.

Henry's judgment eventually got the best of him and, with no new models in mind, competition forced him to shut down all his manufacturing plants in despair. Fortunately, Henry's son Edsel had collected design materials behind his father's back, and eventually the Ford Motor Company came back to life with the Model A, but not before Henry's closed mind had needlessly forfeited the company's once dominant position in the American automobile market.

The human mind contains a door, not one carved of wood, but an invisible door, one that either opens to new ideas or closes them out. The door swings on hinges like any other, opening as it searches for understanding and closing as it makes judgments. Herein lies a crucial truth. Sharp thinkers do not take open minds for granted. They concentrate on keeping their minds open long enough to gather all the relevant information needed for making sound judgments. Mediocre thinking begins judging at the outset, and often confuses preconceptions with real understanding. As the old saying goes, "Some people never learn anything because they understand everything too soon."

The mind's door, even those of the greatest thinkers, can open and close seemingly on its own without the slightest conscious nudge. Sharp thinking thus requires intentional *effort* at keeping the door open, especially in trying circumstances where tough problems arise.

Great Britain's most trying time, its darkest hour, occurred in the days following retreat of the British army across the English Channel at Dunkirk during World War Two. France lay defeated at Germany's hands, and England stood alone against Hitler, nearly defenseless to invasion. British troops possessed only a handful of bullets each, and volunteers—trained with broom handles as rifles—were in short supply. Germany torpedoed a British ship with over 3,000 lives lost, an incident not disclosed to the British people until after the war.

Only Prime Minister Winston Churchill knew the full extent of his nation's peril, and his private agony took a heavy emotional toll as he grew increasingly judgmental of well-intentioned ideas offered to help save the day. Seeing this, his wife, Clementine, penned Winston a note that she immediately tore up and decided not to give to her husband. The note read:

My Darling,

I hope you will forgive me if I tell you something that I feel you ought to know. . . . One of the men in your entourage (a devoted friend) has been to me & told me that there is a danger of your being generally disliked by your colleagues & subordinates because of your rough & overbearing manner . . . if an idea is suggested (say at a conference) you are supposed to be so contemptuous that presently no ideas, good or bad, will be forthcoming. . . . My Darling Winston—I must confess that I have noticed a deterioration in your manner; & you are not so kind as you used to be. It is for you to give the Orders & if they are bungled—except for the King, the Archbishop of Canterbury & the Speaker you can sack anyone & everyone. Therefore with this terrific power you must combine urbanity, kindness & if possible Olympic calm. . . . Please forgive your loving devoted & watchful

Clemmie

Four days later, Clementine pieced the note back together and handed it to Winston. History does not record Churchill's response, but shortly after receiving Clementine's note he concentrated on and won the Battle of Britain, giving his country its first victory against Hitler's juggernaut. While the temptation to grow closed-minded and judgmental challenged Churchill throughout his life, he ultimately earned a lasting reputation as a sharp-minded thinker open to innovative ideas. Adolf Hitler's monumentally arrogant, judgmental attitudes, on the other hand, played a leading role in Germany's eventual defeat. No one questioned the Führer to his face. Sharp thinkers, like Churchill, on the other hand, cultivate friends and associates who can comfortably do what Clementine did for her husband, and, given the perils of the moment, for the whole world, too.

The poet William Wordsworth called open-mindedness "the harvest of a quiet eye." The mind's eye responds instantly to mental commands, and forms the gateway through which all understanding must flow. A sharp mind's eye forms *no judgments* about what it sees. Rather, it simply gathers and transmits information accurately to the brain, which, once possessing all the relevant facts about a situation, makes the best possible judgment.

Judges in the first-century Celtic legal system received this charge before taking the bench to hear cases: "Listen with each ear, then render judgment." The Celtic charge contains two separate, yet complementary imperatives. First, use all your faculties when gathering and absorbing information. Do not close down any senses; keep them all open. Second, judge only *after* listening, not during or before. Stephen Covey correctly observes in his insightful book *The 7 Habits of Highly Effective People* that successful individuals, like wise judges, "seek *first* to understand."

Allowing judgment to follow understanding requires patience, and no one ever achieves perfect patience or flawless understanding. Yet, we can come close if we resist the temptation to judge too quickly. Learned Hand, one of America's most respected jurists, called suspending judgment a "painful effort of the will." While withholding judgment, even for an instant, runs counter to human instinct, sharp thinkers strive to consciously override that instinct.

Prior to taking the oath as a judicial officer, I lunched with Bill Masterson, one of California's most highly regarded jurists, hoping to gain his advice about my new duties. He remembered doing the same with one of his favorite judges, who admonished him, "There are only three things a wise judge must do. Be patient. Be patient. And be patient." Ben Franklin, one of the sharpest thinkers of all time, put it this way: "Genius is nothing but a greater aptitude for patience." Patiently delaying judgment generally leads to more fully informed thinking and, over time, earns a reputation for real genius, not the genius measured by IQ, but an intelligence gained through strenuous mental effort.

A potential for impatience accompanies all difficult thinking tasks. Tough situations come with built-in pressures, and a sense of urgency often intensifies the ever-present temptation to jump to conclusions. Why endure the tedium of listening to everything a person has to say when, from the outset, you believe he is mistaken or not telling the truth? Why interview all five persons who saw an incident when the first two agree precisely on what happened? Why waste time listening to opposing points of view when the first argument sounds highly convincing? Why probe deeper when the first idea coming to mind solves the problem?

Mature judgment, like maturity in life, needs time to develop fully. With thinking, the proper growth and development springs from concentration applied in sustained deliberation, which enables and enhances full understanding. Judging too soon, on the other hand, short-circuits thinking, leaving us wondering when things go wrong, "Why didn't I concentrate on that?"

Achieve understanding *before* judging as you consider this problem.

──────────────────────────── Mental Aerobics

The Oracle

You're Croseus, king of Lydia in 547 B.C. The neighboring nation of Persia (now Iran) grows stronger with each passing day, and you fear the Persian army may soon become powerful enough to attack and defeat your country. Schooled in Greek customs, you decide to take your problem to an Oracle for advice. These spiritual mediums, when presented with important questions, consult the gods and return with answers that, although often difficult to decipher, seem to contain real truth. The most famous of all oracles, Pythia, the Delphi Oracle, lives in neighboring Greece. Many believe Pythia speaks for the most powerful of all gods, Apollo.

You send a delegation to ask Pythia whether you should launch a preemptive military strike against Persia's army. When your representatives arrive, they find Pythia sitting on a golden tripod centered over a bottomless pit where no human can physically touch her. Pythia listens to your question, then responds, "Attack Persia and you will destroy a mighty nation."

On hearing the news of Pythia's answer, you assemble your huge army and march toward Persia, where you soon run into Cyrus of Persia and his significantly smaller and less experienced force. An emissary from Cyrus rides up to your lines with a message. "We will not surrender under any terms. If you attack, we will fight to the death."

Although you assume Pythia indeed speaks for the truthful and infallible Apollo, you hesitate. Should you order your army to attack?

Consciously suspend judgment long enough to understand the situation before reaching a judgment.

Practice Makes Perfect

Cultivate Mature Judgments

Hindsight reveals cases when suspending judgment would have spared us from unwelcome consequences. Think of three occasions when you leapt to premature judgments without fully understanding the situation, occasions when the results of your thinking, or lack of it, adversely affected you or others. Select an example in each of the following realms:

1. Your work or profession
2. Your home or family
3. Something not involving work or home

For each occasion, answer these questions:

- What unwanted consequences did my premature judgment produce?
- What caused me to judge prematurely?
- What could I have done at the time to guard against jumping too soon to judgment?
- Having learned from the experience, what specific changes in my thinking habits will I now make to safeguard against future premature judgments?

FOCUS ON DIAGNOSIS BEFORE ATTEMPTING TO CURE

Avoiding snap judgments grows increasingly difficult as pressures mount for quick solutions; yet, as Gandhi proved, pressure signals sharp minds to think with as much deliberation as the situation permits. For Gene Kranz, that signal came through loud and clear on the evening of April 13, 1970 when Apollo 13 astronaut Jack Swigert radioed: "Houston, we've got a problem." Moments before, a thumping shudder had alerted Swigert and his fellow astronauts to a possible problem. Although it sounded like a sticky valve popping open, all three men instinctively sensed the possibility of something far more threatening.

At Mission Control, Engineer George Bliss looked at his monitors and punctuated Swigert's radio message: "We've got more than a problem!" Ground readouts from oxygen tank two, which held half the mission's oxygen supply, indicated flat zero. As pressure readings from the spacecraft's three power-supplying fuel cells plummeted toward zero, the reading for the only remaining cell edged in the same direction, and Apollo 13 teetered at the precipice of catastrophe.

NASA Flight Director Gene Kranz found himself facing one of the most complicated and urgent situations in history. During four long days, he stood in the global spotlight, making one crucial choice after another. His minute-by-minute thinking became a matter of intense interest to people watching live television and listening to radio broadcasts around the world, as the lives of three American astronauts rested on his every thought.

After quickly gathering preliminary information, Kranz ruled out any possibility of faulty data or malfunctioning indicator lights. He briefly considered the possibility of a stray meteor strike on the spacecraft, but ruled that out, too.

The situation became increasingly grave as minutes passed. Oxygen hissed out of the only remaining main tank; the electrical busses controlling all power faded like flashlights slowly dimming on run-down batteries. Apollo 13's mission, and the lives of the three men on board, would end tragically if the cause of the sudden troubles continued to evade Kranz and his Houston team.

Under mounting pressure, Kranz privately gathered his team in a closed, windowless room and urged everyone to "keep cool." Knowing that any mistake could prove fatal, he cautioned the group not to base their thinking on surmise: "Let's solve the problem, but let's not make it any worse by guessing." Despite the gravity of the situation, he refused to allow himself or his team to rush to judgment, and admonished everyone to concentrate on diagnosing the

problem before attempting any cure. "Let's try to see if we can't figure out just what went wrong with this spacecraft in the first place,"
he said. "For the next few days we're going to be coming up with
techniques and maneuvers we've never tried before. I want to make
sure we know what we're doing."

Rapid loss of oxygen and electrical power posed the first problem: How to save enough oxygen and power in the Command
Module for use days later during Earth reentry. Without immediate
action, lack of vital resources would soon transform the Module into
a freezing death chamber. With this in mind, Kranz now exercised
his best judgment: He directed the astronauts to turn off the oxygen
and power in the Command Module, move into the tiny attached
Lunar Excursion Module (LEM), and seal the hatch between the
two vehicles.

With the transfer completed, diagnosis resumed as Kranz confronted a new set of problems created by his initial decision. The
LEM's limited onboard oxygen and electrical power supplies were
designed to last only about two days and support only two astronauts. Now the cramped LEM carried three men who needed to
survive four long days before returning to Earth.

Once he understood this new set of issues, Kranz focused his
team on finding ways to stretch the LEM's resources beyond all
design specifications and to select an optimal flight path to bring
Apollo 13 home before the LEM quit functioning. Kranz ultimately
directed the astronauts to power down the LEM to a level never
before attempted. In the absence of electrical power, the inside temperature of the LEM dropped to near freezing, and the astronauts
struggled to remain alert in the spine-shivering cold. Knowing he
could not help the astronauts stay warm, Kranz left them to cope
with the problem as best they could.

Next, Kranz concentrated on finding the best flight path, the
shortest and safest route back to Earth. He first considered a risky
"direct abort," a maneuver that involved firing the main rocket
motor attached to the Command Module for five shuddering minutes, slowing the spacecraft on its way to the Moon from 25,000
miles per hour to a dead stop, and then propelling it back toward
Earth. If successful, the radical maneuver could return Apollo 13

before the remaining supply of electricity bottomed out, but it involved an enormous risk. Vibrations from firing the rocket motor in this way could tear the craft to pieces.

After weighing risks against benefits, Kranz eliminated the direct abort option. Instead, he settled on a maneuver that used the Moon's gravity to sling the spacecraft back home, a tactic that would send Apollo 13 even farther away from Earth as it circled once behind the Moon and then swung back on a flight path home. This approach, while physically less risky, left the astronauts facing the very real possibility of running short of electrical power before reaching Earth. Still, Kranz considered this their best hope. In the following days, the loop maneuver succeeded and Apollo 13 headed home. The astronauts eventually reentered the Command Module, turned on its dangerously low oxygen and power, separated the Module from the LEM, and prepared to enter the Earth's atmosphere.

Kranz, for his part, continued diagnosing problems to the very end. His last gut-wrenching decision occurred when it appeared Apollo 13 was approaching Earth on an inexact trajectory. Reentering the atmosphere too steeply would incinerate the spacecraft in a ball of fire. If Apollo 13 entered on too shallow a course, it would bounce off Earth's atmosphere and careen into deep space. Lacking sufficient information and any means to fashion a better solution, Kranz made his last carefully deliberated judgment. He ordered his flight controllers not to inform the astronauts of the danger and held his breath as Apollo 13 plunged into Earth's atmosphere. Radio communications with the Command Module shut down during the perilous reentry, and Kranz could only wait to hear if the astronauts survived.

When on Friday, April 17, Apollo 13 splashed down safely into the Pacific Ocean within sight of its recovery ship, the aircraft carrier USS *Iwo Jima,* Mission Commander Jim Lovell turned to his fellow astronauts, Jack Swigert and Fred Haise, and said, "Fellows, we're home." Gene Kranz, on the other hand, lighted a large cigar in Mission Control and smiled with a joy known only to those who accept the full responsibility of life-and-death decisions. His insistence on concentrating first on diagnosis before attempting cures left no doubt that Gene Kranz indeed "knew what he was doing."

Yes, sharp thinking requires concentration, but concentration on what? Concentrating on the wrong information, or indeed on the right information at the wrong time, can cause as many problems as not concentrating at all. When looking back on some of our worst mistakes, asking, "Why didn't I concentrate on that?" we can often see the "that" is "diagnosis" rather than "cure." Anyone who has used a personal computer knows the sinking feeling you get when you have crashed the system blindly punching keys trying to cure an undiagnosed problem. One of my most vivid law school memories involved a similar experience in the days when lawyers performed legal research manually in libraries rather than electronically on computers.

On a hot Friday afternoon in August 1972, I walked into the Tarlton Law Library at the University of Texas Law School to complete a first-year legal research assignment. I held in my hands a written problem that my instructor said would not take more than two hours to research.

As I wandered around the library, trying to find books that might lead me to an answer, I soon became thoroughly lost among the hundreds of thousands of volumes that make up one of the largest law libraries in the world. The smell of musty old books stacked on shelves hidden deep in the library remains an unforgettable memory even today. As I dove into my research, the windows soon turned dark and the library lights flickered on. Students gradually departed, and I eventually sat alone, surrounded by law books piled high on my reading desk. Realizing the project might require hours more to complete, I pulled myself away long enough to call my wife and tell her not to expect me home any time soon.

A janitor turned out the lights at midnight. I waited a few minutes in the darkness, then switched on a small reading lamp, hoping to avoid detection. Although law students were allowed after-hours privileges, I did not want to argue the point with a janitor who might see things differently. One hour led to the next, and, before I knew it, I had spent the entire night reading excerpts from dozens and dozens of books. The sun's rays peeked through the tall windows at dawn and fell on a confused student sitting beneath the gold-framed portraits of some of the greatest lawyers in Texas history. Exhausted and nowhere close to a complete answer, I thought I might never become a lawyer, let alone a great one. Stuffing a pile of disorganized notes into my briefcase, I walked into the brisk morning air and collapsed on a park bench.

After indulging in a few moments of self-pity, and glancing one last time at the assignment sheet, I noticed at the bottom an instruction I had previously dismissed as unimportant. It said: "Write a precise, one-sentence statement of the issue before starting your research." By now I was desperate, willing to try anything. My all-nighter in the library had been a complete waste of time. A few minutes more could not make matters worse. So, I swallowed my pride and tried writing out a sentence. The sentence made absolutely no sense. I tried again. The second effort proved even more obtuse. Was I too tired even to write a simple sentence? Unwilling to give up, I continued to draft and redraft until I finally wrote a sentence that satisfied me.

After coming up with a workable statement that seemed to express the issue coherently, I stumbled back into the library one last time to search for an answer. In less than 15 minutes, my tired eyes landed on a case that solved the problem.

That morning, I learned a lifelong lesson far more important than any answer to a legal question. Diagnosing issues, precisely articulating *real* problems, must always precede any attempt to find solutions. Albert Einstein once said, "The mere formulation of a problem is far more important than its solution." When asked what he would do if he had only one hour to figure out how to save his own life from near certain death, Einstein said he would concentrate 55 minutes on diagnosing the problem and trust the solution to follow easily in the remaining 5 minutes. To find correct solutions, we must first ask the right questions, or answers will remain hidden in a sea of information.

Most people know diagnosis must precede cure, but impatient for a cure, they do not concentrate enough on diagnosis. While this quick-fix mentality may find remedies, it does not always supply the most effective and lasting ones. Superficial diagnosis allows us to remedy symptoms, but often leaves the underlying disease to fester.

Focus on diagnosis, frame the issue, before you try to solve this problem.

Distance, Rate, and Time

You're purchasing a building located in Fort Worth, Texas. You live in Dallas, 35 miles away. When your Fort Worth lawyer calls to say she urgently needs your signature on certain escrow papers, you agree to meet her along the highway between the two cities. You both start driving toward each other at the same time. Your lawyer averages 65 mph; you average 70.

Which car is closer to Dallas at the point where the two vehicles meet?

Diagnose Deeper Problems

While an incorrect diagnosis does not necessarily prevent you from finding a cure, it nearly always excludes finding the best. You're the chief design engineer for a wireless phone manufacturer. A memorandum arrives from quality control alerting you to faulty hinges on the handset of your most profitable line of flip phones. The company has used the same basic hinge design for nearly six years, yet, almost overnight warranty claims have skyrocketed as a result of hinge failures, costing the company hundreds of thousands of dollars and harming its hard-earned reputation for reliability. Entrusting the problem to one of your best designers, you instruct her to fix the problem as soon as possible.

Five days later she reports back, recommending a complete redesign, with a new beefed-up structure at the point where the hinges have been cracking. The fix will definitely prevent all future hinge failures, but the change will require about four months before the first units with strengthened parts arrive in retail stores. In the meantime, the company must either ship products with the problematic hinges or stop making its most profitable line of phones.

You decide to ask a few probing diagnostic questions of your own, as skilled managers often do, to make sure you understand the problem before accepting the cure recommended by your trusted designer. Write down at least five insightful questions before turning to the Notes.

Put It All Together

Now let's apply all you've learned in this chapter to a practical problem.

Give Mature Advice

Your son attends one of the top universities in the nation on a full scholarship. You cannot afford to send him to such a prestigious institution on your income alone. After three years of college, he ranks near the top of his class in pre-med. From early childhood, he's always wanted to become a doctor, and now it appears he can get into any medical school in the country. His teachers all predict a bright future in medicine.

Your son calls one evening in early May and, out of the blue, says he no longer wants to become a doctor. Indeed, he's tired of school and intends to take a year off to think about what he really wants to do with his life. He's coming home in three weeks after his last final and he'd like to talk it over with you. He insists, however, that he's made up his mind. You do not react immediately, but merely say you look forward to seeing him. As soon as you hang up, you walk to your den, open a file drawer, pull out a copy of your son's scholarship agreement, and read that it terminates automatically if he voluntarily misses even one semester or drops out of the pre-med program.

Add to and build on the following questions as you concentrate on how you will advise your son:

- *Deliberate.* What will I do to make sure I think through this matter completely, no matter how obvious the answer may appear at first blush?

- *Accept responsibility for your thinking and its results.* What might happen if I push him too hard to stay in medicine, and later the profession ultimately turns sour for him? On the other hand, what will happen if I acquiesce to his choice without accepting my responsibility as a parent to tell him things he may not want to hear?

- *Understand before judging.* I will feel greatly disappointed if he quits school and loses his scholarship. How can I avoid blaming him as I try to understand why he thinks he wants to quit? How will I prevent my own views of what I think he should be from clouding my understanding of what he wants for himself?
- *Focus on diagnosis before attempting to cure.* He will probably stay in school if I insist. That may achieve a "quick fix," but what will I do to remain open to the possibility of deeper, compelling reasons for him to take a year off, and even quit pre-med?

THINK FOR YOURSELF

Apply what you've learned about deliberative thinking to an actual recurring challenge in your own business or professional life.

Improve the Quality of Your Concentration

Identify *the* most important category of decision you make as part of your business or professional responsibilities, a recurring type of decision you will certainly face again in the future. Apply the lessons learned in this chapter as you prepare a list of at least five specific steps you will take to improve your concentration when making this type of decision.

THINK ABOUT IT

Pause for a while to examine what you've learned about deliberative thinking and how you can apply the lessons to problems and decisions you encounter every day. Ask yourself:

- What circumstances in my life require my most deliberative thinking, and what specific steps will I take in those situations to improve my concentration?
- What pressures and temptations most often prevent me from adequate deliberation, and what will I do to resist them?
- How will I create space in my life for needed concentration on important matters?

- How will I effectively assert my need to think when others demand answers I'm not prepared to give?

- When am I most likely to judge people or circumstances prematurely, and what will I now do to concentrate first on understanding before making judgments about these people and circumstances?

- Why specifically do I sometimes start throwing cures at problems before concentrating on obtaining an accurate diagnosis? How has this impaired my effectiveness on occasion, and what will I do to concentrate, when necessary, on diagnosis before attempting to cure?

ALWAYS CHECK TO MAKE SURE

Make sure you apply your deliberative thinking skills to monitor and improve the quality of your thinking.

THINK DELIBERATELY:

Deliberate

Accept Responsibility for Your Thinking and Its Results

Understand Before Judging

Focus on Diagnosis Before Attempting to Cure

Notes to Chapter 2

The Crystalline Web

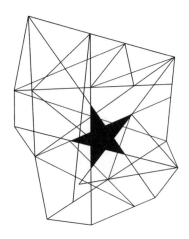

Tangled Hearts

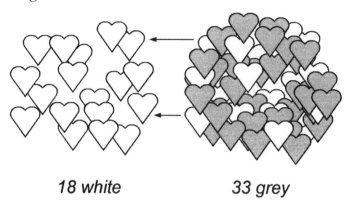

18 white   **33 grey**

The Sacrifice

If you fully concentrated on the problem, you focused on the first three words: "You're the engineer." You cannot do anything to change the situation because no one on board the train, including the engineer, knows the bridge has malfunctioned. Sometimes real concentration reveals tragic circumstances entirely beyond our control.

Chickens and Foxes

Deliberation reveals that placing chickens in the outer squares effectively bars foxes from using certain avenues of approach. The Supplemental Solutions at the end of the book contain the ultimate answer, but *do not* turn there until your deliberations generate a solution you have fully tested and consider correct.

The German Submarine Fleet

Did you consider the possibility that the spy you nabbed may not be the only source of British Intelligence? The German Navy in World War Two faced this exact problem. When they caught not one but several spies, they executed them and assumed this closed the security breach. It did not. The German Navy made the mistake of not concentrating on every conceivable leak. The prime cause of German submarine losses remained hidden in the unthinkable: The British had secretly cracked Germany's ultra-secret naval code. If the Germans had concentrated on the possibility of decryption, they likely would have discovered the breach and used the opportunity to lure British ships into positions of certain destruction. Instead, the Germans renewed their search for spies.

The Oracle

Croseus gave the order to attack and the Persians quickly demolished his army. The Delphi Oracle spoke the truth. A "mighty nation" would be destroyed by the decision to attack: Lydia, Croseus's nation, not Persia. The Oracle did not specify which "mighty nation" would suffer destruction. Croseus failed to concentrate on fully understanding the problem before rushing to judgment. How about you?

Distance, Rate, and Time

If you attempted to calculate the answer using the distance/rate/time formula, you failed to first concentrate on diagnosing the problem. The problem assumes two cars meeting at the same location. With this crucial fact understood, you easily see that both cars are equidistant from Dallas. The two cars could meet anyplace on Earth, yet they would still be the same distance from Dallas. In this instance, as Einstein predicted, accurate diagnosis leads quickly to the correct solution.

Diagnose Deeper Problems

Robert Lutz, President of Chrysler, once encountered a similar situation when he visited his Toledo plant, which manufactured Jeep Cherokees. After several years of near flawless performance, the car's sun visors were now ripping open at the seams soon after shipment to dealers. Lutz learned that a full redesign of the visors was in progress and would require time to complete. The company had to continue shipping cars with defective visors until the redesign could be brought on line.

Rather than focusing on the new design and asking whether it would in fact cure the problem, Lutz asked a straightforward diagnostic question. Why had the visor functioned flawlessly for so many years prior to now? To his surprise, the engineers had not asked this basic question. When they did, at Lutz's urging, they discovered that a tool used by their sun-visor supplier had worn down over the years, and a simple tool repair instantly cured the whole problem.

Does your list of questions relating to flip-phone hinges include: "Why has the hinge defect only recently appeared in newly shipped units?"

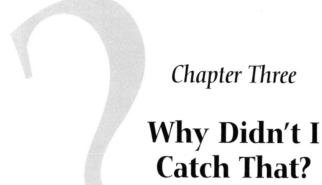

Chapter Three

Why Didn't I
Catch That?

Control the Quality of Your Thinking

President John F. Kennedy set a goal in 1961 for the nation to land a man on the Moon by 1970. His successor, Lyndon Johnson, who as Vice President had helped establish NASA, resolved to achieve Kennedy's goal. As Johnson's presidency progressed, he faced growing political pressures stemming from his handling of the Vietnam war. With his reelection in real jeopardy, Johnson quietly passed the word to NASA to move quickly on the Apollo moon-landing program. The administration and the nation, he reasoned, needed a triumph to counterbalance the ongoing tragedy of Vietnam.

Johnson's strategy, coupled with competition from Russian space successes, drove Apollo's managers and engineers to think and work at near breakneck speed. Quality eroded. Over 20,000 failures occurred during assembly of Spacecraft 012, scheduled to fly as Apollo 1. Worse yet, some engineering work listed as "complete" was *not* actually done in the headlong rush to stay on schedule. Thomas Baron, an Apollo quality-control inspector, stamped the spacecraft "sloppy and unsafe." Rocco Petrone, director of launch operations, called it a "bucket of bolts." Spacecraft manager Joe Shea added, "We hope to God there is no safety [risk] involved in the things that slip through." Astronaut Gus Grissom, who would command Apollo 1, said, "I've got misgivings. We've had problems before, but these have been coming in bushelfuls." Still, NASA continued with plans to launch the craft with a crew of three: Grissom, Ed White, and Roger Chaffee.

On January 27, 1967 the astronauts climbed aboard Spacecraft 012 atop its Saturn rocket booster for a final "all-up" test before the scheduled launch date. As the cabin filled with highly flammable pure oxygen, the crew sealed the escape hatch, which would take over 90 seconds to open in the event of an emergency. Erratic communications between the spacecraft and outside controllers plagued the test from the outset. Hour by hour the number of failures mounted. Eventually an engineer suggested, "Let's cancel out today. . . . We're better off if we shut down and do the full test again." Instead, the team pressed ahead.

Suddenly Ed White shouted "Fire!" Grissom followed with "I've got a fire in the cockpit." An unidentified voice from within the sealed craft yelled "Get us out!" Then a last chilling scream reverberated over the failing communications line, followed by dead silence. Within eight seconds, the lives of three astronauts ended in a ball of smoke and fire fed by pure, pressurized oxygen.

Looking back, astronauts Alan Shepard and Deke Slayton said of the incident: "No one . . . imagined it could happen; dreamed in their worst nightmare that it would happen. Or dared contemplate what was virtually inevitable. . . . NASA engineers had become complacent about the possibility of a fire." Flight Director Chris Kraft added, "It was unforgivable we allowed that accident to happen." The apparent inevitability of the fire left many NASA managers and engineers wondering, "Why didn't I catch that?"

In the wake of the disaster, NASA shut down all flight operations and did not attempt to place another human in space for nearly two years. In that time, the agency redesigned the spacecraft almost from the ground up and conducted a brutally honest, thorough investigation that exposed failures at every level, from shop floor to top management. Taken together, the failures added up to sloppy thinking that sacrificed quality for expediency. To their credit, however, Apollo's engineers and managers learned from their mistakes, held their thinking to much higher standards, and ultimately produced a flight-worthy craft that successfully navigated the vast expanse between Earth and the Moon without further loss of life.

Quality thinking has always required courage, honesty, and determination. In 399 B.C., the 500-member ruling Council of Athens charged one of the city's most unpopular inhabitants with sham offenses and placed him on trial for his life. The accused, a penniless old man clad in threadbare clothing, confronted the Council and suggested they should honor rather than punish him. Outraged, the rulers sentenced the man to death, threw him in prison, and forced him to swallow a bowl of deadly hemlock.

Why did the Council, and many Athenians, so vehemently detest Socrates? He exposed the shabbiness of their thinking. No person, however prominent, escaped the critical scrutiny of the philosopher's sharp mind. His technique, now called the "Socratic Method," remains a model of top quality thinking even today.

Socrates asked questions that challenged people to clarify their thoughts, eliminate inaccuracies, think more comprehensively, make better sense, and achieve intellectually honest results. One of his contemporaries, Meno, likened Socrates's questions to a stingray's barb, a penetrating weapon with equally numbing effects. His probing forced people to reevaluate their thinking, an activity some would rather avoid at all costs.

The high standards demanded by Socrates separated sharp-minded thinking from its dull counterparts. Sharp thinkers ask:

- Is it clear?
- Is it accurate?
- Is it comprehensive?
- Does it make sense?
- Is it intellectually honest?

Run-of-the-mill thinking, like that of many Athenians, fails to apply such vigorous standards, operating something like a production line without established quality controls, and with the same shoddy results. Thus, "Why didn't I catch that?" usually translates into "Why didn't I pay attention to the quality of my thinking?"

This chapter presents five standards sharp thinkers continuously use to monitor and improve the quality of their thinking. The next chapter, using these standards as guides, presents a series of reliable thinking methods that will sharpen your thinking. With this combination of rigorous quality controls and systematic methods, anyone can attain genuinely sharp-minded thinking.

Optical illusions provide vivid metaphors illustrating the need for reliable thinking standards to keep our thinking on track. Observe how this figure appears to bulge its center, warping the two horizontal lines.

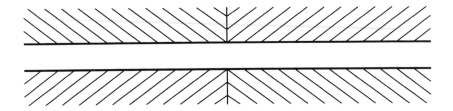

Take a straight edge and slowly move it alongside one of the horizontal lines, observing how the line appears to straighten as the edge nears. Now slowly move the straight edge away and notice how quickly the horizontal line again appears to bend. You need a standard (your straight edge) to keep your thinking straight, and the moment you abandon your standard warping begins.

Warm up your thinking with this exercise.

Mental Warm–Up
Championship Chess

You attend the world chess championships in Oslo, Norway. Your friends cannot imagine spending good money to travel so far only to sit for days watching people think. While your friends do not appreciate the challenges and intricacies of the game, you love to sit and think along with the masters, trying to anticipate their every move.

On returning home, you tell a friend that you watched two grand masters play six matches over the period of one week. No contests were held on Sunday. One master won three matches and the other, four. "How can this be?" your friend asks. Tell her how.

IS IT CLEAR?

Clarity, the first of five sharp-thinking standards, could have saved many lives when Avianca Airlines Flight 52 entered the airspace surrounding New York City with fuel enough to remain airborne for little more than one additional hour. Bad weather and crowded air traffic conditions on the evening of January 25, 1990 forced ground controllers to place Flight 52 in a 15-minute holding pattern, followed by a 27-minute hold, and finally a 46-minute pattern. At this point the cockpit crew informed controllers the plane would run out of fuel before it could reach a suggested alternate airport in Boston and requested a Kennedy landing. Controllers gave Flight 52 priority and placed it in line to land at Kennedy.

During the descent, the captain kept the nose of the plane pointed downward as much as possible to avoid the draining effect that might further deplete precious fuel if the nose remained tilted up at the conventional landing angle. Ground controllers knew Flight 52 was low on fuel, but not how low. Nearing the airport, the captain asked his flight crew, "Can I lower the landing gear yet?" The co-pilot replied, "No, I think it's too early now. If we lower the landing gear, we have to hold a very high nose attitude."

On final approach, an unexpected wind shear suddenly caused Flight 52 to drop 500 feet, setting off an automatic cockpit alarm: *"Whoop whoop, pull up! Whoop whoop, pull up!"* The captain, losing visual contact with the runway, frantically asked other crew members if they could see it. When no one did, he abruptly aborted the landing and headed skyward to circle for another attempt.

"I don't know what happened with the runway, I didn't see it," the captain said. "I didn't see it," said the co-pilot. "I didn't see it," added the flight engineer. The captain instructed the co-pilot to radio ground controllers that he was declaring an "emergency," and the co-pilot broadcast, "We'll try once again. We're running out of fuel." He did not utter the word "emergency" as instructed, a term that would have conveyed the situation more clearly to ground controllers. Later, the captain again instructed the co-pilot, "Advise him [air traffic control] we are emergency!" "Did you tell him?" he asked the co-pilot. "Yes, Sir," answered the co-pilot, "I already advised him."

While the co-pilot may have felt he communicated the situation clearly, he had not and, as a result, traffic controllers continued landing other planes ahead of Flight 52, placing it on a path that would take about 15 minutes to return for a landing. Eventually Flight 52 turned in behind another incoming plane and entered final approach.

"Flame out!" the flight engineer shouted. "Flame out on engine number four. . . . Flame out on engine number three." The whine of jet engines rapidly losing power dominated the cockpit voice recording as all four engines on the Boeing 707 shut down. Within seconds, Flight 52 slammed onto a tiny two-lane road in secluded Cove Neck, Long Island and plowed into a tree line, killing 73 of 158 people on board.

As with most aircraft accidents, many factors combined to cause the crash. At the top of the list in this case would be unclear thinking and unclear communications. The crew never declared a fuel emergency, which would have triggered a much more vigorous response from the ground. At the critical moment when the captain wanted to declare an emergency, the co-pilot failed to clarify the captain's intentions in his communication. Instead, the co-pilot radioed, "We're running out of fuel," apparently assuming ground controllers would take it as declaring a fuel emergency. They did not.

All sharp thinking depends on clarity. Without it, thinking deteriorates into ambiguity and confusion. Just as unclear language leads to miscommunication, so unclear thoughts result in misconception and misjudgment.

You can rigorously test for clarity by applying a series of Socratic questions, which you can ask yourself when wrestling with crucial decisions or perplexing problems. Such inquiries include:

- Does this thinking contain significant ambiguities?
- Is it too vague?
- Is it intelligible?
- Have I clearly defined key terms and concepts?
- Does it need further elaboration?

- Can I better illustrate or explain it?
- Can I depict it graphically?

I routinely test the thinking of others by asking questions or making statements that require clarifying responses, such as:

- What do you mean by this?
- Define this term for me.
- Can you be more specific?
- Give me examples.
- Illustrate your point.
- Can you explain this more clearly?
- Describe this a different way.
- Can you draw me a picture?
- Show me this in graphic form.
- Can you organize and present this more simply?
- Let me repeat this back to make sure I clearly understand what you mean to say.

Questions and statements of this sort, when applied to yourself, people you work with, and those in your private life, can greatly improve thinking quality because the technique provides a real mechanism for monitoring and improving clarity. Practice on yourself, and then try using the technique at work and in your dealings with people in other settings.

Test the clarity of your own thinking with this exercise.

Mental Aerobics
Fine Wine

You and a companion travel to the Napa Valley to sample the fine American wines produced in that region of Northern California. You dine at a local bistro known for serving world-class wines at amazingly reasonable prices. The waiter explains that local vintners often test new selections at the restaurant before marketing their wines nationally and internationally.

With the waiter's help, you choose a full-bodied Cabernet Sauvignon priced at exactly $10 per bottle. The waiter uncorks a bottle and places it on your table to "breathe." Your taste buds anticipate the flavor as you smell the wine's hearty aroma. When the waiter returns, he pours the customary sample into your glass. You roll the wine in your goblet, examining its clarity and color. Then you take a sip. "Wonderful!" you exclaim.

Near the end of the evening, the fun-loving restaurant owner approaches and, after a few minutes of small talk, invites you to answer a question. "If you get it right, I'll give you a case of that Cabernet to take home with you," he offers. Why not? You have nothing to lose. The restauranteur continues, "I produced this Cabernet in my own vineyard and sold it to you at cost. It cost me $9 more to produce the wine than I paid for the bottle. How much did it cost me to produce the wine?"

Remember to require clarity in your thinking just as you would if examining a fine wine.

──────────────────────────────────── Practice Makes Perfect

Find the Right Marriage Partner

This exercise provides an opportunity to clarify your thinking in circumstances where emotions can cloud your best judgment. You've met a wonderfully interesting, exciting, and lovable person, one with whom you can commit to an intimate, life-long relationship. But, one day over lunch, a close friend asks, "Are you thinking clearly about this?"

As you ponder that challenge, you begin asking yourself a series of penetrating questions. Later, at home, you write down the first question that comes to mind: "Have I let my emotions overrule reason?"

Continue the exercise by listing all the questions you can ask that will help you clarify your thinking about this most important person.

Is It Accurate?

While clarity, the first standard, promotes plain thinking, it does not guarantee accuracy, as illustrated by this colloquy taken verbatim from the court reporter's transcript of a real-life drunk-driving trial. The arresting police officer testified on direct examination that the defendant was drunk because he "fumbled around." The defense attorney then cross-examined the officer.

> Q: Now, Officer. You instructed my client to produce his registration certificate, didn't you?
>
> A: Yes.
>
> Q: And he went to the glove compartment to find it, didn't he?
>
> A: Yes.
>
> Q: And it was a large glove compartment, full of papers, right?
>
> A: Yes.
>
> Q: And it would be difficult for anyone, drunk or sober, to find anything in that glove compartment, wouldn't it?
>
> A: Yes.
>
> Q: And my client looked like he was drunk because he "fumbled around"?
>
> A: Yes.
>
> Q: Now, Officer, how could you possibly conclude my client was drunk because he fumbled around in that glove compartment?
>
> A: Because that glove compartment was in *my* patrol car!

Certain he could win the case, the defense attorney made a crucial mistake that quickly produced an unwelcome and surprising outcome. He thought, without double-checking with his client, that the glove compartment was in his client's car. The defense attorney received more accuracy than he bargained for when he challenged the accuracy of the officer's observations.

Accuracy aligns thinking with reality and requires more than just attention to detail. Adding up numbers correctly does not, for example, guarantee accurate results if you have not determined the true significance of the numbers. You could be adding apples and oranges. Complete accuracy exposes reality and discovers truth, both objective and subjective. While reality and truth often remain elusive, sharp minds tenaciously strive for as much accuracy as possible.

Precision and accuracy depend on applying exacting standards and measures. Imagine a carpenter building furniture to precise measurements only to discover later that the foot-long ruler he relied on is only eleven inches long. Just such an error occurred in the building of NASA's space-based Hubble telescope. Placed in orbit by the Space Shuttle in April 1990, Hubble aimed its primary mirror at the cosmos and began returning images to expectant scientists on Earth below. But when the images came back blurred, NASA engineers soon discovered a flaw in the satellite's primary telescopic mirror. While manufacturing engineers had painstakingly ground the 1,820-pound mirror to exact specifications, the instrument used to measure progress of the work consistently had produced inaccurate readings. Engineers had placed so much faith in the "reflective null," as the instrument was called, that they apparently ignored other testing equipment that might have revealed the error. The tiny, but crucial flaw, forced NASA to plan and execute one of the most complicated in-space repairs ever attempted, installing, in effect, corrective lenses on the telescope's eyes.

To avoid making such mistakes, we can use a variety of questions to monitor the accuracy of our own thinking. For instance:

- Does this match reality?
- What assumptions have I made?
- Can my thinking be corroborated, verified, validated, confirmed?
- What sources of error may exist, and what can I do to minimize or eliminate them?

I continuously test the accuracy of others' thinking by asking questions and making statements, such as:

- Can you prove this?
- Be more precise.
- List your assumptions.

- Have you proofread this?
- Show me how you checked your work.
- What did you do to test this?
- Confirm it by some other reliable means.
- Can you find a way to improve the accuracy of this?

Make accuracy your paramount goal as you solve this problem.

Mental Aerobics

The Disappearing Dollar

You're flying home to Chicago for Thanksgiving after a business trip to New York City. A sudden northern blizzard forces the pilot to land in Wichita, Kansas, where you're stuck for the night. When you call a long list of hotels, you discover they're booked solid. A traveling salesman specializing in shower curtain rings who sat next to you on the plane says he knows the owner of a small motel out on the interstate highway.

You and your new companion take a long cab ride to the motel and, sure enough, one cabin remains vacant. You agree to share the cabin, and each of you pays $25. Soon the clerk knocks on your door and hands you and your roommate $1 each, saying he accidentally over-charged for the cabin. The total overcharge was actually $3, but the clerk secretly pockets the $1 balance as a "tip." You and your companion paid $25 each and received back $1—with the refund you each paid $24, for a total of $48. The clerk kept $1.

Where is the missing $1?

Practice Makes Perfect

Think Through Statistical Claims

Accuracy is a hallmark of top-quality news reporting. You're a newspaper reporter in 1936, the year Democrat Franklin Roosevelt ran for President against Republican Alf Landon. A competing paper just scooped your publication with a front-page story reporting the results of a telephone poll that shows people called at random overwhelmingly favor Landon over Roosevelt. You've covered politics for many years, and

your instincts tell you Roosevelt, not Landon, has assumed a commanding lead. You arrange an interview with the pollster, and on the way over
jot down a few questions to test the accuracy of the poll's results. Your
first question reads: "What is the poll's margin of error?" What other
questions will you ask? Remember, real accuracy often involves much
more than simple precision.

Is It Comprehensive?

While clarity and accuracy provide a correct picture, when the focus of
our thoughts becomes misplaced, our thinking can miss the mark
entirely, as illustrated by the Metropolitan Museum of Art art experts
who failed to realize they had a genuine van Gogh on their hands.
William Goetz made enough money in Hollywood to allow him to dab-
ble in expensive art. In the years following World War Two he purchased in Europe a self-portrait by Vincent van Gogh, *Study in
Candlelight*, for about $50,000 and brought it to the United States. A van
Gogh relative later claimed his uncle never painted the work. Goetz,
not wanting to lose the entire investment on one person's word, com-
missioned four experts associated with New York's prestigious
Metropolitan Museum of Art to examine the work. In the end, they
seriously doubted the painting's authenticity for a variety of reasons.

Despite this setback, the ever resourceful Goetz shipped his
painting outside the United States and then reimported it. As
expected, the Customs Service sought to collect a $5,000 tariff
because only original art could come into the country duty-free. As
he had planned all along, Goetz declined to pay the tariff on
grounds the painting was an original van Gogh, thus forcing customs officials to tackle the question of authenticity. On examining
the piece, customs experts spotted Japanese character writing
among the details of the portrait. Treated as unimportant by the
museum experts, these characters contained mistakes identical to
similar errors made by van Gogh in other works of undisputed
authenticity. They proved the Metropolitan's experts wrong!

Looking beyond the superficial, the customs experts peered
deep into the details and then took a broad view, asking whether
those details were consistent with van Gogh's era and life experi-

ence. They examined the whole scene, both the trees and the forest. By thinking both deep and wide, their comprehensive analysis solved the problem. Comprehensive thought, deep and wide thinking, leads to greater wisdom than shallow, narrow thinking. The principle dates back to the beginnings of recorded history.

During his many years as king, Solomon advanced Israel's power and prestige beyond anything the nation achieved either before or since. His reign, beginning in about 970 B.C., remains unexcelled in peace and prosperity. Indeed, his name meant "peace" in Hebrew.

Best remembered for his unrelenting pursuit of wisdom, Solomon authored over 3,000 proverbs, many of which continue to influence thinking today. According to Biblical records, Solomon possessed "great insight, and a breadth of understanding as measureless as the sand on the seashore." Widely admired for his thinking skills, people traveled long distances to obtain Solomon's thoughts.

One event stands out as history's most vivid memory of Solomon's wisdom, his brilliant handling of a dispute between two prostitutes. In Solomon's day, many prostitutes were slaves sold into harlotry by their own parents. By any measure, the two prostitutes who entered Solomon's Court of Justice that day ranked very low on the social ladder. But Solomon personally rendered justice to all his people, no matter their station in life.

The women brought with them two infants, one living and one dead. Each woman claimed to be the rightful mother of the living child. One told the king: "This woman and I live in the same house. I had a baby while she was there with me. The third day after my child was born, this woman also had a baby. We were alone; there was no one in the house but the two of us. During the night this woman's son died because she lay on him. So she got up in the middle of the night and took my son from my side while I was asleep. She put him by her breast and put her dead son by my breast. The next morning, I got up to nurse my son, and he was dead! But when I looked at him closely in the morning light, I saw that it wasn't the son I had borne." The other woman vehemently denied this claim, calling the whole story a lie fabricated to steal her child.

Solomon faced one of the most difficult cases imaginable brought by two disreputable people on utterly contradictory facts.

Neither woman could corroborate her story or prove the other woman a liar. Instead of casting lots to decide this perplexing matter, Solomon looked deep into the motives of the two women in an effort to uncover a clue to the truth. He also took a wider view, considering how genuinely honest mothers would behave in such circumstances. Solomon wrapped his mind around the whole problem.

"Bring me a sword!" the king commanded. "Cut the living child in two and give half to one and half to the other." The Roman historian Josephus reports that people standing nearby openly "laughed" at Solomon's decree. But one of the two women instinctively begged for mercy. "Please, my lord, give her the living baby! Don't kill him!" The other woman only retorted, "Neither I nor you shall have him. Cut him in two!"

With one bold mental stroke, Solomon exposed the deepest motivations of both women and from there inferred the truth. While he could not know truth with absolute certainty, he knew enough to feel certain of his thinking. Solomon gave the baby to the woman who begged for mercy. While no contemporary judge would resort to such a method to discover the truth, we do appreciate the underlying brilliance of Solomon's approach. The Bible says, "When all Israel heard the verdict the king had given, they held him in awe, because they saw he had wisdom from God to administer justice." Solomon's comprehensive thinking, like a mighty river, ran both deep and wide.

The word "comprehensive" shares the same root as "comprehend." To mentally grasp something fully, we must probe the depths, heights, and breadth—the past, present, future, front, back, inside, outside, up, down, all sides. Comprehensive thinking searches beyond the first "right" answer to find the "best" solution. It explores beneath superficial explanations and conventional wisdom, and considers situations individually and as part of a larger whole. It thinks in many directions.

You can achieve the deepest and widest perspectives by asking comprehensive questions. Such questions might include:

- Does this thinking reach the roots of the problem?
- Does it approach the matter from multiple perspectives?
- Does it appreciate possible complexities?

- Does it oversimplify things?
- Have I formed conclusions too soon?
- Is this the best solution?
- What biases might adversely affect this thinking?
- How does this situation interrelate with the broader context in which it occurs?
- Does this thinking exhaust all significant possibilities?

I test the comprehensiveness of others' thinking by asking questions and making statements, such as:

- Give me your insights.
- Let's approach this from a different angle.
- Have you taken too narrow a view?
- What have you done to eliminate or guard against bias here?
- How does this fit into the larger scheme of things?
- Tell me how others view this situation.
- Have you checked with all the stakeholders here?
- Tell me what you've done to try and come up with a better solution than this.

Think comprehensively as you wrap your mind around two riddles created by Lewis Carroll, author of *Alice in Wonderland*.

Mental Aerobics
Untimely Clocks

These two riddles contain four descriptions of inaccurate clocks. Rank the descriptions in order of time-keeping reliability, from best to worst.

- Which is better, a clock that's right once in two years or a clock that's right twice a day?
- Which is better, a clock that loses a minute a day or one that doesn't run at all?

Practice Makes Perfect

Purchase a Dream

This exercise requires your most comprehensive thinking. Your dream house has just come onto the market. The bank will lend you the needed money, but the purchase will stretch your finances to their limits. You've run all the numbers accurately. While your financial prospects look good both now and in the future, a major financial setback might cause you to lose the home. Still, if you do not buy the house now, you may not see another opportunity like this for years to come. You and your spouse want very much to buy the home, and your children can't wait to move into a big new house with a large back yard.

After tucking the children into bed, you and your spouse sit down to discuss the matter. Beyond financial details, you talk about deeper and broader issues to make sure you make the right decision for the right reasons. Your first question is: "What will life be like living in the home of our dreams, but with a heavy debt load on our shoulders?" What other questions might you ask to insure a comprehensive discussion?

DOES IT MAKE SENSE?

Clarity, accuracy, and comprehensiveness are building blocks of sound thinking, but pulling them together requires good sense. Sound thinking by definition makes sense, even though it may at first appear illogical or counterintuitive. When people look back asking, "Why didn't I catch that?" they must sometimes admit they failed to apply this most basic test. It can happen to anyone, regardless of mental prowess or station in life.

Computer scientists have been struggling for years to reproduce the most rudimentary common sense displayed by humans. It is a uniquely human trait. All the argument in the world cannot defeat it. All the analyses and calculations of a hundred mathematicians cannot override it. For most of us it comes rather naturally as we mature and gain experience in the world. When we use it conscientiously, it provides the best safeguard of reason. When it fails, we inevitably make mistakes.

Robert McNamara, Secretary of Defense under President Lyndon Johnson during the Vietnam war, possessed remarkable statistical skills. Few could match his capacity to keep track of millions of minute details. McNamara tried to manage details of the war much as he had run Ford Motor Company when he served as its President. In his new governmental capacity, the numbers he compiled daily all indicated the United States was making progress in the war. North Vietnamese casualties far exceeded those suffered by the U.S. or South Vietnamese armies. While McNamara served as Secretary of Defense, the North retreated after every major battle. But for a long time McNamara, with all his proven management skills, missed one fact that common sense told nearly every American soldier who fought in Vietnam: Many South Vietnamese soldiers lacked the will to fight while the North Vietnamese troops would sacrifice almost anything to win the war. As one historian accurately summed up McNamara's failing: "McNamara's statistics and calculations were of no value at all, because they never contained the fact that if the ratio was ten to one in favor of the government, it still meant nothing, because the one man was willing to fight and die and the ten were not."

To his credit, Secretary McNamara later changed his mind, but by then the U.S. was fully engaged in a tragic war that he had helped escalate. When McNamara voiced his changed thinking to Lyndon Johnson and the President's inner circle conducting the war, he was at first politely ignored, then isolated, and finally forced to resign. Johnson unfortunately insisted on pursuing his chosen course, even though it defied common sense.

Seldom do people consciously abandon common sense. It slips away almost unnoticed as the sly imposter takes center stage before an uncritical audience. The uncritical audience leading to Watergate was the Republican National Committee, and the sly imposter was G. Gordon Liddy. Originally employed by the Nixon reelection campaign to help with "intelligence" activities, Liddy developed and presented a $1 million plan that envisioned: breaking into and wiretapping the Democratic National Headquarters at Watergate; using a Florida yacht to entrap Democrat politicians with prostitutes; and deploying an electronic surveillance plane to snoop on the opposition. When party officials flatly rejected the plan as ridiculous, Liddy carried on undaunted, returning with a scaled down $500,000 version that eliminated the airplane but retained the prostitutes and the break-in. When this version also went down to defeat, Liddy returned with a so-called "modest" plan for $250,000 that involved only break-ins. What followed resulted in the first resignation in American history of a sitting U.S. President, a fiasco that common sense could easily have prevented.

Every person, regardless of IQ, education, or occupation, can fall prey to the sly imposter, especially when passion for results overwhelms reason. Robert McNamara wanted passionately to prevail in Vietnam; the Republican National Committee felt the same way about Richard Nixon's reelection. Sharp-minded thinkers make sure common sense overrides emotion. In the end, when people belatedly ask, "Why didn't I catch that?" they've usually abandoned the sort of logic people gain from ordinary experience and replaced it with unreliable emotions.

When I first took the bench as a judge, my more experienced colleagues told me again and again to use the "smell test." By that they meant a decision might seem right and still not be right. All our specialized training does not make us better judges if we do not test our decisions with common sense.

As a lawyer I first learned the value of the "smell test" when I visited one of my client's-tuna canning plants. As large, gutted fish were removed from cold storage and placed on a conveyor belt headed to the processing facility, a worker leaned down and briefly smelled the inside of the fishes' body cavities. Every now and then he removed a carcass from the line and tossed it away because it did not pass this simple test which relied on the ordinary human nose's ability to detect rotten meat more accurately than any machine. Likewise, my senior judicial colleagues wanted me to understand that a similar smell test remains the fail-safe mechanism that most reliably protects wise judges from issuing ill-conceived decisions that leave them belatedly wondering, "Why didn't I catch that?"

Sharp thinkers, like wise judges, test their thinking to make sure it makes sense, and the testing involves more than just paying lip service to the worn-out statement "I'll think about it." Thoughtful judges, for example, often commit their decisions to writing. A decision that "won't write," as judges say, probably requires significant rethinking. What seems logical in the mind sometimes makes no sense on paper. Illogical thinking produces awkward sentences and tangled paragraphs. Writing aids sensible thinking. The mind often works best in close cooperation with the hand's unique ability to organize and express thoughts. Albert Einstein once said that people could spot him in any crowd by the fact he always carried a pen and paper in hand. Einstein's ever-present writing materials assisted in the discovery of secrets of the Universe that even today appear counterintuitive and illogical, but which make perfect sense when committed to paper and examined, such as $E = MC^2$. The great English thinker John Stewart Mill put it this way: "If you want to know whether you are thinking rightly, put your thoughts into words." If not in writing, then at least vocalize them to a trusted friend or colleague.

You can thoroughly test whether or not common sense supports your own thinking by asking pointed questions during the process, such as:

- Is this plausible?
- Is it consistent?
- Is it credible?
- Is it realistic?
- How will this stand up to reasoned scrutiny?

I test the sensibility of others' thinking by asking these sorts of questions:

- What did you do to test the validity of your reasoning?
- What other logical approaches did you explore?
- What assumptions and inferences did you make to reach this conclusion?
- On what facts do you base your opinions?
- What are the weaknesses of this line of reasoning?
- Give me the best arguments against this conclusion?

Exercise your common sense as you take on the following challenge.

———————————————————————————————— Mental Aerobics

Library Lights

You're spending the night in an English bed and breakfast near Yorkshire. After dinner, you wander into a windowless, oak-paneled library lighted by three bulbs, each connected to its own switch outside the doorway. Your host leads you out of the room, closes the solid oak door, and offers you a challenge.

"I'll let you stay free tonight if you can figure out which switch controls which bulb."

"That's too easy," you say.

"Yes," your host chuckles, "but I'll only allow you to open the door and enter the room one more time. You can flick the switches as much as you want, but I won't let you touch them again after you open the door."

How will you solve the problem? All it takes is a little common sense.

———————————————————————————————— Practice Makes Perfect

Consider Opportunities for Public Service

You've always wanted to devote more time to public service. When the congressional representative from your district announces her retirement, many of your best friends encourage you to run for the office. You privately ask yourself, "Does this make sense?" You choose to write a list of questions you feel you must answer before deciding whether to make the many sacrifices required of those who run for and serve in the U.S. Congress. Your first question is, "Why do I think I want the office?" List other questions designed to reveal whether running for Congress makes sense.

IS IT INTELLECTUALLY HONEST?

Bright minds can construct clear, accurate, comprehensive, sensible thoughts that, while marvels of mental acuity, are just plain *wrong*, wrong because they lack intellectual integrity. Honesty is the glue that holds sound thinking together and makes it not only well-constructed but wise, as Judge Learned Hand demonstrated when he decided one of the most controversial cases handed down during

World War One. A surprisingly large number of Americans opposed the nation's involvement in the war, which they saw as a continuation of long-standing European hatreds they and their ancestors had hoped to escape by emigrating to America. Sometimes boisterous and often vocal opposition to the war prompted Congress to pass the Espionage Act of 1917, criminalizing certain forms of open criticism of the government's war policy.

Enforcement of the new law first targeted *The Masses,* a politically provocative periodical read by 30,000 intellectuals. Its contributors included the renowned poet Carl Sandburg. When the postmaster of New York, Thomas Patten, refused to mail *The Masses,* saying it violated the Espionage Act, the publication sued him in federal court to lift the ban. The case, titled *Masses Publishing Co.* v. *Patten,* was assigned to Judge Learned Hand.

The government justified the postmaster's ban by, among other things, pointing to a *Masses* cartoon captioned "Congress and Big Business." The spoof portrayed businessmen inspecting a document titled "War Plans" with Congress standing on the sidelines asking, "Excuse me, gentlemen, where do I come in?" The businessmen replied, "Run along now! We got through with you when you declared war for us."

Since the Espionage Act made it unlawful for a publication to promote "insubordination" or "refusal of duty," Judge Hand contemplated whether words, such as those used in the cartoon, violated the Act and, if so, whether Congress could constitutionally ban them. Many considered *Masses* v. *Patten* an easy case to decide. Certainly, Judge Hand would quickly dispatch the matter. Hand not only privately and publicly supported the nation's decision to enter the war, as a judge, he also firmly believed that the courts should not second-guess congressional actions such as the Espionage Act. Favoring restraint, he abhorred judicial activism and staunchly opposed what he saw as a growing tendency of some judges to inject their own social preferences into their deliberations.

Intense national attention and political pressure could have swayed Judge Hand to rule in favor of the government. Not only were the lives of American soldiers on the line, but court insiders, and Hand himself, knew he might suffer personally if he blocked the postmaster's ban on mailing *The Masses.* At the time, many considered Learned Hand a leading candidate for elevation to the U.S. Court of Appeals and a possible future nominee to the U.S. Supreme Court. Who in Congress would support his elevation if he ruled in favor of an anti-war magazine and against Congress in wartime?

Most legal scholars at the time believed that the Constitution allowed Congress to prohibit and even punish speech that might lead people to violate any law, something *The Masses'* cartoon might do if it prompted someone to resist the draft. However, Judge Hand disagreed. Banning *The Masses* would render the First Amendment essentially meaningless, he thought. In the end, Hand issued a well-reasoned decision in favor of the publication and blocking enforcement of the Act.

Reaction to Hand's decision proved swift and hostile. The Court of Appeals quickly reversed his ruling, and Hand instantly lost his otherwise near-certain elevation. In the following months the government indicted the editors of *The Masses* for criminal conspiracy but failed to obtain convictions after two trials ended in hung juries. The ordeal succeeded in driving *The Masses* out of business, but Hand's intellectual honesty survived, persuading the U.S. Supreme Court fifty years later to embrace a portion of his original thinking. Hand was ultimately elevated to the Court of Appeals, but not to the U.S. Supreme Court where many believe he would have become one of the greatest judges ever to sit on the nation's highest court. His judicial decisions, still cited in contemporary cases, rank among the most intellectually honest opinions ever produced.

The highest quality thinkers emphasize intellectual honesty, especially in circumstances where powerful forces might tempt them to succumb to a more popular but wrong-headed decision. The pressure can come from almost any direction: an authority figure at work, a friend or family member, an embarrassing situation, social influences, an overwhelming personal desire, or simple everyday stress. If we do not consciously decide to maintain our intellectual integrity in the face of these pressures, both obvious and subtle, we run the risk of unconsciously compromising the quality of our thinking. Such compromises invariably lead to looking back at wrong-headed thinking and wondering, "Why didn't I catch that?"

Intellectually honest thinking values truth and distinguishes between right and wrong. It realizes the difference between fact and opinion. It adheres to its principles regardless of situations, all the while admitting to its own inconsistencies, weaknesses, and faults. It remains willing to change its mind when presented with new facts. It does not cleverly twist words to evade or deceive. Indeed, it punches through deceptions and relentlessly seeks out the truth.

Intellectually honest minds know the difference between shrewd arguments and sound thinking. Articulate people can easily manufacture rational-sounding arguments on most any point, as TV and talk-show personalities demonstrate daily. Some appear to pride themselves more in their ability to *sound* logical than to *be* logical. However, rhetorical ability does not necessarily reflect sound judgment.

Quite often less capable advocates win in court before intellectually honest judges because these judges properly focus on the merits of cases rather than on the slickness of presentations. For that reason, experienced lawyers resist feeling overconfident when facing inferior opponents. Quality thinkers behave like intellectually honest judges, insisting on reality and searching for truth no matter the source.

You can test the intellectual honesty of your own thinking by asking candid questions, such as:

- Am I avoiding issues that must be addressed?
- Does my thinking freely admit its possible faults and flaws?
- Can I detect inconsistencies in this thinking?
- Does this rationalize rather than reason?
- Am I allowing a desired result to divert me from genuinely honest thinking?
- Have I substituted speculation for facts?
- Does my reasoning pretend to deal with issues, which it actually avoids?
- Does it claim to know more than it really does?
- Am I holding myself to the same rigorous standards I demand of others?

I test the intellectual honesty of others' thinking by asking questions and making statements, such as:

- What are the principles on which you base this thinking?
- You may be entirely sincere, but are you right?
- Is this merely an argument rather than a solid fact?
- Tell me the weaknesses here.
- How might someone legitimately discredit this decision?
- Have you exposed these views to vigorous criticism?
- What opposing views did you seek out and consider?

Exercise your own intellectual honesty as you consider this problem.

───────────────────────────────── Mental Aerobics
Discipline with Integrity

Imagine that you head the marketing division of a major company, and you're a prime candidate to become the next CEO. Jennifer Martin is far and away the most trusted and valuable player on your management team. As you begin deciding year-end cash bonuses for managers, you note that Martin's performance numbers appear better than ever, though you don't understand one particular item involving her results. What, you wonder, does this mean?

The next day you receive disturbing news from the company's Chief Financial Officer. Jennifer Martin's numbers have actually fallen, and the error has greatly inflated her bonus potential. Later, one of Martin's subordinates hands you a memo showing Martin herself created the error. When the subordinate pointed out the problem to Martin, she instructed him to disregard it. You call Martin into your office and confront her with the discrepancy.

Jennifer Martin accepts full responsibility, offers no excuses, and promises never to let anything like this happen again. Her straightforward answers convince you this is a one-time flaw in Martin's otherwise outstanding record.

After Jennifer Martin leaves your office, you stand alone, facing a tough decision. Your most trusted and valuable manager manipulated her bonus numbers. Should you fire her? Losing Martin will hurt your division. You almost certainly will never find anyone else as capable as she, and you may lose your shot at CEO if Martin's departure leads to a serious drop in sales. You can cut Martin's bonus to zero and privately or publicly admonish her.

You recall an event six months ago when you personally fired a sales representative caught falsifying data relating to his commissions. After firing the unrepentant man, you wrote a memo to every sales representative warning that "false commission reporting by sales personnel will automatically result in termination." No one would consider Martin "sales personnel," her misreporting does not involve "commissions," and she, unlike the salesman, sincerely regrets her misconduct.

What will you do in Jennifer Martin's case? Ask yourself: "Is my decision intellectually honest?" Do not settle for a simple "yes" or "no." Make sure you can state "why" one way or the other.

Practice Makes Perfect

Handle Embarrassing Mistakes

You're the principal assistant to the head of your company's internal audit division. She wants to become Chief Financial Officer and recently said she will make sure you receive her present job if she moves up, which most insiders believe will occur within the next two years. Your future at the company appears golden.

When you recently completed an audit of the company's asset management system, you discovered several major properties were significantly undervalued. With corrections made to the books, the overall value of the company increases enough to support a large public stock offering. The Board of Directors authorizes an offering, issues a detailed prospectus, and the price of the company's stock skyrockets as the offering hits the market. All key executives, including your boss, will reap huge profits if the offering succeeds.

Your work papers from the asset audit sit on your windowsill for weeks, until you finally decide to file them away. Several papers fall onto the floor in the process, and, as you pick them up, a note in your handwriting catches your eye. "Double-check these figures," it says. Just out of curiosity, you find the figures on your computer and realize for the first time that they do not check out. You spend the remainder of the day and all night frantically searching through mounds of data, and by daylight you're certain that you made an auditing error. Correcting the mistake will significantly lower the company's asset values, severely depress its stock prices, and cause thousands of innocent shareholders to lose millions in investment value.

The chances of your error ever being discovered are remote. Your boss reviewed your work and did not catch it. The company's outside auditors examined the data in preparing the prospectus, and they also failed to catch it. If your error comes to light a lawsuit will almost certainly be brought by investors participating in the public offering, and the outcome could easily bankrupt the company and cause hundreds of employees to lose their jobs.

Decide what you should do with the information you now possess. If you think the answer obvious, consider what might occur if you make a different decision. The Notes do not suggest an answer. Make up your own mind.

PUT IT ALL TOGETHER

Now let's apply everything you've learned in this chapter to a real-life situation.

Pearl Harbor

You're Navy Admiral Husband E. Kimmel, Commander in Chief, Pacific Fleet, headquartered at Pearl Harbor, Hawaii, in December 1941. You receive top-secret decryptions of Japanese High Command radio transmissions indicating that Japan is preparing for major military activity, but the messages do not indicate where or when. A priority dispatch from Washington, D.C., called a "war warning," says that "an aggressive move by Japan is expected within the next few days." At the same time, your chief of intelligence, Captain Edwin T. Layton, informs you the U.S. Navy has lost all contact with Japan's aircraft carriers.

When you ask your top advisors for their thinking on Japan's military intentions, they dismiss an attack on Pearl Harbor for three reasons: (1) Capital ships berthed at Pearl could not be sunk by air-dropped torpedoes because the harbor is only forty feet deep at most, and torpedoes of this type cannot operate in less than sixty feet of water; (2) concentrating U.S. battleships at Pearl effectively immunizes the base from attack, because the fleet at Pearl is so powerful the Japanese will not risk losing their fleet by bringing it within harm's way; and (3) an approaching Japanese armada would be detected in sufficient time to permit the U.S. fleet to maneuver and successfully engage the enemy.

Listening to your most trusted advisors, you silently evaluate the quality of their thinking using five standards:

- Is this clear thinking?
- Is it accurate?
- Is it comprehensive?
- Does it make sense?
- Is it intellectually honest?

Write down your evaluation of each criterion. Give specific examples for each point.

Think for Yourself

Apply all five standards of quality thinking to a problem of personal importance to you.

Tackle Tough Personal Problems

Think of a real-life, nagging personal problem you have thought about but have not yet resolved. Reconsider the problem, consciously applying all five quality standards as you think it through completely. Ask yourself over and over in the process: Am I thinking clearly, accurately, comprehensively, sensibly, and honestly?

Think About It

Pause to consider how you can apply the quality-control standards presented in this chapter to problems and opportunities you encounter every day. Ask yourself:

- What compromises clarity in my thinking, and what will I do about it?

- What types of inaccuracies most often creep into my thinking, and what will I do to guard against them in the future?

- Why do I sometimes address problems from a single viewpoint when I ought to probe from many directions, and what will I do to improve the comprehensiveness of my thinking?

- Why do I sometimes reach conclusions that, in retrospect, defy common sense, and what will I do to reduce the likelihood of this occurring in the future?

- When am I most tempted to be less than entirely honest in my thinking, and what will I do to resist the temptation when it arises?

Always Check to Make Sure

Monitor and improve the quality of your thinking by holding it to the highest standards.

CONTROL THE QUALITY OF YOUR THINKING:

Is It Clear?

Is It Accurate?

Is It Comprehensive?

Does It Make Sense?

Is It Intellectually Honest?

Notes to Chapter 3

Championship Chess

The masters played other opponents, not each other. If you did not catch that, you probably fell for the ambiguity built into the problem and made a false assumption that the masters played against each other. You can significantly improve the quality of your thinking by spotting and clarifying ambiguities.

Fine Wine

You did not think clearly if you jumped to $9 as the solution. The problem hinges on the words "$9 more." The wine in the bottle costs the owner $9.50 to produce: $9.50 is "$9 more" than $.50. If you did not catch the "$9 more" requirement, you did not clearly understand the problem and tried to answer a question not asked.

Find the Right Marriage Partner

Other clarifying questions might include:

- Is this love or infatuation?
- Is this relationship just too good to be true, given what I've learned about people from other relationships?
- Am I not focusing on subtle doubts that I need to more fully explore?
- What does my mind think about what my heart feels?

The Disappearing Dollar

The total cost is $48 ($47 for the room and $1 for the "tip"). You each paid $23.50 for the room and $.50 for the so-called "tip." If your answer turned out wrong, ask, "Was my thinking accurate?" If not, why not? The problem states that you "each paid $24," but does not say what for. You may have inaccurately viewed the $24 as for the room only, and thus treated the tip as something above and beyond the $24.

Think Through Statistical Claims

If you asked "What assumptions did the pollster make?" you have begun to find the loophole that actually existed in the 1936 telephone poll. In those days polling was an infant "science." The 1936 pollsters knew enough to make calls randomly and recorded results precisely, but they incorrectly concluded that Landon would win by a landslide. When election results were counted, Landon carried only two states, and Roosevelt, not Landon, won by a wide margin. The poll, while precise, assumed that a random sampling of people with telephones accurately represented the voting populace. On the contrary, the nation in 1936 was in the throws of economic depression, and only wealthy people, predominately Republicans, could afford phones.

Untimely Clocks

While the clocks described in the first half of each riddle may seem different because of the way Carroll describes them, a comprehensive view of both riddles reveals that the descriptions at the beginning of each fit the same clock, and the descriptions at the end of each riddle fit another single clock. The two riddles are interconnected, as only comprehensive thinking reveals. If a clock loses a minute a day, then it is right once every two years. If a clock does not run, it is right twice a day. Ranking the clocks in order of reliability results in only two categories. As it turns out, a clock in the second category, one that doesn't run, is more likely to tell time perfectly on any given day than a clock that loses only one minute each day. If your solution did not catch the interrelationships among the clock descriptions, ask, "Did I take too narrow a view of the riddles rather than considering them as an interconnected whole?"

Purchase a Dream

Other comprehensive questions might include:

- What is the worst scenario we can envision?
- What other dreams might we need to give up in order to afford this house?
- Are we purchasing this house to impress others?
- Have we considered all other reasonable alternatives?
- What does this particular house possess that we cannot find for less elsewhere?
- If we end up in financial trouble as a result of this purchase, what will that do to our family and our future?

Library Lights

Use your common sense to consider how light bulbs operate. Remember, they give off more than light. They emit heat. Throw on one switch and wait for the bulb to heat up. Then turn that switch off and throw on another. Now go into the room. The lighted bulb is connected to the switch you just turned on, the warm bulb is connected to the switch you just turned off, and the third bulb is connected to the remaining switch. If your proposed solution did not solve the problem, ask, "Did it make sense?" If not, consider why not.

Consider Opportunities for Public Service

Other sensible questions might include:

- What will I do with the office if I win?
- Do my political views make me a viable candidate?
- Do I have any skeletons in the closet that will harm my candidacy?
- Can I raise the money required to fund a competitive campaign?
- Who will volunteer to do the many campaign tasks I will not have time to perform?
- How will this affect my family and career?

Discipline with Integrity

Is your personal desire to be the next CEO a bias with which you need to deal? What about the fact that the terminated sales representative is a man and Jennifer, a woman? Can you treat Martin differently and remain intellectually honest?

Pearl Harbor

- *Is this clear thinking?* My advisors do not possess any clear indication of the Japanese fleet's location or intentions.
- *Is it accurate thinking?* This thinking assumes the Japanese do not possess a technical solution for the problem of dropping torpedoes from the air into less than sixty feet of water.
- *Is it comprehensive?* Concentrating our fleet at Pearl might make it an inviting target to Japanese commanders.
- *Does it make sense?* This thinking does not seriously consider the possibility that the Japanese might evade detection and gain all the military advantages that come with catching us by surprise.
- *Is it intellectually honest?* My advisors do not give the Japanese military any credit for finding creative ways to limit the effectiveness of the assumed superiority of our fleet.

As it turned out, the Japanese solved the torpedo technicality by attaching an ingenious wooden fin to their torpedoes. They correctly calculated that complete surprise could overcome every advantage the U.S. fleet might possess. The U.S. Navy was so utterly convinced the Japanese would not attack Pearl Harbor that it did not seriously prepare for the contingency. As a final proof of the Navy's incredulity, the general air-raid alarm was not sounded on the morning of December 7, 1941 until well after the first Japanese bombs hit and destroyed their targets.

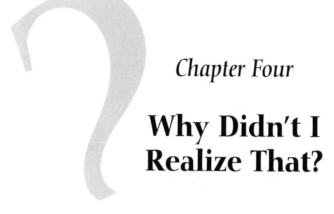

Chapter Four

Why Didn't I
Realize That?

Think Systematically

Scientists discovered in the late 1890s that uranium, a substance then used as a coloring agent in ceramic glazes, emitted invisible rays that left telltale signs on unexposed photographic plates. Fascinated by the penetrating qualities of the beams, similar to X rays, scientists such as Lord Kelvin set out to extract small quantities of uranium from a rocky ore called pitchblende.

An unknown scientist took a different approach when she decided to explore other substances for signs of similar emissions. Marie Curie, working on a shoestring budget, set up a laboratory in a damp, near-freezing brick-and-glass storage room outfitted with dilapidated tables and chairs, using testing apparatus partly made of discarded grocery crates.

Beginning with samples borrowed from friends, Curie systematically examined nearly every element on the then-known periodic table without finding any noteworthy emissions. Some might have stopped here, but not Curie. Instead, she refocused and began exploring the worthless pitchblende remnants left over after better-known scientists had extracted uranium from it. She soon found that the heavy, black pitchblende residue emitted far more active rays than the uranium taken from it. Surprised by this result, Curie double-checked her makeshift testing apparatus and confirmed her readings.

Then she asked, "Does pitchblende contain unknown elements more powerful than uranium and, if so, what are they?" To answer her question, Curie systematically removed as many known elements as possible from the pitchblende residue in an effort to find the source of the rays. As the reduction process continued, she found that the remaining product became more and more powerful, up to 900 times more powerful than uranium. Could a single, as yet unidentified, element be producing these extraordinary emissions? Yes, she concluded, naming that element "radium," Latin for "ray." She called its rays "radiation."

Curie's discovery astonished the scientific world. Radium burned like a fire without end. It apparently violated the first law of thermodynamics by endlessly producing energy without seeming to consume anything in the process. Just one gram could continuously produce nearly 100 calories of heat per hour, a property that ultimately led to the creation of today's nuclear reactors.

Curie next set out to isolate radium in its purest and most potent form. The daunting task involved distilling ten tons of discarded pitchblende. One batch at a time, she repeatedly pulverized, dissolved, filtered, precipitated, and crystallized the substance. The task included boiling material in large cast-iron cauldrons that Curie personally stirred with a heavy iron rod as long as she was tall. In her words: "I had to work with as much as twenty kilograms of material at a time so that [the lab] was filled with great vessels full of precipitates and of liquids. It was exhausting work to move the containers about, to transfer the liquids, and to stir for hours at a time. . . ."

Three years of backbreaking effort eventually produced a fingertip-size quantity of radium weighing one tenth of a gram. Science acknowledged discovery of the new element after its atomic weight was accurately measured in 1902, and, soon afterward, Marie Curie became the first woman to win a Nobel Prize. Her notebooks, preserved in archives today, remain too radioactive for humans to handle without special precautions. Doctors attributed her final illness, aplastic anemia, to prolonged radium exposure.

Marie Curie surprised the scientific world by hypothesizing that what she called radioactivity originated from inside the atom, a property we now call *atomic energy*. Her systematic investigation of radium overturned the existing belief that atoms could not be broken into smaller components, parts containing amazingly vast quantities of hidden energy. Soon Albert Einstein quantified the newly discovered energy with his equation $E = MC^2$, and he later asked rhetorically: "If every gram of material contains this tremendous energy, why did it go so long unnoticed?" He, like others, wondered, "Why didn't I realize that?" His answer: No one ever observed nuclear energy until Marie Curie systematically discovered radium.

By taking the right mental steps in the correct sequence and consciously controlling the quality of her thinking every step of the way, Marie Curie's systematic thinking had revealed an amazing scientific truth. All sharp minds apply some form of systematic thinking to problem-solving and decision-making. Even seemingly creative "free thinkers" use methods, often unique, to control the quality of their thought process. The best structured thinking, however it operates, invariably encompasses two essential components: a *methodology* coupled with *quality controls*.

Systematic thinking produces better results because it brings all our mental talents to bear on problems and opportunities. In its absence, loopholes easily develop that leave even the Einsteins of this world asking in hindsight, "Why didn't I realize that?" The word "realize" in this context means literally to "find truth through the power of reason." While the previous chapter presented standards for controlling the quality of our thinking, this chapter focuses on exercising our power of reason with various reliable, structured thinking methods. The combination of systematic methods and rigorous quality standards consistently produces sharp thinking, not just for brilliant scientists like Marie Curie, but for all of us.

Warm up your systematic thinking with the following exercises.

Mental Warm–Up

Flip Flop

Reverse the triangle to point to the right rather than to the left by changing the position of only three diamonds.

Now try another warm-up, this time thinking systematically as you search for a way to save three lives.

Mental Warm–Up

Survival

You're a bush pilot operating a small two-seat pontoon plane deep in the Alaskan wilderness. As the first winter storm heads toward your summer base camp, you take off for the safety of Fairbanks, many miles away. Flying about 2,000 feet above a wide river, you see three men waving frantically from an opening in the dense vegetation along the river bank. Sensing an emergency, you land and soon learn the men are hunters stranded in the wild after their boat sank nearly two months earlier. The men, named Art Boyle, Jess Dunn, and Sully McClean, say they had nearly given up all hope of rescue before winter set in.

After you tell the hunters you can fly only one man at a time back to safety in your small plane, you ask who will go first. The three begin arguing vehemently. Boyle suddenly picks up a heavy stick and almost strikes Dunn before you intervene. As Boyle drops the stick, Dunn grabs an axe handle and heads for McClean. Two months alone in the wilderness have turned these three hunters into near savages. Boyle shouts he will kill Dunn if he ever gets a chance, and Dunn threatens to do the same to McClean.

As snowflakes begin falling lightly, you realize you must immediately start flying the men back to your base camp where you and the group can weather the approaching storm. You cannot possibly reach Fairbanks and return with a rescue party in time to save the group.

How can you fly all three, one at a time, to your base camp without any dying at the hands of another? How should you sequence your passengers? Those you leave behind must remain free to defend themselves against the wild as they wait for your return. You saw a hungry grizzly bear roaming upriver as you landed. Boyle will kill Dunn if left with him, Dunn will likewise kill McClean, but McClean will not harm either Boyle or Dunn. Think systematically as you figure out how to rescue all three men.

A METHOD BEHIND EVERY MASTERPIECE

Although we do not realize it at the time, learning to think systematically is an important reason we attend school, and all our teachers cover the subject, not just those teaching science and math. As a schoolboy in London, England, I found myself stuck in an art appreciation course that I saw as a complete waste of time. Our teacher took us on endless field trips to galleries filled with paintings she called "masterpieces." To me they just looked like pretty "pictures." Back in the classroom, she propped a blank canvas on an easel, squirted various oil tints onto a wooden pallet, held up a slender brush, and asked, "How do you think the masters did it?" Big deal, I thought. Dip the brush into the paint and slosh it onto the canvas. But she considered the task far more complicated. "You've got to start with an *idea*," she said, "something you see with your mind and want to make real."

My perceptive teacher went on to explain that no artist reproduces perfectly what we see with our eyes. I accepted that, but argued that a really "good" painting should closely match reality. "No," she insisted, "good paintings create new realities. Artists start with something in mind, then come up with a way to make it real." To illustrate the point, she held up an attractive portrait she had recently completed and asked what we thought lay underneath the surface of the fresh paint. "Canvas," the class answered in a chorus. "Yes," she responded, "but there's something much more valuable than canvas under there, something *between* the canvas and the

paint." No one had a clue what she meant, so she handed us a photograph taken of a charcoal sketch drawn on the canvas before she
started applying paint to her portrait in oils.

Over the next few weeks our art teacher, who now had our
attention, showed us many techniques the masters had used to
transform ideas into reality. Some made numerous sketches on separate slips of paper; others sketched directly on canvas; some drew
with charcoal; others with light oil; and some began with no sketch
at all. But in every case, the artists formulated plans before dipping
brushes into paint.

Sharp minds work like great artists. They never wander aimlessly through important thinking projects but, rather, envision the
steps they will take in order to think matters through completely.
They sketch the thinking process, even if the blueprint remains only
in their minds.

A sharp-minded Chief Executive Officer, for example, leans
back in her chair, alone in her office, and tangles with hard realities.
The facts appear obvious. Her Florida subsidiary has been hemor-
rhaging red ink. Unless it spends a fortune redesigning and retooling
its product line, mounting competition will crush it. On the other
hand, the Florida workforce is highly skilled, motivated, and loyal.
While the CEO can lay hands on sufficient capital to make changes,
she sees little margin for error. The odds of success? Less than fifty-
fifty. Potential profits? Huge. What should she do? Call it quits and cut
losses *or* move ahead and develop the new product line?

Reaching for her pen, the CEO takes out a blank notepad.
Several hours later, the pad remains empty, save for a few meaningless doodles. One question dominates her thinking: "How should I
think this matter through?" That central issue sparks several more
questions:

- What specific steps must I take to make sure I think this through
  completely?
- In what sequence should I perform the steps?
- How much time should I allow for each step and the whole
  process?

- What resources, human and otherwise, will I invest in making this decision?
- What information do I need, and how can I efficiently gather it?
- Which other persons should I involve?
- What documents must I gather and review?

The CEO answers these questions and asks even more until she feels she has sketched out her thought process in sufficient detail to provide a roadmap to the best solution. Sharp thinkers, like this CEO, think systematically from start to finish, performing the right mental steps in the right sequence. They take command of situations by immediately assessing circumstances, setting goals, and establishing priorities, just as Gene Kranz did when the Apollo 13 mission suddenly shifted from landing on the Moon to finding a way safely back home. They invest quality time early in planning the whole process. They realize plans may change, but each project possesses a definite structure and direction even in the most topsy-turvy circumstances.

In *Alice in Wonderland,* Alice asks the Cheshire Cat for directions. "Where are you going?" the Cat inquires. "I don't really know," Alice answers. "Well," offers the Cat, "I suppose then any road will do." But when you've set your course toward sound thinking, you want to map out just the right route: the right mental steps taken in the right order.

Use a systematic approach to think your way through this exercise.

Mental Aerobics

The Near-Perfect Game

You're a cub reporter recently assigned to the sports desk at a major newspaper. When the lead reporter takes a summer vacation, you must write your first column describing this afternoon's baseball game lost by the home team 0–4. Your brief description reads:

Billy Yamata, the hottest pitcher in baseball today, squared off against only 27 hitters and struck them all out 1-2-3, a feat never before achieved by any pitcher in baseball history. Fans watched breathlessly as batter after batter failed even to make contact with Yamata's fastballs. Strong to the end, Yamata's last pitch for the home team was clocked at 101 mph. The stadium erupted as Billy bounded off the mound surrounded by his teammates, but the excitement ended on a bittersweet note, because the home team had lost the game 0–4.

The phone rings as you turn off your computer for the evening. The newspaper's Editor-in-Chief growls on the line: "I've seen lame columns in my career, but this wins the prize. Either you rewrite it before tonight's deadline, explaining how the home team lost that game, or you're fired."

The sound of the crusty editor's handset slamming on its receiver still rings in your ear as you switch on your computer and begin to rewrite the story. What will you write?

SYSTEMATIC METHODS

Let's look at a variety of different systematic methods that, when combined with the quality controls (clarity, accuracy, comprehensiveness, sensibility, intellectual honesty) learned in the previous chapter, can produce sharp-minded results in most any thinking situation. The methods are:

- Start with what you know is true.
- Connect it up.
- Weigh pros and cons.
- Consider the odds.
- Pursue the critical path.

START WITH WHAT YOU KNOW IS TRUE

I vividly remember my first nonjury civil trial, not because the case was unique, but because it taught me how best to uncover truth and find facts in a mass of confused evidence. After hearing all the testimony and the closing arguments of the opposing lawyers in a medical malpractice case, I went into chambers with a stack of carefully taken notes and all the documents introduced into evidence. The defendant doctor had insisted he warned the plaintiff patient of possible allergic reactions involved with taking a medication he prescribed, and his chart contained an entry in his handwriting saying "Explained possible complications." The patient, who nearly died from an allergic reaction to the medication, testified she had not been cautioned about the possibility.

I expected a decision to come quickly as I reviewed my notes. It did not. Instead, the evidence was completely contradictory, with everything twisted in circles and tangled together in tight knots. Witnesses on opposite sides testified differently on every important point. The harder I tried to see the forest, the more I became lost in the trees. The deeper I went into the woods, the more I became tempted to flee by calling it a draw and deciding for the defendant, who wins when the facts are evenly divided.

That night at home I remembered my high school algebra teacher, a man raised in the deep South who spoke with a heavy southern drawl. When students approached him after class asking for "help" (that is, the *answers* to particularly hard problems), he would reply, "Ah cain't hep ya if ya don't hep ya'self. Start with whatcha know." He made us recite the facts of problems, singling out what we thought most important, and, somehow, almost miraculously, the solution often came quickly to mind. Of course, our teacher had simply taught us how to think more systematically. Why not, I thought, apply my algebra teacher's method to this perplexing case? There had to be a key somewhere, one I could use to unlock the truth. Thinking about that key, I gradually realized that, up to now, I had not consciously thought about exactly where to start, trusting instead a hit-and-miss approach leading nowhere. I needed to start in the right place, then journey back into the forest one careful step at a time.

The next day in chambers I compiled a short list of significant facts that seemed undeniably true. Searching among them, I found several that appeared particularly important. Ten years earlier, the patient had almost died from an allergic reaction to a bee sting. The incident occurred while she was living in another state where she had a different doctor. The plaintiff and defendant both agreed she never told him of her allergy to bee stings. She claimed he never asked.

"Given these truths, what else must be true?" I wondered. People rarely hide life-threatening allergies from their doctors. Since the defendant doctor admittedly did not know about the bee-sting allergy, he may not have raised the general subject of allergic reactions with his patient before giving her the medication. But what about the "Explained possible complications" entry on the doctor's chart? A photocopy of the chart had been entered into evidence during trial. I now asked for the original and, sure enough, the color of ink used to make the crucial entry was slightly different from that used to make other entries concerning the office visit involved. The notation had been added as an afterthought, likely after the patient suffered an allergic reaction to the medication prescribed by the doctor. I awarded judgment to the patient.

This first experience in finding truth, repeated countless times over the years, taught me a valuable thinking method. Proceed from the known, however small, to the unknown, however large. Huge doors often turn on small hinges. How often have you allowed nagging, difficult problems to remain unsolved for too long, thinking to yourself, "I just don't know where to begin." When this happens, remind yourself to search out the right starting point. That point is truth.

Each year I teach trial practice to students at two local law schools. Cross-examination remains the most difficult skill my students must learn in their quest to become effective trial lawyers. Time and again students flounder when confronted by skilled liars. Effective cross-examination exposes liars in open court, but the task requires far more effort than portrayed in the movies or on TV. Seasoned trial lawyers develop a knack for sensing when a person may be lying. "But how can we sense it?" my students ask. "It's like fishing for albacore," I reply.

Albacore is the expensive "white meat" tuna you buy in supermarket cans. Sport fishing for albacore off the coast of California involves an all-night trip by boat to locations where the wily fish school. On my first excursion, the fish nearly outsmarted me, but a skilled fisherman, who felt sorry for me, showed me how to catch the critters. First, he helped me place a live, wiggly, six-inch sardine on my hook. Next, he showed me how to lower the sardine into the water and let out my line to the point where I could no longer see the little fish. At this depth, an approaching albacore could not see me either.

My skilled instructor reached for the line running from the tip of my pole into the water and placed the thin strand in my hand.

"Hold it gently between your thumb and index finger," he said. "Can you feel anything?"

"No," I answered.

"Good," he went on, "that means the sardine's calm. Now, when you feel the line jiggle slightly in your fingertips, that means the sardine's getting nervous, and sardines get jittery when they see albacore. When you feel a nervous twitch, give the line a yank. An albacore's swallowing your sardine."

"But, how do I know it's an albacore, and how do I know just when he's taking the bait?" I asked.

"When you know that," the man replied, "you'll be a real fisherman."

Sure enough, my line jiggled, I gave it a yank, and I caught one of the fattest albacore landed that day.

"What does catching liars have to do with all this?" my students ask.

"Well," I say, "pay close attention to your witness, and when you sense him starting to twitch, hit hard with a few barbed questions, and you might just catch a big fat lie."

Experienced albacore fishermen and seasoned trial lawyers have at least one skill in common: They start with something they know is true, in this case a wiggle, and use it to solve the larger problem of catching a wily fish or crafty liar. Beyond this, only practice makes perfect.

Start with what you know is true as you systematically solve the following mystery. Remember to think clearly, accurately, comprehensively, sensibly, and honestly.

—————————————————————————————— Mental Aerobics

Midnight Murder

You're a rookie on the local police department's homicide squad. The phone rings in the middle of the night reporting a possible murder of the wealthiest person in town. When you arrive at his home around 3 A.M., you meet your highly experienced partner, Detective Holmes, who leads you to the upstairs master suite where you see Doyle Grimes lying face up in bed with a foot-long butcher's knife buried in his heart.

The only other person home that night, the wealthy man's butler, indicates he was sleeping soundly in his quarters at the other end of the house and heard nothing until awakened by his master's electric call bell at 2 A.M. Responding to the call, he discovered Grimes lying dead in bed. Since the dead man's finger still rests on the button next to his bed, you assume that summoning his butler was Grimes's last living act.

The victim's son and daughter arrive while you search the house for clues. They will inherit the man's entire fortune. Neither appears overly upset by what has happened. Grimes made so many enemies during his lifetime that even his own children find it hard to grieve. As you talk to the son and daughter, a Doberman suddenly charges out of a basket in the master suite and begins barking madly at the son and daughter. The butler grabs the dog by his collar and pulls him away.

The son tells you he visited his father earlier in the evening, departing before midnight. The butler escorted him to the front door and set the alarm as the son left. The patrol officer who later responded to the butler's 911 call says he found the alarm still set when he arrived. You check all the doors and windows and find them closed and securely fastened. You learn, however, that unlike the daughter, the son possesses a key to the front door and knows how to disengage the alarm before entering.

A forensic team finds no fingerprints on the knife. When your partner offhandedly points to a small hole in the wall of the master bedroom asking "What's that?" the son answers: "It's a pinhole for a security camera." You quickly find the system console and remove a videotape that you and your partner insert into a player and begin watching. Numbers on the running tape show it was actively recording in the bedroom throughout the night of the crime. Unfortunately, the camera did not take in the bed or record sound and only showed a large basket in a corner of the room where the dog slept soundly without disturbance.

Detective Holmes smiles and says in a low voice, "Well, Watson,"—your name is Watson—"I think we have our killer." "We do?" you respond quizzically. "Why don't you slip a pair of handcuffs on the butler?" Holmes instructs. As you do that, the butler mutters, "How'd you know?"

Holmes details his reasoning on the way back to the police station. "Elementary, my dear Watson," he says. "I started with what I knew was true, and went from there." How do you think Holmes figured out that the butler did it?

Practice Makes Perfect

Make Sense of Contradictory Facts

Imagine you decide to attend law school. On the first day of your course on evidence, an intruder suddenly bursts into the classroom and dashes to the front. He scrawls something on the board and erases it, mutters incoherently, takes items out of his pockets and returns them, speaks wildly to the professor and a few students, and then runs out as abruptly as he came in. The whole event lasts no more than five minutes. You and the other students fall back in your chairs, wide-eyed and stunned.

The professor grins a knowing smile. She picks three students and sends them out into the hallway with instructions not to talk to anyone else until asked to return. One by one she calls the three back and instructs them to describe everything they saw and heard during the intrusion. A volunteer records the observations on the board. The three try hard to remember. No student wants to look stupid in front of the whole class. None of the stories match. One student recalls the intruder wanted the professor to change a test grade. Another recalls only a request to retake a test. One remembers the intruder writing "Let's party tonight" on the board. Another recalls the words "Let's study tonight." Not one remembers the whole incident. All fail to agree on virtually every detail.

The professor instructs you and the class to take out a blank sheet of paper and write, as best you can, exactly what occurred, bearing in mind what you saw and heard, plus the observations of the three students recorded on the board.

How will you decide what to write down?

Connect It Up

Not only must you start in the right place to think efficiently, you must also chart a mental path that ultimately leads to sound choices and correct solutions. In the popular 1970s movie and television series *The Paper Chase*, Professor Charles W. Kingsfield Jr. of Harvard Law School gruffly orders students to stand and recite the pathways they charted in finding their solutions to tough legal questions. Understandably, students rise hesitantly, hands shaking, voices trembling before a crusty professor obviously in command of every facet of the facts and law involved. The students prove no match for Kingsfield. Time and again they jump to wrong conclusions, failing to see vital connections between key facts and the law. Hollywood did not invent this painful scene. Every day, in classrooms across the nation, law students struggle with the daunting task of mastering their cases, and law professors demand that students fully digest the pertinent facts and law before discussing the meaning of any given judicial decision. As one of my first-year professors once snapped, "I refuse to joust with unarmed persons."

Professor Kingsfield taught Harvard's course on contracts to first-year law students. My own first-year contracts professor was Robert Hamilton, who, on the first day of class, walked in several minutes late holding a large piece of cardboard. On it he had fastened snapshots of every student in the class arranged in the form of a seating chart. Laying the chart on top of his desk, Hamilton opened his textbook to our first assigned case and remarked, "I assume everyone read the materials." Running his index finger slowly across his chart, he matched a photo with a face in class, called out the student's name and instructed, "Give us the facts, please."

Although the student recited the facts as best he could remember, Hamilton appeared dissatisfied. Pinpointing another student on his chart, he called her name, and commanded, "Complete the facts, please." This student remembered a few more facts, but soon ran out of anything new to add. Hamilton then called on another student, and another. Soon no one, including me, could say anything but "I can't think of anything more."

Finally, Professor Hamilton smiled wryly and launched into his own enthralling recitation. The case came alive, wholly unlike the lifeless words written on the pages of our book. When Hamilton finished, I felt connected with the people and events involved. I understood not only what happened, but felt I might know why. The jumbled mass of facts and law in my head now fit together as a coherent whole.

At the end of his recitation Professor Hamilton paused and gently stroked his full beard, possibly reflecting on the long road ahead for our class. Then he broke the silence, explaining that every case we would study in the coming year involved real people with real legal problems. Before we could ever hope to appreciate the significance of a case, we must work hard to understand the interrelationships among the people, their problems, and the legal principles that applied to the situation. In short, Hamilton wanted us to "connect it up," starting with small bits of knowledge and methodically assembling them to form a larger coherent whole.

Another Professor, Sir Isaac Newton, used the same skill when he proved that a strange force associated with the mass of objects holds the entire universe together. Newton's genius, like Galileo's, and many others before and after, sprang from his capacity to make connections among facts and concepts that at first appear unrelated. What, for example, connects the Moon orbiting Earth with an apple falling from a tree? Before Newton, no one knew or even thought to ask that question. Now we know that what feels like "weight" is actually gravitational attraction between two masses. Neither the Moon nor an apple, studied in insolation, reveals gravity, but taken together they expose a deep, fundamental truth about the entire Universe and how it operates, a truth revealed only by systematic thinking that makes sound connections.

We all learned in school how to "analyze" problems, the craft of breaking things apart to examine individual pieces (the literal meaning of the word "analysis.") The strategy works well in many settings, but not where relationships and interconnections matter most. "No man is an island entire to itself; every man is a part of the whole," wrote poet John Donne. The verse applies not only to humanity, but equally well to how humanity must view and think about the world of problem-solving and decision-making. To succeed at these tasks, we must learn how to "connect it up" as well as how to take it apart with analysis.

Can you make all the right connections as you ponder these exercises?

Long-Distance Thinking

Prior to the 1950s, long-distance calls required human operators to make the necessary connections. Area codes, introduced in the mid-1950s, substantially reduced the cost of calls by effectively eliminating long-distance operators. Looking back, it appears that the phone company assigned area codes randomly. New York City, for example, received 212; Chicago, 312; Los Angeles, 213; Hawaii, 808. However, the phone company actually used logic to assign these area codes. Can you figure it out?

Deal with Group Dynamics

Think of a current situation in which you must work with three or more people, all with differing interests and views, to solve a problem or accomplish a goal. Perhaps you're thinking about changing certain procedures at work. Maybe you're involved in a family dispute. Make sure you select a situation that requires you to consider how multiple individuals interrelate with each other.

Begin with a blank sheet of paper and write the names of the key individuals at different locations on the sheet. Draw a large circle around each name; then, within each circle, list that person's relevant interests and views. Starting with the first circle, draw a line to another circle and consider how these two individuals will interreact on the matter in question. Write your thoughts on the line between the two circles. Continue connecting circles this way until you feel you have exhausted all important connections.

With a different color pen, write down a proposed solution for the problem or task you have in mind. Write inside the prior circles and on

the lines how you believe the individuals and group will react to the solution. Continue the process until you find a solution that works best in
light of all the interests, views, interrelationships, and interactions you've
identified and considered.

WEIGH PROS AND CONS

Making all the right connections does not always lead to correct
solutions because the importance of individual connections differ.
We must evaluate the worth of each factor individually *and* as part
of the larger whole, as Benjamin Franklin demonstrated with a system he called "prudential algebra."

Benjamin Franklin did far more than fly kites in electrical
storms. Widely applauded as one of the great philosophers of his
day, both in America and abroad, he does not fit the stereotype of a
philosopher–recluse cloistered among his books, lost in abstract
thought. Franklin's thinking originated in the "Age of Reason." He
insisted, as did his contemporaries, on systematic reasoning. When
Franklin demonstrated with his kite the electrical properties of
lightning, some contemporaries undoubtedly wondered, "Why
didn't I realize that?"

Franklin developed a favorite method of thinking, which he
used most impressively in 1787 as a delegate to the nation's
Constitutional Convention in Philadelphia. All went well at first as
the delegates worked on what ultimately became the United States
Constitution. Within several weeks, however, a deep rift developed
between representatives of the large and small states. States with
smaller populations, such as Connecticut and Delaware, feared that
larger states would overwhelm their interests if representatives in
Congress were elected in proportion to population. Larger states,
such as Virginia with 420,000 inhabitants, considered it unfair to
give a state such as Delaware, with a population of 37,000, an identical number of votes. The more the delegates discussed the issue,
the wider the gap grew. Soon it appeared the whole Convention
would collapse under the weight of this one question.

Ben Franklin, who had remained remarkably quiet up to this
point, rose to the occasion. First he proposed that all remaining ses-

sions begin with prayer, something that had not occurred until then. All agreed. Having brought the delegates together on the common ground of cooperative prayer, Franklin made a speech that squarely framed the crucial political issues dividing the Convention. "The diversity of opinions turns on two points," he said. "If a proportional representation takes place, the small states contend that their liberties will be in danger. If an equality of votes is to be put in its place, the large states say their money will be in danger." All agreed Franklin had hit the nail on the head.

At Franklin's urging, the Convention formed a special committee with one delegate from each state to address the seemingly intractable problem. Ben Franklin served as Pennsylvania's delegate on the committee. Following several days of heated debate, Franklin made a motion in committee that broke the deadlock, and the committee later recommended Franklin's motion to the full Convention, which adopted what we now call the "Great Compromise." The U.S. government would include two legislative bodies: a Senate with equal representation from each state and a House with representation proportional to population. Only the House of Representatives would possess the power to initiate bills raising or spending money. The Senate could vote on money bills, but not amend them.

On September 17, 1787 Ben Franklin made the most stirring of all speeches at the Convention, urging every delegate to sign the completed Constitution, saying, "There are several parts of this Constitution which I do not at present approve . . . [but] . . . The opinions I have had of its errors I sacrifice to the public good." After weighing the many pros and cons on each side, Franklin said he believed the new Constitution provided the best government on which the delegates could agree. All signed.

History proved Franklin's balanced reasoning brilliant. The United States Constitution remains today the most highly regarded political instrument of all time. Its pros, as Franklin concluded, outweigh its cons. While this may seem obvious today, it certainly did not in 1787.

Ben Franklin's remarkable systematic thinking skills had won respect in both America and Europe long before 1787. Fifteen years before the Constitutional Convention, Franklin described his pro-and-con method in a letter to Joseph Priestly, the British scientist who discovered oxygen. In it Franklin said that sound thinking begins with finding ways to hold entire problems in the mind long enough to think them through completely. He customarily deliberated for several days. During that time he kept the whole matter at the front of his consciousness, constantly weighing pros and cons and reducing the field of issues down to those of greatest importance before making a final choice.

London, September 19, 1772

Dear Sir,

When those difficult cases occur, they are difficult, chiefly because while we have them under consideration, all the reasons pro and con are not present to the mind at the same time; but sometimes one set present themselves, and at other times another, the first being out of sight. Hence the various purposes or inclinations that alternatively prevail, and the uncertainty that perplexes us.

To get over this, my way is to divide half a sheet of paper by a line into two columns; writing over the one Pro, and over the other Con. Then, during the three or four days' consideration, I put down under the different heads short hints of the different motives, that at different times occur to me, for or against the measure. When I have thus got them all together in one view, I endeavor to estimate their respective weights; and where I find two, one on each side, that seem equal, I strike them both out. If I find a reason pro equal to some two reasons con, I strike out the three. If I judge some two reasons con, equal to some three reasons pro, I strike out the five; and thus proceeding I find at length where the balance lies; and if, after a day or two of further consideration, nothing new that is of importance occurs on either side, I come to a determination accordingly.

And, though the weight of reasons cannot be taken with the precision of algebraic quantities, yet when each is thus considered, separately and comparatively, and the whole lies before me, I think I can judge better, and am less liable to make a rash step, and in fact I have found great advantage from this kind of equation, in what may be called moral or prudential algebra.

Wishing sincerely that you may determine for the best, I am ever, my dear friend, yours affectionately.

B. Franklin

Ben Franklin called his pro-and-con system "prudential algebra," in which "prudential" means gaining insight through the exercise of reason. Not incidentally, we use the word juris*prudence* to describe the process of sound judicial thinking.

Ben Franklin's prudential algebra offers a sound method of systematic thinking even in today's complex world. Some call it "cost and benefit analysis." Regardless of what you name it, the process requires reasoned judgment using a scale held in the mind's hand. A single major cost can tip the scale against any number of less important benefits and *vice versa*. When balancing the scales, we do not simply count the number of pros and cons, but weigh the relative importance of each. As Franklin made clear in his letter to Priestly, we find the correct balance only when "all the reasons pro and con are . . . present to the mind at the same time. . . ."

Identify and weigh the pros and cons as you make up your mind in this tough situation.

─────────────────────────────────── Mental Aerobics

A Spicy Problem

You're the president of an up and coming spice company with several products distributed nationally. Two FBI agents visit your office requesting an immediate private meeting. They show you an anonymous handwritten note in which the writer claims to have purchased bottles of your powdered cinnamon in Seattle, mixed the contents with a deadly and tasteless poison, and then returned the bottles to an undisclosed supermarket shelf. Have you, the agents ask, received any reports of illnesses or poisonings associated with your cinnamon? No, you haven't. The agents tell you that similar claims of food adulterations, not reported in the press, have occurred in Seattle and, in every case, the anonymous writers were bluffing. Nevertheless, can you provide a list of all stores in the Seattle area that carry your product? Of course. After the agents depart, you quickly convene a meeting of your key advisors to discuss the situation. During the meeting, a member of the customer relations department dashes into the room with an anonymous note claiming that poisoned cinnamon bottles have been placed on the shelves of three unspecified grocery stores scattered around the country. The handwriting on this note matches that on the one the FBI showed you.

Since you distribute your product to tens of thousands of outlets nationwide, from small convenience stores to huge supermarkets, a total recall will cost many millions of dollars and might bankrupt the company. Adverse publicity alone could ruin the growing brand's reputation, not just for cinnamon, but all spices. No consumer has been harmed yet, and only the FBI, your company, and the anonymous writer know about the situation.

Is the letter writer bluffing? Should you order a total nationwide recall? Do not jump too quickly to any particular conclusion. Write out the pros and cons, balancing them as Ben Franklin would do.

Practice Makes Perfect
Make Crucial Career Choices

You're a senior manager in a top accounting firm, one step away from becoming an equity partner. A client unexpectedly offers you a chief financial officer's job at double your present salary. If you stay with your firm and make partner, you will eventually earn more money than you can as a corporate CFO. But if you accept the offer and later advance to company president, your earnings will far exceed anything an accountant makes. Less than half of senior managers make partner. On the other hand, CFOs rarely advance to presidencies. You love to spend time with your spouse and young children, and your current position places heavy demands on your time, far more than you anticipate with the CFO job. Still, you enjoy your present position and love working with the exacting details of professional accountancy. As a CFO, you would be less involved with technical accounting issues and more focused on management duties, which you consider burdensome.

Will you accept the CFO position? Writing down pros and cons, you quickly realize that you need to ask yourself some tough questions about what belongs on the pro and con sides of the ledger. For example: "Am I thinking about changing jobs for the wrong reason, such as running away from a difficult problem I need to stay and solve?" What other questions might you ask to develop a meaningful list of pros and cons?

CONSIDER THE ODDS

Weighing pros and cons involves more than simply balancing the relative importance of various factors and outcomes. We must also correctly judge the probability that these will or will not occur. Since every decision contains elements of risk, those who understand the odds generally make the best bets, and vice versa, as I observed one evening at a blackjack table in Laughlin, Nevada.

Following a long day of boating on the Colorado River that runs through Laughlin, I went to my hotel room, cleaned up, and walked downstairs to the casino for a few hands of blackjack before dinner with my wife. I know just enough about counting cards in single-deck blackjack to pose a danger to myself and anyone who mimics my bets. Blackjack odds change as the dealer passes out cards and then returns them to the discard pile. Highly skilled players bet small sums when the odds run against them and boost their bets when the odds shift in their favor. The trick is to somehow know the odds.

Sometimes players sitting next to me make the mistake of thinking I know how to consistently calculate the fluctuating odds. On this particular occasion, just such a person sat beside me and placed several tall stacks of $100 chips on the table. He broke even on his own for a while, but then started copying my betting patterns after he noticed I had won more dollars than he had. When I upped my bet from $5 to $10, he increased his from $100 to $200. In the next few minutes his stack of chips grew by as much as $5,000. Then the bottom dropped out, and we both lost a long string of hands.

Up to now my neighbor had not said a word to me. Eventually, however, he broke the silence with "Look's like we've got some catching up to do. I'm down a thousand." I don't remember what I said in response, but I wondered what he meant by "catching up." I soon found out. He started betting $500 every hand. Lucky at first, he won a few hands when the odds were obviously against him. The dealer smiled as the man tipped him for the good fortune, but I saw something less complimentary behind the dealer's grin. He was amused by the high roller's foolishness. Over time the man lost more hands than he won, but a few miraculous wins against all odds fueled his enthusiasm for higher bets, even though his stack of chips steadily diminished.

As the man counted his chips between hands, he muttered "gotta get back to even." When that did not happen, he asked the pit boss to raise the table limit so he could place even larger bets. The pit boss happily obliged. When the man ran out of chips, he bought more with cash from his wallet. Next, he asked a companion standing behind him to bring a bag down from his room. From that bag he pulled out bank-wrapped packages of large bills and bought more and more chips, all the while upping his bets even higher, saying, "I've lost so many hands, my luck's *gotta* turn around."

When the man eventually ran out of money, he called the pit boss over and said, "How about upgrading my room for the night? That's the least the hotel can do." The pit boss said he would "check into it," and the man stood up from the table empty-handed. As he turned to leave, I heard his companion say, "We just lost a ton of money." About then my wife came up, I put my chips in my pocket, and we went to the casino restaurant for an enjoyable meal.

This unlucky gambler fell victim to one of the worst errors the human mind can make. He mistakenly believed his odds of winning increased each time he lost another hand. In his own words: "I've lost so many hands, my luck's *gotta* turn around." If this man flipped a coin and saw heads five times in a row, he would conclude the odds of flipping a tail on the next try had increased. In reality, the odds remain the same on each flip, no matter what has occurred before. Blackjack odds change as cards are dealt and discarded, then instantly return to favor the casino the moment the dealer picks up the discards and reshuffles the whole deck, which, as might be expected, occurred frequently while the high roller played at my table.

To win consistently at blackjack, you must use a system that correctly accounts for the odds. The same holds true for all decisions and problems involving costs and benefits.

Fully consider the odds as you solve this problem.

Let's Make a Deal

On a visit to California you decide to attend a taping of the television game show *Let's Make a Deal*. The host, Monty Hall, picks you out of the audience as a contestant, shows you three large doors, and says a Rolls Royce hides behind one door and two goats behind the others. Impulsively, you choose Number 2. Telling you the car is worth $200,000, Hall opens Door Number 1 to reveal a goat with a long fuzzy beard. Hall then asks if you want to keep Number 2 or switch to Number 3 before he opens both doors to see if you win the car. You think about the choice while the audience shouts out suggestions, and Monty prompts you for a quick answer.

Should you switch to Door Number 3? Avoid giving a seemingly easy answer. Concentrate on your odds. You can win a Rolls Royce. Earn it with your mind rather than letting pure chance, and crowd mentality, determine your fate.

Make Your Best Bet

Think of a current problem in your life that involves risk and money: a tempting, speculative investment opportunity, or maybe a business strategy you're thinking of recommending to your boss. Perhaps you think you've found a chance of a lifetime, but can't decide whether to take it. On the other hand, your business may be in trouble, and you need to decide whether to carry on or quit.

Make a list of pros and cons associated with the choice. Place the pros in the order of relative importance, from top to bottom, and do the same for the cons.

Now, estimate the odds that each pro and con will occur.

Once you've written down the odds for each pro and con element, weigh the elements, taking into account not only their relative importance, but the odds that each will or will not occur.

PURSUE THE CRITICAL PATH

The relative importance and odds of various considerations do not always point directly to a correct answer, especially when problems are nested within problems. To achieve the best overall solution in these situations, you must decide which problem to solve first, second, and so on.

In my first litigation assignment, I had the good fortune to work with a wise thinker named Gordon Hampton, one of the founders of the law firm where I eventually became a partner. After spending a good hour describing the details of a very complicated case, Gordon instructed me to "frame the issues" and gave me several days to accomplish the task.

The next morning I walked into his office ahead of schedule and proudly presented my list of issues. Glancing at my ten items, Gordon graciously handed them back with an understanding smile. I was not the first rookie lawyer trained by Gordon Hampton nor would I be the last. "Too many," he said without further elaboration. I took another stab at it and the next day arrived at his office with three issues. This time, Gordon looked at my list with some approval, although he reworded my statements and penciled in a fourth issue.

Gordon then handed the completed list to me, saying, "There, I think we've covered all the bases." Relieved to finish the project, I stood to walk out of the office. "Wait," he said, "we're not finished. Now comes the most important part." Gordon reached for the list, leaned back in his chair, and looked the document over from top to bottom. After several minutes of intense thinking, he removed an old pair of long-bladed scissors from his top drawer and cut the page into four pieces. He then asked me to piece our list back together with the issues in the most useful sequence. "We'll start at the top of the list," he said. "Don't change anything without checking first with me."

When Gordon Hampton had scissored the issues and asked me to put them back together, I'd assumed he wanted them arranged in logical order from top to bottom. However, I soon discovered he had something else in mind: He wanted me to *sequence* the issues strategically in the order they should be litigated. Gordon rearranged my order and placed the most crucial issue *last* in sequence. It was what lawyers call a "case breaker," an issue he frankly wanted to delay, one that spelled certain defeat if lost. Gordon wanted to go after easier-to-win and less risky preliminary matters first in an effort to avoid letting the outcome of the case turn on the harder-to-win, more difficult issues. His sequencing made perfect sense once his strategy came clear. As in warfare, smart generals pick their fights so that the sequence of engagements provides the critical path to ultimate victory. In this way, they can loose a few battles and still win the war.

The written sequence Gordon and I completed became our strategic map throughout the remainder of the case. Although it required revision from time to time, the document served as one of our most effective management tools in litigating the case to a successful conclusion.

Complex thinking tasks such as Gordon and I faced often involve multiple interrelated problems. Sequencing them correctly requires careful consideration of the urgency, gravity, and logical fit of each, something Gordon spent many years teaching me how to do well.

Decisions on a single issue can open and close doors leading to others. Computer programmers call these "logical gates." The first logical gate confronting Apollo 13 involved the Command Module. Gene Kranz had only 15 short minutes in which to decide whether and how to power down the Module. If he failed at the outset to solve that pivotal problem correctly, his subsequent options would have been reduced to a series of extremely unpleasant and sad efforts at comforting three courageous men in the final moments of their lives. Knowing which problem to solve first spelled the difference between life and death.

Look for the critical path as you think through this exercise.

Mental Aerobics
Trains and Planes

Planes did not travel much faster than trains in the early days of aviation. You're the pilot of one of the first biplanes, flying across the desert by the "seat of your pants." Since your plane lacks navigational instruments, you must find your way using landmarks on the ground. You're following a railroad track that runs straight across the Mojave desert from Needles to Barstow, California. The instant you pass over a train going in your direction, another train exactly 200 miles away is moving toward you on a parallel track. One train is moving at 60 mph, the other is chugging along at 40 mph and your ground speed is 120 mph. How many miles will you fly between now and when the two trains meet?

Practice Makes Perfect
Establish Top Priorities

One of history's all-time great thinkers, Plato, used a triangle to establish and sequence goals and priorities. Draw a large triangle on a sheet of paper, with the point at the top of the sheet.

Focus on some part of your life where goals and priorities mean a lot, such as your job, profession, or business. List at the bottom of the triangle five or more goals you most want to achieve in this realm. Be specific. For instance, instead of writing "I want to feel satisfied with my work," list specific items you want to accomplish so that you can feel satisfied, such as, "I want to close a certain deal." Take time to prepare a well-considered, comprehensive list. Once you complete the bottom-line list, decide which of the items you consider more vital than others. Write the group you've selected higher in the triangle. Repeat the process until, in the end, you write only one item at the very top.

You have now identified your most important goal and given it top priority. From now on, when you make decisions, think with your identified top goal squarely in mind. Always consider how the specific problem at hand may or may not affect achievement of your most vital objective.

Now, work downward in the triangle sequencing lesser goals and priorities. Consider how you will achieve these lesser items in light of the higher priorities you've listed above them.

Put It All Together

Apply the lessons of this chapter to this intensely practical problem.

Make Tough Budget Cuts

Focus on either your personal or business budget. Quickly estimate your total expenses for the past 12 months. Imagine that your
income for the coming 12 months will be 25 percent less than your
expenses for the same period last year. Assume you cannot draw on
any alternative resources, such as savings or borrowing, and you must
somehow cut basic expenses by 25 percent. If the 25 percent goal does
not force you to make hard choices involving real sacrifice, increase
the percentage.

Use a systematic method to decide what expenses you will trim
or eliminate. Identify all potential cuts. Establish priorities. Weigh the
pros and cons of each cut. Consider cuts individually and together as
a whole—connect them up. Pursue the critical path from cut to cut
until you achieve your goal. Do not settle for the first possible solution. Continue thinking until you find the best answer. Remember to
keep your thinking clear, accurate, comprehensive, sensible, and
intellectually honest.

When you complete the exercise, ask yourself whether you
should indeed make one or more of the identified cuts in real life,
not just hypothetically. If that requires further thought, use a systematic method to achieve the sharpest possible thinking in making
your real-life decision.

Think for Yourself

Use all you've learned in this chapter to deal with a real-life situation.

Make Decisions Systematically

Think of an important problem or decision you now face at
work or home involving *people*.

1. Select a systematic method learned in this chapter or elsewhere to solve the problem or make the decision.

2. Write down the steps of your process before beginning to think through the problem or decision.

3. As you complete each step, *stop* and consciously evaluate the quality of your thinking for: *Clarity, Accuracy, Comprehensiveness, Sensibility,* and *Intellectual Honesty.*

THINK ABOUT IT

Pause for a while to examine what you've learned about systematic thinking and how you can apply these methods to problems and decisions you encounter every day. Ask yourself:

- What systematic methods do I most often use to think through problems and opportunities, and what methods will I use in the future?

- Do I consistently plan my important thinking projects at the outset?

- Do I need to become more systematic in my thinking and, if so, how will I better structure my thinking in the future?

- Do I monitor the quality of my systematic thinking to assure clarity, accuracy, comprehensiveness, sensibility, and intellectual honesty, and, if not, what will I do to correct the situation?

ALWAYS CHECK TO MAKE SURE

Make sure there is a method behind all your thinking masterpieces. *THINK SYSTEMATICALLY:*

Start With What You Know Is True

Connect It Up

Weigh Pros and Cons

Consider the Odds

Pursue the Critical Path

Notes to Chapter 4

Flip Flop

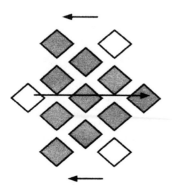

Survival

Fly Dunn to base camp, then return for Boyle. Take Boyle to camp, leave him there, pick up Dunn, and return with him to McClean. Drop off Dunn, fly McClean to camp, leave him with Boyle, then return alone for Dunn and fly him to safety.

The Near-Perfect Game

Billy did not open the game. Arturo Capistrano started for the home team and pitched the worst game of his career, allowing home runs on the first four pitches he threw. Billy came in as a relief pitcher in the first inning and proceeded to throw his perfect game, but the home team never managed to score a single run in support of Billy's amazing feat.

Midnight Murder

The dog paid no attention to the murderer. Only the butler and the son apparently had an opportunity to commit the crime. The dog dislikes the son and would likely have been aroused by the son's presence in Grimes's bedroom. Not so with the butler, who appears to get along with the dog. Grimes may have seen his murderer and placed his finger on the call button as a way of pointing police to the killer. The butler may have adjusted the camera so he would not appear on tape as he entered the room to commit the murder, never thinking that pointing the camera toward the dog would give him away. Any similarities between this exercise and Arthur Conan Doyle's *Hound of the Baskervilles* is entirely intentional!

Make Sense of Contradictory Facts

This demonstration, often performed in beginning evidence classes, shows that human beings do not see, hear, or remember events the same. Honest testimony always comes with rough edges, sometimes very rough. No one owns a flawless memory, and innocent misrecollection occurs quite often. Only one truly accurate version of the staged classroom incident exists, but it can elude even the sharpest mind.

How will you begin to decide what actually occurred? If you start by comparing and contrasting what the three students say, you can quickly bog down in irreconcilable contradictions. Instead, start with what *you* know. You witnessed the scene yourself. Write down your recollections before considering conflicting memories of the other students. You know the strengths and weaknesses of your memory better than you do the memories of others. How well were you paying attention? Your personal knowledge and self-understanding, while imperfect, will supply a base with which you can eliminate many items not in substantial controversy and then move to the more difficult conflicts. The base you build may provide crucial clues for deciding among the significant disagreements. *Where* you start thinking can make a big difference in whether you end up at the correct destination.

Long-Distance Thinking

Touch-tone dialing only became widespread in the 1960s and 1970s. Until then, phone users dialed rotary disks, a task more time-consuming than punching buttons, especially when dialing the higher numbers. Lower digits require less time for the rotor to return to the starting position so that a user can dial the next digit. The phone company assigned the faster-dialing numbers to highly populated metropolitan areas such as New York City (212) and Los Angeles (213), while tiny Hawaii received (808).

A Spicy Problem

When listing pros and cons, you may find more reasons *not* to order the recall. For instance, making the situation public could invite copycat crimes and even prompt an otherwise bluffing person to carry out the crime for real. But, in weighing pros and cons, consider what might happen if even one person later dies from using your company's cinnamon, and the public learns you had sufficient advance warning to recall the product and prevent the death. Sometimes one factor can outweigh all on the other side.

In 1982, when Johnson & Johnson learned that several people had died after taking Tylenol capsules injected with cyanide by a psychopath, the company recalled its product from every store shelf in America (32 million bottles) and placed a new safety cap on containers to help prevent similar criminal acts in the future. The incident cost Johnson & Johnson over $100 million, but the company's decisive action earned it more goodwill than dollars can buy. Your problem involves only threats. No poisoned cinnamon has yet appeared on store shelves, and no one has reported any ill effects. Do these distinctions make a real difference in your mind?

Make Crucial Career Choices

Your systematic questions might include:

- Which boss will be more supportive?
- Is there another job beyond accountant, CFO, or company president that I want most of all?
- What exactly are my near-term and long-term goals both professionally and privately?
- Do I possess a real chance of success in the new position with a different company?

Let's Make a Deal

Your odds of picking the car are 1 in 3 when you choose your first door. The odds remain 1 in 3 if you stay with your original choice after Monty opens a door. However, if you switch, you improve your chances of winning to 2 in 3. Thus, you should accept the offer to switch doors. If you find this hard to believe, look at the following chart.

				Odds of Winning

Monty opens a door
with a goat, and behind
the unopened door you
first selected is . . . . The Car. . . Goat A . . . Goat B

First Option:
If you **stay** with the door
you first selected, you. . . . . Win . . . . . Lose. . . . . Lose   1 in 3

Second Option:
If you **switch** to the
other unopened door,
you. . . . . Lose. . . . . Win . . . . . Win   2 in 3

Experiment using objects or slips of paper to make sure you realize these odds are real.

Trains and Planes

The critical path in this problem is not the one you take while flying your plane. Rather, it is the path of the two trains and how long it will take for them to meet along the way. The trains will meet in two hours, with one train having traveled 120 miles and the other 80. Since you are traveling at 120 mph, you will have flown 240 miles when the trains meet.

Chapter Five

Why Didn't I Come Up With That?

Use Your Imagination

People worldwide instantly recognize the *Intel Inside* logo, even though they have never seen the product itself. In the years following its founding, Intel, and all its competitors, remained unknown to consumers. Since the companies sold their products directly to computer manufacturers, they never needed to advertise to the general public. Intel dominated its competitors, hiring marketeers not for their marketing skills but for their engineering talents. These marketing people effectively communicated the technical features of Intel's innovative semiconductors to computer design engineers who, in turn, incorporated them in their new systems. Consumers, on the other hand, bought computers without paying much attention to who made the internal components.

In the early 1980s Intel and its competitors concentrated on memory chips, which only store information, and not on microprocessor circuits, which function as the logical brains of computers, because memory chips produced far greater revenues and profits. Computers use many memory chips but only one microprocessor. Competition in the memory segment of the market grew fierce, and by the mid-1980s the Japanese shocked the U.S. semiconductor industry by capturing the lion's share of memory-chip sales worldwide. This forced many U.S. semiconductor companies out of business and cut deeply into Intel's revenues and profits. Working hard to improve its manufacturing efficiency, the company came up with numerous innovations, but its upper management recognized that it would take more than efficiency to restore Intel's competitive prowess.

With only a 5-percent share of the memory chip market, Intel detected a shift in its revenue base away from memory and toward the logic side of the business, where the company had recently introduced the 286 microprocessor. After much internal soul-searching, Intel, under CEO Andy Grove's leadership, took a gigantic gamble and invested over $100 million in developing new microprocessor technology. Some observers and company executives worried that this shift could lead to disaster.

Soon, however, Intel's engineers came up with the revolutionary, and far more costly to produce, 386 microprocessor. Now the company possessed a product far superior to everything else on the market, including its own 286. Would computer designers adopt the more expensive 386 technology or would they continue using cheaper 286s, which accommodated most existing software? The initial answer to that question was disheartening. Although computer design engineers eagerly built 386s into the relatively few machines produced for technically sophisticated users, they shunned 386s for less expensive, mass-produced computers. Intel's engineer-to-engineer sales force could not break through the barrier, even with a less expensive version of the 386. At this point, Andy Grove turned to his trusted technical advisor Dennis Carter, for fresh ideas.

Hired from Rockwell in 1981, where he had designed Intel products into flight-control systems, Dennis Carter fit comfortably into Intel's engineering-oriented marketing culture, and he rose quickly through the ranks to become one of Andy Grove's personal assistants. When Grove asked Carter to solve the 386 marketing problem, Carter did something startling: He reached beyond design engineers and directly contacted consumers who buy computers. The home market for personal computers had not yet blossomed, so computer buyers were mostly corporate information technology (IT) managers who purchased large numbers of business machines. Carter believed IT managers could tremendously influence the mix of components placed inside computers. Could Intel improve 386 sales by radically altering the company's marketing strategy to focus on IT managers? Andy Grove saw promise in the idea and authorized Carter a temporary effort, with a limited budget and a support staff of three.

Carter immediately hired a two-person ad agency with his small budget and worked with them to come up with a catchy concept that would grab the attention of IT managers and communicate the superiority of the 386. Some inside Intel doubted Carter's approach, arguing "it will kill our own baby—the 286." To that, Carter responded, "That's what we do. In pushing the edge of technology, we kill what we did before."

Carter's controversial approach did not end in words. During internal briefings on his idea, he astounded many by spray-painting a big red "X" across the number 286. Some in the company called the idea "graffiti," fearing it might negatively associate Intel's products with socially undesirable behavior. Carter, however, stuck with his idea and convinced Grove the message had to be simple and bold. Only then, Carter believed, would IT managers start exerting real pressure on manufacturers to incorporate 386s in their computers. Since Grove himself welcomed controversy as an indispensable companion of innovation, he gave Carter a green light to proceed with the creative, controversial, and undeniably risky idea.

Carter first tested his new marketing strategy in Denver during May and June of 1989 with a modest billboard campaign and a few newspaper ads. The ads displayed the number "286" with a bright red "X" spray-painted across it. "What could it be?" many asked. The answer appeared one week later when Carter added "386" beneath the red-X'd 286. Then Carter and his small team personally visited IT managers in Denver to ask if the ad had caught their attention and, if so, what message, positive or negative, it had communicated. To his delight, the message had come through loud and clear. Denver's IT managers now expressed real interest in upgrading to 386 technology.

Given the Denver results, Grove authorized Carter to spend up to $5 million on a nationwide blitz in ten major cities. Intel's controversial campaign drew instant attention, some of it quite nega- tive. A *USA Today* article headlined "Intel Ads Pure Foolishness" blasted the company for eating its own baby. Nevertheless, Intel's 386 sales to manufacturers took a significant upward jump. Thanks to Dennis Carter's imaginative thinking and the efforts of many oth- ers at Intel, the 386 ultimately penetrated the less expensive, mass- produced computer marketplace where Intel very much wanted to go. But an even greater challenge soon appeared on the horizon.

Competition from other microprocessor makers, such as Advanced Micro Devices, began to erode Intel's dominance. Intel's advertising had opened up opportunities that others exploited. With competitive pressure mounting, Andy Grove shot a Friday afternoon memo to Carter saying, as Carter now remembers it, "Oh, by the way, Dennis, you're spending a lot of money on advertising and it's all kind of wasted and it's helping our competitors as much as us. Why don't you fix this really fast?" That weekend, Carter thought long and hard, and hit upon a solution. Intel had success- fully gone straight to consumers before. Why not do it again?

When, on Monday morning, Andy Grove came looking for an answer to his Friday memo, Dennis Carter was ready. Carter laid out a bold new strategy in the space of ten minutes. "If the end user is making the decision, we want them to decide on our technology," Carter began. "If they're going to decide on our technology, then they have to know our technology is inside the product. '386' doesn't tell them anything. We want a logo on the computer that says *Intel Inside.*"

With that, Carter proposed a new cooperative advertising pro- gram that would encourage computer manufacturers to add a small *Intel Inside* to their print ads. From this small beginning, Carter hoped to eventually persuade manufacturers to prominently display Intel's logo on the outside of their computers. When Carter later presented the idea to Intel's Executive Staff as instructed by Grove, the room resounded with a collective: "What the heck are you talk- ing about?" Still, Grove supported the concept and directed Carter to proceed as soon as possible.

Intel Inside quickly progressed from print ads to TV spots to computer logos, and, in short order, *Intel Inside* took its place as a truly worldwide trademark on a par with Coca-Cola. That accomplishment has left Intel's competitors shaking their heads, wondering, "Why didn't I come up with that?"

Creative thinking of the sort that generated *Intel Inside* requires imagination—and lots of it. George Bernard Shaw, one of the most creative thinkers of his day, put it this way: "Imagination is the beginning of creation. We imagine what we desire; we will what we imagine; and at last we create what we will." Perhaps the single greatest creative thinker of the twentieth century, Albert Einstein placed imagination at the pinnacle of creative thought. From experience, he concluded: "Imagination is more important than knowledge." He himself used it when he came up with the theory of relativity, imagining himself riding on a light beam. As hard as that may be to envision, Einstein began his thinking by constructing in his mind what he could not see any other way. Imagination plays a crucial role in all genuine creative thinking, because it allows the mind to see the unseen, envision the invisible, and transform ideas into reality.

Creativity by definition brings into being something that did not exist before. It most often begins with what we know, but soon moves to what we do not know. A creative person need not possess Einstein's IQ or Picasso's talent, but all creative people do display keen imaginations.

If you want to see imagination at work, spend some time with children. They revel in it. Then, as they mature, some sharpen their imaginations, while others let it atrophy. Einstein, who never lost his childlike curiosity, candidly admitted that most of his great discoveries began with childlike questions that sparked his imagination.

To become highly creative thinkers as adults, we must energize our inborn imagination. Sounds easy, doesn't it? Just adopt the wonder of childhood. However, developing and exercising imaginations of the sort that consistently produce creative ideas requires hard work. In the words of one of America's most creative innovators, Thomas Edison, imagination is "ninety nine percent perspiration and 1one percent inspiration." Dennis Carter of Intel, and creative thinkers like him, would all agree.

A common myth claims that people either possess creativity or they do not, that they were born with it or not, and that few can obtain and sharpen it. Yes, imagination may start at birth, but creativity only happens when people apply their imaginations to creative ends. In adults, creativity is a skill like any other. As we'll see, anyone can learn it, albeit not easily. Genuine creativity often requires raw courage; never flees from adversity, frustration, or even failure; challenges conventional wisdom; and vigorously explores beyond the first workable answer to find the very best solution imaginable.

Warm up your imagination with this creative challenge. Remember to think systematically and maintain the quality of your thinking with clarity, accuracy, comprehensiveness, sensibility, and intellectual honesty.

Mental Warm Up

Make a Chocolate-Covered Candy Bar

You hit upon an idea for a new chocolate-covered candy bar you believe can one day become more popular than traditional favorites such as Snickers and Milky Way. It will wrap a thick layer of specially formulated milk chocolate around a unique soft filling. You need to mass produce about 10,000 bars as samples but cannot afford to hire a candy maker. You design your bar in a familiar rectangular shape: 3 inches long, 1 inch wide, and 1 inch deep. The outside chocolate layer must be 1/8 inch on all sides to achieve the desired flavor combination. Hardening the chewy center, even for an instant, will destroy its wonderful flavor.

Use your imagination to solve the problem of inserting your soft filling into its delicious chocolate wrapper, all in the desired rectangular shape.

EXERCISE A VIVID IMAGINATION

Many of our greatest treasures began as a dream in someone's imagination. A grand dream inhabited Martin Luther King Jr.'s mind in August 1963 as he sat exhausted on the steps of the Lincoln Memorial, gazing out at crowd of 250,000 worn down by the heat of a sweltering summer day. All had come to town for the civil rights

"March on Washington." About one-fourth of the crowd was white. President John Kennedy watched the event on television along with millions of Americans. The President would meet with Dr. King and a small group of march leaders in the Oval Office immediately following the Lincoln Memorial speeches.

Scheduled last in a long procession of speakers, King had been given only eight short minutes on the program. A friend protested, "There's no way in the world, Martin, that you can say what needs to be said in eight minutes." That friend underestimated Dr. King, who had stayed up the entire night before drafting and redrafting the written text of his short but historic speech. Copies had been proofed and distributed to the press early that morning.

Press reports at first indicated only 25,000 people assembled at the Washington Monument for the march to the Lincoln Memorial. Disappointed by the reportedly low turnout, Dr. King and his wife, Coretta, drove to the site. On arrival their spirits lifted as they looked out across an immense crowd surrounding the Washington Monument, the largest single gathering in the history of the civil rights movement to that point. The procession grew so massive that leaders, including Dr. King and Coretta, could not march at the front as they traditionally did.

Once at the Memorial, Dr. King took his place on the rostrum and concentrated privately on his speech text, scratching out words and adding new phrases up to the last moment before his introduction at the end of the program. Finally, as King approached the microphone, some at the edges of the crowd began drifting slowly toward waiting busses and cars. Coretta remembers thinking how hard it might be for him to arouse the audience so late in the proceedings.

Not to worry, however, because her husband's familiar voice instantly caught everyone's attention. "Five score years ago," he began, "a great American, in whose symbolic shadow we stand, signed the Emancipation Proclamation. This momentous decree came as a great beacon of light and hope to millions. . . ." The mood of the crowd swelled. Then King paused and, in a surge of deeply felt emotion, he set aside his written text. What followed remains forever embedded in the memory and conscience of America: *"I have a dream.* I have a dream that my four little children will one day live in a nation where they will be judged not by the color of their skin but by the content of their character." These vivid words sparked a nation's imagination, creating a vision of an America that did not yet exist. Over and over King described his dream, and time and again the crowd cheered. They shared the dream and, for a moment, dared to imagine it coming true.

The crowd fell silent as Martin's oration ended. Coretta, who had seen crowds respond to her husband's speeches countless times before, called it "the awed silence that is the greatest tribute an orator can be paid." Then the crowd went wild, shouting, clapping, and dancing with joy.

Dr. Martin Luther King Jr. saw a better future with his mind's eye. In describing what he so vividly imagined, King did more to make it a reality than any other single figure in American history.

Of course, not everyone appreciates what creative minds such as King's imagine, as Walt discovered when he shared his dream with Art. Walt and Art were best friends living in Los Angeles. In the 1950s, Walt took Art on a 50-mile drive south of the city to the farm country of Orange County, where he turned off the main highway onto a narrow paved road, then onto a dirt road, and finally onto a pair of tractor ruts running into the middle of a huge field. Pulling up beside a dilapidated barn, Walt hopped out of the car and said, "Art, look at all this. Isn't it wonderful? I'm going to buy it all and build a place where dreams can come true. I want you to be my partner."

The whole world now understands the image Walt Disney had in mind as he stood with his friend in that Orange County field, but Art Linkletter did not. He declined the invitation and could only later ask himself, "Why didn't I realize that?" as he and millions of others saw Walt Disney's dream become one of the most joyous and profitable places on Earth. Today the Walt Disney Company leads the world in "imagineering," every day applying the lesson learned from its founder: Creativity begins with imagination, and vivid imaginations create best.

Exercise your most vivid imagination as you think about the following problem.

Mental Aerobics
What Do You See?

What does this photograph depict? Come up with as many imaginative ideas as you can.

Practice Makes Perfect
20/20 Hindsight

"Congratulations on your 20/20 hindsight!" we retort sarcastically when critics point out our obvious errors. But hindsight really is a wonderful thing when used creatively. Suppose, for example, you want to improve the profitability of your company, so you assemble your most trusted advisors to help think through the problem. By using "imagined hindsight" to frame the profits question, the group may well come up with many more workable ways to achieve your goal than if you frame the problem in traditional form.

- *Traditional form asks:* "How can we increase profits 50 percent next year?"

- *Imagined hindsight asks:* "Imagine this meeting is happening one year from now and we just learned company profits have increased 50 percent. How could this have happened?"

Think of a problem in your business or private life that requires a creative solution, one for which you want to generate a number of workable alternatives before selecting the best answer. Use imagined hindsight to come up with those alternatives, and then decide among them. Remember to think systematically, and keep your thoughts clear, accurate, comprehensive, sensible, and intellectually honest.

IMAGINE COURAGEOUSLY

An imagination, however vivid, may not produce truly creative ideas unless we exercise it courageously in the face of those opposed to innovation, as Navy Lieutenant William Sims realized when he thought about ways to improve how the U.S. Navy waged battles at sea. Prior to the twentieth century, rival ships fought at close quarters using smooth-bored cannon and boarding parties armed with swords and muskets. Near the turn of the century, high-velocity, rifled guns replaced old cannons, and these far more accurate and powerful guns allowed warships to commence firing at greater distances, generally up to one mile. Accuracy, however, remained a serious problem for guns fired from rolling ships at sea. The slightest movement at the instant of firing would throw a projectile far off target, especially at long ranges. When it came to firing the new rifled guns, a "pointer" estimated the range to the target, turned a heavy crank to elevate the gun to achieve the desired range, and then looked through the gunsight until his ship hopefully rolled the gunsight into line with the target. In effect, the ship, not the pointer, tried to align the weapon on the target. Complicating matters, a successful shot required the pointer to push the firing button before the sight moved onto target, because the human finger does not react instantly to what the eye sees. Thus, even with the new guns, naval tactics did not change. Ships and their crews closed to within a few yards and pounded away unmercifully. The strategy of sea battles remained essentially unchanged from the glory days of John Paul Jones, and no one in the U.S. Navy could imagine it being any other way. Then along came a fledgling Lieutenant named William S. Sims.

While assigned to China duty, Sims observed gunfire practice aboard the British ship HMS *Terrible*. The ship's captain had come up with a surprisingly simple way to keep the barrels of his guns continuously trained on targets as his ship rolled at sea. First, he modified the elevating gears of his weapons, making it easier for crews to raise and lower the heavy gun barrels. Then he instructed his pointers to look steadily through their sights and continuously adjust, using the new gears to stay on target throughout the firing process. It all boiled down to basic physics: When the HMS *Terrible* rolled down, inertia worked with pointers to keep weighty gun barrels up on target, and when the ship rolled up, the opposite occurred. When Sims saw the technique in action, he imagined the unimaginable: naval battles fought and won at distances of one mile and beyond.

Believing that the innovation would revolutionize warfare at sea, Sims wrote a detailed report to the Navy Department in Washington. When it disappeared in the bureaucracy, Sims wrote a second report, and a third. Because the reports threatened a centuries-old navy fighting culture, they foundered in a sea of closed bureaucratic minds. The navy's whole way of life centered on its weapons and how they were used at sea. Up to now, gunnery officers held relatively unimportant positions onboard ship. If the navy's guns suddenly became lethal at long ranges, the status of these officers would inevitably rise. Among crewmen, the now highly respected gun pointers would be replaced by technicians, expected to hit their targets at long distances rather than acclaimed in the rare instances when sheer human talent, and a bit of luck, hit the mark. Anyone with average hand–eye coordination could now do the job.

Two years and thirteen reports later, a frustrated Sims upped the ante by writing his missives in more confrontational language and circulating copies to officers outside his chain of command.

This forced the Chief of the Bureau of Ordinance in Washington to conduct a rigged "experiment" on dry land which "proved" continuous-aim firing "impossible." The Chief knew from the outset that a land-based test would fail. One man acting as a pointer could not possibly move a heavy gun barrel up and down fast enough on dry land to adjust for a simulated ship's roll. The land-based experiment eliminated the positive effect of inertia generated by a rolling ship. To make matters worse, the Washington brass made their pointer work with an old, unmodified gear mechanism. Following the failed experiment, senior navy officers set out to discredit Sims personally, labeling him a crackpot, egotist, and, worst of all, "dishonest," the most ruinous of all epithets in a military culture that prized honor above all virtues.

Nevertheless, Lieutenant Sims stiffened his resolve, risking everything by writing a letter directly to the President of the United States, Theodore Roosevelt. The President at once saw the potential significance of Sims's vision, ordered the Lieutenant home from China duty, and made him Inspector of Target Practice. Within six short years naval gunfire and the tactics of surface battle at sea changed radically, in large measure due to the courage and imagination of one person. Over the years, Sims rose in rank and stature within the navy, and he earned a lasting place in history as the man who "taught the U.S. Navy how to shoot." Looking back, many in then navy had to grudgingly wonder, "Why didn't I come up with that?"

Lieutenant Sims's story does far more than add an interesting anecdote to navy lore. It shows why creativity often eludes the fainthearted. The, Navy, like many successful organizations, exists as a tightknit society, a unique culture in which people find their identity and purpose in life. Anything threatening to alter the existing social order becomes a candidate for passive and even active resistance. People instinctively protect their settled ways of living and thinking.

Breaking ranks always requires courage, in the navy and elsewhere. Those who muster the courage to rock boats quite often invite the suspicion, resistance, and even sabotage of shipmates who prefer a comfortable ride. Those in the comfort zone dislike and fear change. They avoid risk—and, given their presence, even dominance, in some organizations, they let conformity trump creativity whenever new thinking threatens the status quo. It's all quite natural because we all find it easier to criticize than create. Critics need not take personal responsibility for ideas, since they only invest themselves in finding fault in the ideas of others.

Creative minds must march courageously to the beat of a different drum, one not always pleasing to those with trained ears. As a person exposed constantly to the fiercest criticisms, Bill Cosby, one of America's most creative comedians, said, "I don't know the key to success, but the key to failure is trying to please everybody." Imaginative thinking inevitably displeases some, friends and enemies alike.

Battling naysayers and idea killers takes heart. The razor-sharp weapons they use to defend the status quo can destroy more than ideas—they discredit creators of ideas as well, as nearly happened to Lieutenant Sims. To his credit, though, Sims's courage ran deeper than sword-swinging bravado. He knew how to *think* courageously, and he never shied away from using his imaginative courage to make big waves in an organization comfortable with smooth sailing. Truly creative thinking always involves risk, sometimes huge risks.

Be prepared to take real risks as you face this problem.

_____ Mental Aerobics
Besieged

You're a benevolent feudal lord during the Middle Ages. A barbarian army invades your land, forcing you to take refuge in your sturdy castle, where you and your subjects survive a steady onslaught for many months. The barbarians intend to kill everyone in the castle, but so far have mostly allowed starvation to do their dirty work. Peering over the parapet of a castle wall, you detect a growing restlessness among the barbarians. They will likely take the castle if they attack because your malnourished soldiers cannot turn them back. Only two sacks of grain remain in the storehouse.

Soon the barbarian leader boldly rides up to the castle gate to demand your surrender, saying he will spare the lives of the women and children in return. You know from past experience that the barbarians will not honor this pledge. They always kill every man, woman, and child, no matter what. You sense, however, that despite his bluster, the barbarian does not feel fully confident that he can win if he attacks. He does not know the extent of your soldiers' weakness. For all he knows, you possess enough food to survive for years.

How can you use your depleted food supply to prevail over the barbarian army? Remember to think courageously in the face of near certain death.

Practice Makes Perfect

Summon Your Courage

Identify a problem in your life that you've been avoiding, something you would rather not face, a problem that requires courage to confront and solve. Perhaps you're involved in an unhappy relationship, bottling up feelings that may someday explode and destroy what you would rather save. You may not have grappled with a sensitive problem at work because taking on the matter involves personal risks you would rather avoid. Maybe you long to break a bad habit but haven't found the courage to do so.

Exercise a courageous imagination as you think of creative ways to deal with the problem. Given the risks involved, make sure you think clearly, accurately, comprehensively, sensibly, and honestly.

IMAGINE YOUR WAY THROUGH ADVERSITY, FRUSTRATION, AND FAILURE

Sometimes in the darkness of adversity, frustration, and failure, we can only see light at the end of the tunnel with a vivid, courageous imagination. The University of Notre Dame owes its existence to the imagination of one man who saw through adversity when others could not. Father Edward Sorin and the Catholic Congregation of Holy Cross, which had originally established educational institutions in France following the French Revolution, dreamed of extending their mission to the people whose love of liberty had inspired the French quest for freedom. Father Sorin and seven Holy

Cross brothers arrived in Indiana in 1842 to begin building the University of Notre Dame. Starting in a snow-covered log cabin originally occupied by fur traders, the group slowly began to make their dream a reality on a 640-acre parcel of donated land.

One adversity followed another. A cholera epidemic killed many in the 1850s. Then, when the Civil War broke out in the 1860s, many of the sisters, priests, and brothers went off to work for the Union cause. Father Sorin dispatched seven priests from his already small faculty to serve as battlefield chaplains, and he himself later served at Gettysburg, giving absolution to Union troops just before they marched into one of history's bloodiest battles.

Father Sorin and his colleagues had managed to construct a number of major buildings, including space for colleges of liberal arts, science, and law, by the late 1870s. Then, one night in April of 1879, the work of nearly forty years went up in smoke as a raging fire wiped out all the university's major buildings, save its stone church. In the aftermath, Father Sorin gathered his despondent colleagues and students in the church for mass. "The fire is really my fault," he said. "I came here as a young man and dreamed of building a great university in honor of Our Lady. But I built it too small, and she had to burn it to the ground to make that point. So, tomorrow, as soon as the bricks cool, we will rebuild it, bigger and better than ever." Brick by glorious brick, Father Sorin and those who followed in his footsteps built Notre Dame into the grand American institution we see today.

Imaginative thinkers often suffer anxiety, frustration, and even failure, setbacks that can ensnare even the most determined thinkers and eventually quench every creative fire. Trapped in the jaws of defeat and seeing no way out, imagination may stagger and die. To escape, it must somehow see beyond the snare. That, in itself, requires imagination, as Father Sorin demonstrated in the aftermath of the Notre Dame fire. Just as he imagined his way through a crisis that might have stopped a less determined soul, we, too, must force ourselves to see beyond immediate setbacks and visualize future success.

Winning isn't everything, and even winners carry scars. Their wounds remind them of losses incurred along the road to success. Indeed, failure happens more often than success on creativity's path. Most of Thomas Edison's 1,093 patents, for example, involved inventions that proved utterly worthless, but he never let them stall his quest to innovate. As Edison proved, even the most creative minds can fail a dozen times before they succeed just once.

Fred Smith, creator of Federal Express, received a "C" on a college economics paper he wrote describing his idea for a nationwide distribution system. Lou Holtz, Notre Dame's enormously successful and creative college football coach in the 1980s, lasted only eight months as coach of the New York Jets. Walt Disney was fired for incompetence. Leo Tolstoy flunked out of school. Abraham Lincoln began serving in the Blackhawk War as a Captain and ended up as a lowly private. Albert Einstein's professors at the University of Bern rejected his doctoral dissertation on the special theory of relativity. Thomas Edison's teachers thought he was stupid, and Winston Churchill's considered him a "slow learner."

You cannot succeed until you feel free to fail, and imagining future success does more than anything else to set you free. It treats adversity, frustration, and failure as growth opportunities. Soon after his failed 1952 attempt to climb Mount Everest, Sir Edmund Hillary pointed to a picture of the treacherous mountain and said, "Mount Everest, you beat me the first time, but I'll beat you the next time because you've grown all you're going to grow, but I'm still growing." One year later Hillary stood on top of Everest basking in the bright sunshine of success.

Georgia Tech played UCLA in the Rose Bowl on January 1, 1929. Roy Regals grabbed a fumbled ball, ran across field to avoid being tackled, and turned toward the goal 60 yards away—the wrong way. Fortunately for Regals, his own teammate tackled him just shy of the opposing goal line. During half time, Regals sat in a dark corner of the locker room far away from his teammates. Not a player or coach said a word. Everyone kept Regals's failure in mind, especially Regals himself. Then head coach Nibbs Price stood and said, "The team that started the first half will start the second." Regals responded from his dark corner, "No coach. I can't do it. I'm too ashamed." He could not imagine even showing his face in the stadium, let alone playing on the field. "Regals," Nibbs said, "get back in the game. It's only half over." Regals did just that. People

called him "Wrong Way Regals" for the rest of his life, but he finished the game, something only Coach Nibbs imagined possible.

For those engaged in a creative task, such as building a winning team, imagination remains the most effective conqueror of
adversity, frustration, and failure. Imagine your way through adversity as you tackle the following exercise.

——————————————————————————————— Mental Aerobics
Losing Proposition

You're escaping with your child from a country dominated by a tyranni-
cal regime. Following an exhausting trek over perilous mountain terrain,
you arrive at the border, where a narrow bridge spans a deep chasm and
ends in freedom. As you begin crossing, armed border guards suddenly
appear from behind and give chase as guards from the opposite side
rush to greet you. You and the guards from both sides meet at the center of the bridge, and, rather than engaging in a gun battle, the leader of
the pursuing guards proposes a terrible bargain. He will let you escape
to freedom if you will leave your child behind. You refuse, of course, so
he offers a second alternative. He will place a copper and a silver coin in
his large fur hat. You will reach in and blindly pick out one coin. If you
come up with silver, you and your child will go free. If you pull out copper, you must return for trial and the gulag, but your child will go free. If
you refuse the proposition, the guard will order his unit to take you and
your child by force, which will likely prompt a gun battle between guards
on both sides in which you and your child will be the first to die.

Lacking any real choice, you accept the proposition. The guard
holds a copper and a tarnished silver coin in his open palm and places
them in the deep folds of his cap. From the corner of your eye you see
the guard switch the silver coin with a second copper coin. Standing
next to the rail of the bridge, and peering into the deep chasm below, you
realize that to assure survival you must pull one of the copper coins out
of the hat. You cannot accuse the guard of dishonesty, or he will order
his unit to take you and your child by force. The guard moves his hat in
your direction and demands that you reach in for a coin as he inspects
your hand to make sure it is empty.

Imagine your way through this adversity. What can you do to assure
that both you and your child go free?

Practice Makes Perfect
Find Hidden Treasures by Learning from Failures

You're a treasure hunter in search of a fortune in buried gold on the lost island of Tompatu, a map of which you recently discovered in a water-tight container inside the wreckage of a sunken seventeenth-century pirate ship. Mounting a secret expedition to Tompatu, you arrive on a tiny square patch of sand and coral. Since your map does not show where on the island to dig for the treasure, you soon realize that finding the trove amounts to locating a minuscule needle in a giant haystack. Frustration takes its toll as every attempt to find the gold ends in failure.

Tempted to abandon the search, you take a long walk on a deserted beach. There you find a bottle floating at the waterline. Curiosity leads you to pick it up and pull out its tight-fitting cork. Whoosh! A column of smoke pours out of the bottle and then clears to reveal a pur-ple-colored figure looming over you on the beach. "I am the Genie of Tompatu," she says, "and I know where the pirates buried the treasure." She hands you the following grid which divides the island into 64 squares, each about 50 feet on a side.

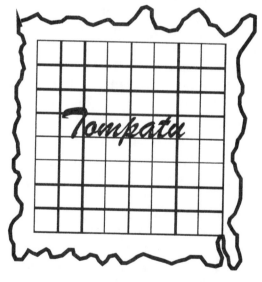

"The treasure lies six feet under the sand inside one of those squares," she says, "but you may ask me no more than eight ques-tions to locate it." The genie promises to tell the truth when asked a "yes" or "no" question. Otherwise, she will say whatever protects the treasure from discovery, be it the truth or a lie.

Using your most creative imagination, develop eight "yes/no" ques-tions that will inevitably lead to the correct square. Do not give up. Imagine your way through all the adversity, frustration, and failures along the way.

THINK BEYOND THE BOUNDS
OF CONVENTIONAL WISDOM

To generate truly creative ideas, imagination must often break through conventional "wisdom" of the sort that John Sculley penetrated when he led Pepsi to victory over Coke. When, in 1978, Pepsi beat Coca-Cola's market share for the first time ever, Pepsi's president, John Sculley, achieved a personal goal he had set eight years earlier when he became the company's youngest marketing vice president at age thirty. When Sculley set out to beat the world's best-known trademark, conventional wisdom considered the task impossible. Over the years, Pepsi's executives had tried everything from price cutting to redesigning the bottle, all to no avail. What could young Sculley know that they did not?

Coke's dominant trademark had become more than just a household name. The distinctive hourglass shape of a 6.5-ounce Coke bottle had become a part of American culture, something instantly recognized by sight and feel. As a result, Pepsi's executives believed they could only compete by imitating their rival. In the late 1950s Pepsi spent millions developing its own distinctive "swirl" shaped bottle, but the new design did not really differ all that much, and it did little to cut into Coke's dominance.

Into this climate of conventional wisdom came John Sculley, who believed Pepsi must radically change the way it played the game. Could Pepsi somehow make an end-run around Coke's image, embodied largely by the unique way Coke packaged its product? To gain a better understanding of the game, Sculley launched an ambitious consumer study involving 350 families. The research revealed that people consumed far more soda than they were taking home from the supermarket. That gave Sculley an idea: Pepsi would make it easier for people to take home more Pepsi than Coke. Sculley figured, beyond all traditional thinking, that the size of soda containers meant more to consumers than shape, no matter how distinctive. Pepsi could cancel out the advantage of Coke's distinctive packaging by competing on size rather than shape, an unexpected maneuver that would catch Coke completely off guard.

Soon much larger Pepsi containers and packages crowded supermarket shelves. The strategy worked, knocking Coke back on its competitive heels, a position the company had never experienced and one from which it took time to recover. Coke itself found it hard to transcend conventional wisdom. It continued, for example, counting sales in terms of 6.5-ounce increments. John Sculley, on the other hand, tallied total ounces sold. Worst of all for Coke, Sculley's larger containers and packages ultimately rendered Coke's small 6.5-ounce glass bottle largely irrelevant, a stunning development no one had thought possible in any scenario.

Today the Coke bottle that once assured dominance for a century-old company has joined the ranks of sacred Americana. As before in the world of American enterprise, the creative thinking of one person has taken a whole industry beyond the bounds of conventional wisdom into an entirely new competitive era. Sculley's thinking left many in his industry, and not just those at Coke, wondering, "Why didn't I come up with that?"

Pepsi's executives before John Sculley consciously or unconsciously accepted Coke's supremacy as a fact of life. That assumption proved false, of course, when Sculley abandoned traditional thinking, as Alfred Sloan had done before him with General Motors to beat the unbeatable Ford.

In Sloan's day, industry experts assumed that buyers must pay in full before driving cars off the lot. When Sloan set aside the assumption, he found ways for customers to take possession of General Motors cars before they could afford to pay for them, and his imaginative thinking gave birth to a whole new way of doing business: buying cars on the installment plan. John Sculley likewise abandoned an entrenched assumption that Pepsi must mimic Coke's image.

Thinking beyond conventional wisdom requires more than pure logic. Indeed, logic often digs thoughtful people into deeper and deeper ruts. Yes, logic can improve the inhabitability of an existing rut, but it can also entrench us so deeply we cannot see over the rim. Imagination propels people into a whole new groove. This, of course, is more easily said than done. We've seen earlier in this book how our minds think in "logical" patterns—and jumping out of existing, established patterns to see new perspectives takes real effort. Look at this pattern, for instance.

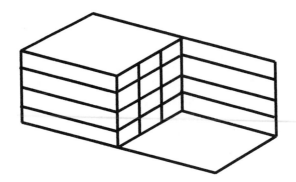

What perspective does your mind adopt: looking down from above or looking up from below? Whichever you choose, look at the pattern until you can see it from the opposite view. Look up if you started by looking down and vice versa.

Now comes the most difficult part. Try to switch *rapidly* back and forth from one view to the other. See how your mind struggles? The instant you relax your thinking, your mind settles on one view and remains there until disturbed by a conscious prod in the opposite direction.

We must consciously switch our perspective to escape the established view. Otherwise, our minds simply continue reproducing in kind. Benjamin Cordozo, one of the sharpest minds ever to hold a seat on the U.S. Supreme Court, once said, "In the life of the mind as elsewhere, there is a tendency toward reproduction of kind." Cordozo included himself in that phenomenon. Even the sharpest mind reproduces conventional wisdom unless consciously nudged in new directions.

Moving the mind in new directions takes a lot of practice. You cannot turn the skill on and off like tap water. Rather, creativity requires continuous use, lest it dry up and refuse to flow when needed most. Leonardo da Vinci kept creativity flowing by studying both art and science, sometimes thinking of art as a science, and at other times seeing science as an art, all the while never falling into the conventional ruts of either. He routinely avoided routine thinking. We can do the same, beginning with simple activities and moving to more complex matters where we need imaginative thinking the most.

Here's an exercise to get you started.

Mental Aerobics

Knotty Problem

You're the most successful military general and empire builder in ancient Mesopotamia. You outthink your adversaries at every turn, defeating army after army against all odds. As winter approaches in the year 333 B.C., you march your troops to the city of Gordium for shelter. While there, you discover a knotted rope-ball so tangled and twisted no person has ever been able to untangle it. An old prophesy predicts that the person who unties the knot will rule all of Asia. You have long dreamed of conquering Asia, the crown jewel of the known world. After studying the complicated knot for days, you end up sitting alone with it, wondering whether it will defeat you when all the world's armies could not.

Surprise the people of Gordium by thinking beyond the bounds of conventional wisdom and untying the knot. Good luck.

Practice Makes Perfect

Invent a New Internet Business

A wealthy investor approaches you offering to invest up to $1 million in start-up capital for a new Internet-based business of your choosing. The investor will grant you 50 percent of the equity and profits if you come up with a promising new concept different from any known Internet enterprise to date. You must invent a whole new business, not simply a better way to do what someone else already does, and not just another ".com" that eats up resources without producing a profit.

Stretch your imagination beyond the bounds of all existing business concepts to earn the investment capital and take full advantage of the opportunity. What will you propose? Give specific details.

IMAGINE THE VERY BEST SOLUTIONS

Thinking beyond the bounds of conventional wisdom produces unconventional answers but does not guarantee any one solution will lead to success. Finding the best possible solution requires still more imagination of the sort Tom used when his plans for a glorious summer day of swimming and playing with friends collided with Aunt Polly's orders to whitewash ninety feet of board fence standing nine feet high. Dipping his brush and sloshing a white streak on the wood-planked surface, Tom felt overwhelmed by the huge task ahead and plopped down dejectedly on a tree-box. His day of play having turned into weary work, Tom ransacked his mind for some way out.

Soon Jim bounded out of the house on his way to draw water from the nearby town well, a task Tom ordinarily loathed. But now the chore appeared attractive by comparison to his own, so he offered to trade a few minutes of whitewashing with Jim in return for a trip to the well. Oh, no, said Jim. Aunt Polly had specifically instructed him not to bargain with Tom or help him with the fence. The ever-resourceful Tom tried another approach, offering Jim a pure white marble to seal the deal. When Jim still declined, Tom offered to throw in a look at his sore toe. Unable to resist any longer, Jim accepted the marble and took a peek at Tom's swollen toe. Before he could begin whitewashing, however, Aunt Polly appeared out of nowhere and sent Jim scurrying off to the well, bucket in hand, leaving Tom to his chore and the wrath of his Aunt.

When Aunt Polly departed, Tom emptied his pockets and quickly concluded that all his worldly possessions could not entice enough boys to surrender part of their Saturday to whitewash the whole fence. Tom, of course, did not want to whitewash any part of it. He had to find a better alternative than bartering away all his possessions. But what?

Soon Ben Rodgers came strolling down the middle of the road, imagining himself captain of a mighty Mississippi sternwheeler. As Ben approached, Tom paid him no mind. Ben teased, "You're up a stump, ain't you!" Acting as if whitewashing were a privilege, Tom stroked his brush as an artist creating a masterpiece.

Silently, of course, Tom coveted Ben's freedom and the half-eaten apple in Ben's hand. As Samuel Clements tells the story:

Tom wheeled suddenly and said: "Why it's you, Ben! I warn't noticing."

"*Say*—I'm going in a-swimming, *I* am. Don't you wish you could? But of course you'd druther *work*—wouldn't you!"

Tom contemplated the boy a bit, and said, "What do you call work?"

"Why, ain't *that* work?"

Tom resumed his whitewashing, and answered carelessly, "Well, maybe it is, and maybe it ain't. All I know is, it suits Tom Sawyer."

Soon Ben asked Tom to let him give it a try. Tom refused, saying Aunt Polly wanted the work done right, and she would not trust the task to just anybody. Even when Ben offered Tom the core of his apple to sweeten the deal, Tom showed no interest. Eventually, however, he gave in, accepted the apple, and traded places with Ben. As the day progressed, more and more neighborhood boys tried their hand at whitewashing, while Tom's wealth grew to include a kite, a dead rat and a string to swing it with, two tadpoles, and six firecrackers.

Tom's imaginative solution turned his worst nightmare into a great triumph. Indeed, if Tom Sawyer's enterprise had not used up all the whitewash in Aunt Polly's bucket, he would have owned the combined wealth of all the boys in town. Imagine Aunt Polly's surprise, and pleasure, when she examined the fence and found not one, but three glistening coats of fresh whitewash, making it the best looking fence around. While one might doubt Tom's business ethics, he clearly found the best of all imaginative solutions for both his dilemma and Aunt Polly's fence.

Tom Sawyer understood imaginative thinking. Not wanting to work physically, but fully willing to work mentally, Tom first came up with an idea that failed. That failure just caused him to think harder. Most boys, and adults as well, would have given up at this point and endured the chore. Not Tom. He imagined another, better alternative, and proved what every creative thinker knows. The best ideas, the ideal ones, come from a constant exercising of the imagination. Generating imaginative ideas, searching for multiple alternatives, counteracts the mind's tendency to settle into old existing patterns. And, even when creating new patterns, the mind tends to accept the first pattern that fits. But, even if the first answer appears "right," imaginative minds continue searching beyond right to find the "best" solution.

Finding best solutions requires us to think hard enough and long enough to let go of ideas we would rather not abandon. Conventional wisdom, after all, tells us to "waste not, want not." As we've seen, though, creative thinking defies conventional logic, especially when searching for best solutions. Many alternatives, new ideas, unconventional concepts, even very good ones, end up in the discard pile. Like great filmmakers, who edit their work ruthlessly, imaginative thinkers toss out more ideas than they use in the end.

Just as imaginative thinking includes letting go of some very hard-to-come-by and "interesting" concepts, it also embraces thinking the "illogical." While perhaps not so efficient as logic, genuinely creative thinking generates ideas that can escape the purely logical mind. Indeed, logic can squelch imagination by prompting premature judgment; and any rush to judgment can short-circuit imagination as people settle for second or even third best. Earlier in this book we learned to "understand before judging." That same rule applies to creative thinking, with a slight variation. Here we must "*imagine* before judging." In other words, the creative thinker focuses on generating many ideas—good, bad, and in-between— before selecting the optimal one.

Children display wonderful imaginations but have developed little judgment. As their judgment skills grow, their imaginations tend to wane because the adult process of judgment mostly selects and eliminates ideas, whereas imagination generates them. No wonder children lose over half of their creativity between ages five and seven, and adults over forty years old end up with under 2 percent of what they began with as children. While we cannot recover our childhood, and would never trade mature judgment for it, we can rejuvenate much of the creativity lost over the years by suspending judgment while generating creative ideas in the quest for optimal solutions.

Focus on finding the best possible solution as you think through this problem.

Mental Aerobics
Stuck Truck

You're an independent trucker hauling heavy loads across the nation's highways. Ten years ago you quit your assembly-line job in Detroit and set out on your own, determined to become your own boss. Over the years you saved enough money to buy your own big rig, a sturdy and powerful tractor–trailer combination. Like many independent truckers, you've decorated your tractor beautifully with shiny metallic paint, and you've attached polished chrome accents from hood to exhaust. But unlike many, you've also adorned your trailer with expensive paint and chrome fittings.

On a cross-country trip from Florida to Oregon, you stop at one of your favorite diners in Baton Rouge, Louisiana. After feasting on catfish and hush puppies with plenty of butter and honey, you climb back in the cab and drive under a newly installed concrete overpass toward the highway. Suddenly your truck jerks to a halt as you hear the sound of metal grinding against concrete. Jumping out of the cab, you see the top of your trailer wedged up tightly against the lower part of the overpass girders. With a measuring tape from your toolkit, you discover that the top of your trailer is exactly 2 inches higher than the bottom edge of the overpass.

Within minutes a heavy-duty tow truck arrives and offers to pull your truck out from under the overpass. A police officer presses you to remove your truck so that blocked traffic can begin moving again. Towing the truck will greatly increase the damage by ripping the entire roof off your spiffy trailer. Hoping to unhitch your trailer and somehow lower it under the overpass, you find the hitching mechanism jammed shut. With only a couple of minutes to take action before the police officer orders the tow truck driver to drag your rig from under the overpass, you despair.

What can you possibly do? Don't settle for just a workable answer. Use your creative imagination to quickly find the very best solution.

── Practice Makes Perfect
Make Wise Charitable Contributions

You recently earned $10 million after taxes playing the stock market and
have decided to give $500,000 of your new wealth to charity. You write
the following ground rules on a sheet of paper:

1. Must give to at least five charitable groups or activities.

2. Will not give more than $200,000 to any one group or activity.

3. Neither I nor any relative or friend can receive any benefit from the
   giving.

4. Will not give to any group or activity involving a relative, a friend, or
   me.

5. Will give away all the money within the next six months.

Using your most creative thinking, how will you distribute your
bounty so that it will do the most good?

PUT IT ALL TOGETHER

Use what you've learned in this chapter to solve this complex practical problem.

Solve a Compensation Dispute

You're one of ten partners in a successful law firm. The
founder of the firm has always run it efficiently, but he retired last
year and has been replaced by a management committee of three
partners, including yourself.

Allocating profits among the partners has become an enormously divisive issue. Several of your best partners have threatened
to leave and start their own firm if the management committee cannot solve the problem soon. When the founding partner ran the
firm he personally "divided the pie," as he called it. No one disputed
his decisions, but now, with the days of benevolent dictatorship over,
and the firm operating more democratically, a lot of vocal protest
has broken out.

Profits generated by individual partners vary a great deal. Some produce over $1 million a year, others less than half that. Partner performance also varies from year-to-year. A partner may generate large revenues one year and much less the next. One partner registered only $200,000 in profits last year because she worked mostly on a case for a contingency fee and will not receive anything unless she wins the case when it goes to trial next year. The following chart, prepared the last year the founding partner ran the firm, lists the partners in order of seniority, their individual profits generated and compensation awarded.

Compensation Awarded Last Year by the Founding Partner			
	Seniority (Years with the firm)	Profits Generated	Compensation Awarded
Founder	35 years	$ 600,000	$1,500,000
Partner A	32 years	$ 800,000	$1,500,000
Partner B	30 years	$1,400,000	$1,200,000
Partner C	25 years	$1,500,000	$ 900,000
Partner D	22 years	$ 200,000	$ 700,000
Partner E	18 years	$ 700,000	$ 800,000
Partner F	15 years	$ 800,000	$ 600,000
Partner G	12 years	$1,000,000	$ 600,000
Partner H	10 years	$ 500,000	$ 500,000
Partner I	9 years	$ 600,000	$ 400,000
Partner J	8 years	$ 900,000	$ 300,000

You must fashion a compensation system that will fairly address the interests of all the partners, not just for the coming year, but year-to-year for the foreseeable future. Partner A wants to keep the existing system, giving full authority to make all compensation decisions to the most senior partner. Partners B, C, D and E want a lock-step system that assigns one point for each year of seniority. Individual compensation would be calculated by dividing a partner's individual points by the total of all partners' points and multiplying the result by the firm's total profits for the year. Partners F, G, H, I, and J want a full merit system, with profits distributed by a compensation committee charged with the responsibility to make sure high-performing partners receive substantially more than other partners, regardless of seniority.

Partners A, B, C, D and E threaten to leave the firm if a merit-only system is implemented without regard to seniority. Partners F, G, H, I, and J threaten to leave unless some form of merit system is implemented.

If you do not come up with a creative plan that wins acceptance of the full partnership, the firm will inevitably dissolve and everyone will lose. Think imaginatively as you generate creative solutions and pick the best to recommend to the management committee. Can you fashion a better system than any suggested by the partners? Check the Notes after crafting your best solution.

THINK FOR YOURSELF

Apply the lessons of this chapter to your own life.

Imagine Your Future

You don't need a crystal ball to see your future. Use your imagination, focusing first on your working career and then on your private life.

Starting on the left side of a large blank sheet of paper, write down your working situation today. As an example, write your line of business, job position, compensation, and other key facts. Draw a circle around your present situation. Next, draw short lines to the right, like tree branches, listing alternatives or changes in your career that you want or expect to see in the next five years. Exercise your most creative imagination when coming up with various alternatives, especially for what you *want* to occur. Assign probabilities to each branch. Next, go to the end of the new branches, draw more short lines to the right, and list subsequent alternatives or changes. Repeat the process for the following five years, listing wants, expectations, and probabilities. Write years across the top of the page as you progress. Cover your life up through age 70 or beyond.

When you finish, and not before, go back to the beginning and circle in black the branches representing the most probable path of your life. Then return to the beginning once more and circle in red the branches representing the path you most *want* to take, regardless of probabilities. Now compare the two paths, imagining what, specifically, you can do to change your future from the likely path to the most desired path. Write down the steps you intend to take now and in the future to make what you want a reality.

When you complete the process for your career, repeat it for your private life. Devote as much time as you need to this project. Exercise a vivid imagination; imagine courageously; imagine your way through adversity, frustration, and failure; think beyond the bounds of conventional wisdom; and imagine the very best solutions.

THINK ABOUT IT

Pause for a moment to consider how you can better use your imagination to think more creatively. Ask yourself:

- What prevents me from getting the most out of my imagination, and how will I limit the influence of these negative forces?
- What pressures for conformity must I resist to improve the quality and results of my creative thinking?
- Do any naysayers, critics, and idea killers squelch my creativity, and how will I deal with them to free my thinking from their harmful influences?
- Does fear of failure unnecessarily limit my creativity, and, if so, how will I conquer my fears and set my creativity free?
- How will I make sure I do not accept conventional wisdom when I ought to think beyond it to find better solutions?
- Why do I sometimes settle for the first workable solution that comes to mind when I ought to continue thinking to find the

best, and what will I do to make sure I continue thinking when only the best will do?

- Why do I sometimes judge prematurely rather than think imaginatively while leaving judgment to later? On these occasions, what will I do to withhold judgment in order to promote creativity?

- How will I better apply each standard of quality thinking (clarity, accuracy, comprehensiveness, sensibility, and intellectual honesty) to my creative thought?

ALWAYS CHECK TO MAKE SURE

Think imaginatively when you need innovative solutions and want to make better decisions.
USE YOUR IMAGINATION:

Exercise a Vivid Imagination

Imagine Courageously

Imagine Your Way Through Adversity, Frustration, and Failure

Think Beyond the Bounds of Conventional Wisdom

Imagine the Very Best Solutions

Notes to Chapter 5

Make a Chocolate-Covered Candy Bar

Create a metal mold with cavities matching the outer shape and size of your candy bar. Chill the mold in a freezer, then fill the cavities with milk chocolate. Wait a short while as the cold surface of the mold hardens the outer layer of chocolate. At just the right moment, tip the mold over and pour out the as yet unhardened center portions of the chocolate. Now pour your secret chewy center into the cavities and cover the open bottoms with chocolate. Allow the bars to cool to room temperature, pop them out of the mold, and enjoy sweet success.

What Do You See?

The photograph was taken just as Mary C. Fitzpatrick, on the left, was named Miss Teenage America, 1971, with first runner-up Mary A. Grabavoy on the right.

Besieged

Did you courageously imagine that you could use your two precious sacks of grain for something more important than short-term survival? In a few days you will run out of food anyway. Throw one of the grain sacks over the wall as a display of strength and contempt for your enemy. The barbarians might then abandon their starvation strategy and: (1) depart, not wanting to incur further losses; or (2) attack, in which event your soldiers are better prepared to fight now, even in their weakness, than after the grain has run out entirely.

Losing Proposition

You must become as tricky as the guard. You can, for example, reach into his hat, fumble with the coin you select, and drop it over the side of the bridge, where it will disappear into the chasm below. Then say to the guard: "Reach into your hat so we can figure out which coin I dropped."

Find Hidden Treasures by Learning from Failures

Letter the grid across the top from A to H and along the left side from 1 to 8. Find the treasure by process of elimination, such as: "Is the treasure buried in square A-1?" Of course, a square-by-square approach leaves too much to chance, and you can only try eight times. However, you can reduce the odds by asking, for example: "Is the treasure buried in Column A?" Do not let frustration tempt you to quit, and do not turn to the Supplemental Solutions at the end of the book without having solved the problem on your own.

Knotty Problem

Nothing requires you to take the knot apart in a way that leaves the rope intact in a single strand. Grab a sword, as Alexander the Great did, and hack the knot to pieces.

Stuck Truck

Let enough air out of all your tires to lower your rig a little more than 2 inches. Then drive out from under the obstruction.

Solve a Compensation Dispute

Consider a combination lock-step and merit system. Reserve an agreed-upon percentage of profits in a bonus pool to be distributed solely on merit by an elected compensation committee as desired by Partners F, G, H, I and J. Distribute the remaining profits using a lock-step system, as desired by Partners B, C, D and E. A combination merit and lock-step system possesses features wanted by all the partners. The percentage reserved for the bonus pool can be adjusted to a level that all can accept, even though it may not fully satisfy anyone.

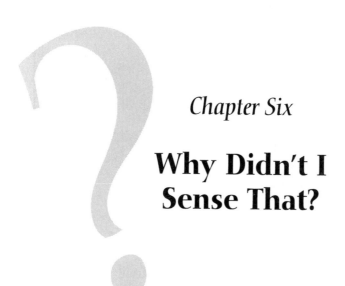

Chapter Six

Why Didn't I
Sense That?

Listen to Your Inner Voice

"Half a league, half a league, half a league onward, all in the valley of Death rode the six hundred." Six hundred seventy-three gallant British cavalrymen dashed headlong through a gauntlet of murderous cannon and musket fire to a certain but unnecessary death on October 25, 1854. *"Cannon to the right of them,"* wrote Alfred Lord Tennyson in his poem recounting the scene. *"Cannon to the left of them, cannon in front of them volley'd and thunder'd. Storm'd at with shot and shell, boldly they rode and well, into the jaws of Death, into the mouth of Hell rode the six hundred."*

The Charge of the Light Brigade occurred during the Crimean War. Russia had attacked Turkey with the goal of capturing Constantinople and thereby gaining unobstructed naval access to the Mediterranean through the Black Sea. Britain and France joined forces to counter the Russian aggression, which threatened the peace of Europe. Early in the war an allied army of 60,000 landed in a territory of the Black Sea known as the Crimea and marched toward Russia's main naval base at Sebastopol.

The allies, led by Commander-in-Chief Lord Raglan, advanced to the outskirts of Sebastopol and laid siege to the city. Raglan then sent his cavalry division, headed by Lieutenant General Lucan, rearward to guard the port facility at Balaclava, the allies' sole source of supply, without which they could not continue the siege. As Lord Raglan shelled Sebastopol with heavy guns, the Russians prepared a surprise attack on Balaclava. Only the British cavalry, a few infantrymen and British cannons stood in their way.

A valley surrounded on all sides by rolling hills dominated the approach to Balaclava. Lord Raglan massed his cavalry division at the eastern end, while along the southern hills he placed artillery guns in a series of redoubts that could bombard any advancing enemy. At dawn on October 25, allied artillery gunners opened fire on a 20,000-man Russian force approaching from the north, commencing the Battle of Balaclava.

Hearing the gunfire, Raglan positioned himself on a hill 600 feet above the valley floor, from which he watched the Russians easily overrun his gun emplacements. Soon Russians occupied the hills on three sides of the valley, with the British cavalry blocking the remaining eastern end. The cavalry commander, Lucan, could not at the time see the battlefield or a single soldier on it. Lord Raglan, on the other hand, saw nearly everything: 8 Russian infantry battalions, 4 cavalry squadrons, and 14 cannons atop the northern ridge; 11 Russian battalions and 30 cannons on the southern hill line; and the bulk of the Russian cavalry force massed at the opposite end of the valley with 12 cannons out front.

Russian soldiers began dragging away the British cannons captured on the southern hill line. Horrified by the prospect of losing his guns, Raglan quickly dictated a written message to his cavalry division commander. The dispatch, scratched in pencil on a thin sheet of paper preserved to this day, read: "Lord Raglan wished the cavalry to advance rapidly to the front—follow the enemy and try to prevent the enemy carrying away the guns. Troop Horse Artillery may accompany. French cavalry is on your left. Immediate."

Captain Lewis Nolan delivered the message to Lieutenant General Lucan by riding at full gallop across perilous terrain. Lucan found the dispatch bewildering. Lacking a view of the battlefield, he shouted to Nolan, "Attack, Sir? Attack what? What guns, Sir?" Nolan, who considered the inexperienced Lucan a coward, threw his head back in evident disgust, pointed to the opposite end of the valley, and retorted: "There, my lord, is your enemy. There are your guns."

Lucan hesitated, as well he should have, intuitively sensing something amiss with the order. Every cavalry doctrine of the era held that charging headlong into a battery of cannons backed by massed cavalry could only end in annihilation. On the one hand, Lucan felt duty-bound to obey orders: *"Their's is not to make reply, Their's not to reason why, Their's but to do or die."* On the other hand, Lucan was a British Lieutenant General, expected to "reason why," to keep his head and think, despite the confusion of battle. After all, relying more on intuition than any "book solution," senior British officers had repeatedly won great victories from Trafalgar to Waterloo.

Unfortunately, Lieutenant General Lucan chose to ignore his intuition. Turning to Major-General Cardigan, Lucan ordered the Light Brigade to lead the charge. Cardigan replied, "Certainly, Sir; but allow me to point out to you that the Russians have a battery in the valley on our front, and batteries and riflemen on both sides." Lucan nevertheless instructed Cardigan to proceed.

While Cardigan formed the Light Brigade into three lines at the valley's eastern end, Lucan lined up the remaining Heavy Brigade to their rear. If the Light Brigade could disable the Russian cannons, the Heavy Brigade might advance on the Russian cavalry massed behind the cannons.

As the Light Brigade began its initial measured trot into the "Valley of Death" with Cardigan out front, an uncanny silence enveloped the scene. No one on either side fired a shot. The Russians could not believe any disciplined British cavalry unit would attempt such a counterintuitive maneuver. Surely, the Russian commander thought, this could only signal the beginning of a much larger British attack from other directions as well.

Suddenly Captain Nolan, who had enthusiastically joined the Light Brigade for the assault, galloped his mount forward across the line of advance and passed in front of Cardigan, frantically waiving his sword overhead and pointing to the captured British guns on the hills to the right. Instantly, the first Russian cannon shell exploded near Nolan, sending a shard of white-hot shrapnel into his chest. Then every available Russian cannon and musket opened up on the advancing British.

Lord Raglan, observing all this from his perch 600 feet above the fray, expected to see the Light Brigade now turn to the right and attack the Russians attempting to drag away the captured British guns. Instead, Raglan watched helplessly as the Brigade quickened its pace to a canter and continued heading straight toward the massed Russians and their belching cannons at the opposite end of the valley.

Gunsmoke covered the hillsides as volley after volley poured into the valley, cutting down horse and rider alike. Only the most disciplined and courageous unit could possibly continue through the dreadful carnage. The Light Brigade never faltered, but Lucan, who followed behind with the Heavy Brigade, now exercised his inherent command authority and withdrew the Heavy Brigade beyond range of the Russian guns, watching in disbelief as the Light Brigade rode on, now terribly alone, into *"the jaws of Death . . . the mouth of Hell."*

Yard by deadly yard the Light Brigade advanced into withering fire. With Major General Cardigan miraculously still alive and leading the way, riders and horses reached the Russian gun position, swords swinging and hoofs tramping.

> *Flash'd all their sabres bare,*
> *Flash'd as they turn'd in air,*
> *Sabring the gunners there,*
> *Charging an army, while*
> *All the world wonder'd:*
> *Plunged in the battery-smoke*
> *Right thro' the line they broke;*
> *Cossack and Russian*
> *Reel'd from the sabre-stroke*
> *Shatter'd and sunder'd.*
> *Then they rode back, but not,*
> *Not the six hundred.*

Surrounded by Russian lancers, the British horsemen could now only fight for their own individual survival. While some managed to break out and head back through the valley toward safety, most did not survive the return trip, as cannon and musket fire continued to rake across the field.

The charge of the Light Brigade had lasted twenty minutes from beginning to bloody end. Miraculously, Major General Cardigan, who had led the charge, reached safety unscathed. Lord Raglan later confronted Cardigan in a rage, "What did you mean, Sir, by attacking a battery in front, contrary to all the usages of war and the customs of the service?" Turning next to Lucan, Raglan fumed: "Lucan, you were a Lieutenant General and should therefore have exercised your discretion, and, not approving of the charge, should not have caused it to be made." Raglan's order, however ambiguous, did not require Lucan to "attack at all hazzards," customary language that would have removed Lucan's discretion.

At the end of the day, the Russians successfully carried away seven captured British guns. Months later, an allied assault on Sebastopol failed and Raglan, saying he could never return home with his head held high, died thereafter in the Crimea. The official cause of Raglan's death was recorded as "Crimean Fever," but many who knew him believed he died of a broken heart.

Cardigan and Lucan returned to England. Cardigan received a hero's welcome, with clothiers copying his wool jacket and selling them as "Cardigan" sweaters, a style popular even today. Lucan, forever vilified, remained unrepentant to the bitter end. The British public and the military refused to accept his claim that he had only followed orders. The Light Brigade, most felt, would not have perished had a senior officer exercised his inherent intuitive discretion. Everyone familiar with cavalry warfare knew that intuition, as much, if not more, than precise logic, could spell the difference between life and death in battle.

Unlike many who, after making a terrible mistake, can only wonder "Why didn't I sense that?" Lucan *did* sense the problem in time to correct it, yet he ignored his inner voice at the crucial instant when it spoke most forcefully. Chalk it up to inexperience? Surely a more experienced battlefield commander would have relied on intuition without needing to know exactly why he felt uneasy.

The word "intuition," rooted in the Latin *intueri,* means to comprehend from within one's own mind. Webster's defines intuition as knowing something without conscious use of reasoning. Some call it a hunch; others, a feeling. "I have a funny feeling about this," one might say. "I can't explain it, but I've just got a hunch."

Until recently, a society enamored with the scientific approach has denigrated intuition as a throwback to less enlightened times. But the tide of thought has turned. We now recognize intuition as a faculty successful people use to their great advantage. Researchers, such as Daniel Isenberg, have brought management theorists back to their senses by showing that highly effective business decision-makers rely on intuition as much, if not more, than pure logical analysis. As Isenberg observed in his groundbreaking Harvard Business Review article "How Senior Managers Think," senior managers often leap across logical difficulties to seize opportunities and solve problems. The higher people climb up the corporate ladder, the more they rely on intuition. While their decisions appear quite logical later on, it turns out that intuition played a decisive role in their original thinking. As Alfred P. Sloan, creator of General Motors, observed, "The final act of business judgment is intuitive." Ray Kroc described his intuitive decision to purchase McDonald's against the advice of his consultants this way: "I closed the office door, cussed up and down, threw things out of the window, called my lawyer back, and said, 'Take it!' I felt in my funny bone it was a sure thing."

A funny feeling. A hunch. Each day Americans carry in their wallets and purses a reminder of the value of intuition: On the back of every dollar bill appears the likeness of an unfinished pyramid, with an intuitive eye resting atop the structure as the essential element needed to complete it.

　　Unlike any other contemporary country, the United States sprang from brilliant thinking, but the founders did not depend on logic alone. They listened to the inner voice of intuition and would urge us to do the same.

　　Intuition allows us to discover unseen realities and hidden truths. It alerts us to problems and warns of risks and dangers we might not otherwise detect. How does it work? No one knows for sure. It apparently derives from subconscious thinking, a level of knowledge not readily perceived by the conscious mind. It often arrives unexpectedly as one of those "aha" moments we have all felt but cannot produce on demand. The subconscious mind spawns insights as spectacular as anything the conscious mind generates, and it appears to continue working even when the conscious mind sleeps, explaining why we sometimes wake up in the middle of the night with great ideas we must jot down.

　　The physical division of labor guided by the left and right lobes of the human brain may also explain intuition. *Both sides think,* but in different ways. Since the left side thinks in verbal terms, we label its results "rational," "logical," or "analytical." The right side, however, can produce equally rational, logical, and analytical results, but not in verbal terms, which leads us to label right-side thinking "intuitive."

　　Even before psychologists identified these differences, Sigmund Freud warned against overestimating the role conscious verbal thinking plays in the minds of highly productive thinkers. Sharp thinkers rely on both verbal and nonverbal thinking, on both logical and intuitive thinking, to achieve sound results.

　　Those who do not appreciate the value of intuition often mistake it for wild guessing. Yes, it may appear irrational because of its nonverbal nature, and random because it emerges unexpectedly from the subconscious mind, but intuition is neither irrational nor random. It is just as valid as any conscious verbal thought. Knowing, without at first knowing why you know, does not make what you know wrong. Coming to a conclusion without being able to say how you got there does not make your conclusion illogical.

　　The sharpest thinkers, as the highly intuitive Buckminster Fuller eloquently observed, "capture the awareness and secure the usefulness" of intuition. Unfortunately, we all too often fail to notice, let alone catch and use, our intuitive inspirations. While intuition may *feel* too spontaneous and irrational, we must learn to capture the valuable insights it produces.

Albert Einstein said, "I never discovered anything with my rational mind." Of course, Einstein knew how to think consciously and verbally, and he did it better than perhaps any other person of his century, but he did not think only that way. John Maynard Keynes wrote of Isaac Newton, who invented calculus and discovered gravity: "It was his intuition, which was preeminently extraordinary. . . . He seemed to know more than he could have possibly any hope of proving."

Thinking based purely on conscious reasoning seldom generates the most creative decisions and solutions. Pure logic assembles knowledge by extrapolating from the past. It abides by the law of noncontradiction, rejecting new possibilities that at first appear to confound existing knowledge. Intuition, on the other hand, often generates contradictory possibilities that initially defy conventional wisdom. Living as we do in an uncertain, ambiguous, even random world, we must blend logical thinking with "funny feelings and hunches." Otherwise, we may end up repeatedly asking ourselves, "Why didn't I sense that?"

Knowing the feel of real intuition, listening to the whispering voice from within and trusting what it says, sharp thinkers allow intuition to achieve what reason alone cannot. Warm up your intuition with this problem.

Mental Warm–Up

Faster Than Any Speeding Bullet

You're a test pilot in the Third Millennium. Chuck Yeager broke the sound barrier back in the 1950s, and you now hope to equal the "light barrier" and become the first human ever to travel at the speed of light. Accelerating your spacecraft for several days, you watch as the digits on your speed indicator approach, and then exactly equal, 186,282,396 miles per second, the speed of light. You and your ship do not vaporize as some experts had predicted. As you peer out a front portal over the nose of your craft, you observe dazzling stars, but you also see your face's reflection on the inside surface of the glass-like opening. Suddenly you suspect you might not actually have matched the speed of light, no matter what your indicator shows. Light reflecting off your face would need to travel *faster* than the speed of light to reach the glass, and that's theoretically impossible.

Should you send a message back to your controllers on Earth telling them your attempt to travel at the speed of light has failed? Let intuition supply you with an answer reason alone cannot produce.

LET INTUITION DO
WHAT REASON ALONE CANNOT

As you discovered while imagining you were shooting through space faster than any speeding bullet, intuition can lead to answers that reason alone does not provide. The most crucial on-the-spot decision made in the final moments leading to the first moon landing may not have been made by Neal Armstrong, piloting Apollo 11's landing craft, Eagle, or by copilot Buzz Aldrin, or by Gene Kranz, directing the flight team at Houston's Mission Control, but rather by a 26-year-old computer whiz named Steve Bales. When Eagle's computer malfunctioned, Bales intuitively made a split-second choice that saved the mission, but could just as easily have caused a catastrophic crash onto the rocky lunar floor.

As Neil Armstrong ignited Eagle's descent engine at 50,174 feet above the Moon's surface, he began his computer-assisted flight to the landing point below. Eagle dropped along an increasingly steep downward arc, its onboard computer gradually adding rocket power to full throttle. Without assistance from a sophisticated computer, no pilot, however talented, could possibly fly the boxy, wingless craft. Second-by-second the system automatically performed a long list of tasks.

Suddenly, at 6,000 feet, a computer alarm sounded in Eagle's cockpit and emergency lights flashed both inside the craft and at Mission Control. Consoles displayed the numbers 12-0-2, indicating Eagle's computer had overloaded under the strain of performing all its required tasks in the short span of each one-second cycle.

Everyone at Mission Control sensed an approaching abort: a dangerous, untried maneuver in which the astronauts would detonate explosive bolts, jettison the descent stage and its burning engine, ignite a separate ascent rocket, and, with luck, return safely to lunar orbit.

Neal Armstrong radioed urgently: "Give us the reading on that twelve-oh-two program alarm."

Flight Director Gene Kranz called for a response from Steve Bales, his GUIDO (space jargon for "guidance officer.") Steve wanted more time to think. Kranz pounded his fist on a metal display console, demanding an answer.

Bales had programmed Eagle's computer so it would perform the most important landing calculations first in each of its preset one-second cycles. Even if the computer overloaded and could not finish all its work in one second, the most vital tasks should have been performed before the computer cycled back to the top of its list of split-second tasks. If the overload continued, however, Bales knew the whole computer might begin slowing down, taking more time to execute. If this happened, the whole system could abruptly halt. Simulations run during the last days before launch had shown the computer could recover from an overload, provided it did not occur repeatedly.

"GO!" Bales shouted back to Kranz.

Moments later, at 4,000 feet, Kranz polled each flight controller on a final GO/NO-GO for landing. Steve paused. His console now showed continuing 12-0-2 alarms. The overload occurred again and again, something no one had expected could happen.

"GO," Steve responded.

At 3,000 feet a 12-0-1 alarm flashed, a new variety of computer overload. At 2,000 the alarm sounded again, prompting Neil Armstrong to call out: "Twelve alarm. Twelve-oh-one alarm."

"GUIDO, what about it?" Kranz snapped at Bales.

A "NO-GO" from Steve at this point would instantly lead to an abort order from Kranz. Alan Shepard, America's first person in space, and Deke Slayton, NASA's Chief Astronaut, recounted the moment best in their book *Moon Shot*. "Program alarms were still leaping onto the monitoring screens. Bales had to judge whether

Neil and Buzz would have a good computer working for them. . . . In a flash of memory and instinct, he reviewed all the practice and simulator runs they'd made. . . . But that was practice. This was it. He had a *gut feeling* . . . that he wasn't jeopardizing the lives of two men so far away. Yet there were those alarms."

Was the computer slowing down? Would it suddenly stop performing vital calculations? Reason alone could not provide a sure answer. No time existed for careful thought. Bales could only allow his intuition to accomplish what reason alone could not, and somehow he had a hunch the computer would accomplish its mission, even though he lacked the time necessary to figure out exactly why.

Deke Slayton saw the confidence in Steve Bales's eyes as Bales shot his answer back to Kranz.

"GO! Just GO!" Bales shouted.

When Bales made his decision, he did not know the remaining 2,000 feet would take much longer for Eagle to descend than planned. The astronauts had omitted a procedural step long before starting the descent, causing Eagle to overshoot the intended flat terrain and hurtle toward heavily-cratered, boulder-strewn territory. As Armstrong extended the flight, skipping over treacherous rocks and craters, Buzz Aldrin caught a yellow "low-fuel" light suddenly flashing in Eagle's cockpit. Eagle had only 30 seconds of fuel remaining.

Bales's computer continued its vital calculations, but Eagle should have landed by now, and the alarms continued. Leaving the computer to Bales, Gene Kranz turned his attention to the dangerously low fuel. If the tanks drained empty before Kranz initiated an abort, Eagle and its two astronauts would crash onto the hard lunar floor before the ascent rocket could fire up. Death loomed only seconds away. Grabbing the handles on either side of his console, and holding on for dear life as if he were now riding Eagle alongside Armstrong and Aldrin, Kranz chose to rely on the instincts of his two astronauts.

"Light's on," Aldrin radioed, as Armstrong continued searching for a safe landing site.

"At such a moment a pilot flies," Alan Shepherd and Deke Slayton later wrote. "Neil could *feel* what fuel they had left," just as Bales could *feel* the performance of his computer, and Kranz could *feel* the wisdom of trusting his astronauts' judgment rather than his own.

The world listened breathlessly, unaware of the peril, as the final seconds before landing ticked away. Then came the words history will never forget.

"Houston, Tranquility Base here," Armstrong radioed. "The Eagle has landed."

Mission Control and millions around the world went wild.

Later, in a calmer moment, Gene Kranz spoke for Steve Bales, Neil Armstrong, Buzz Aldrin, and everyone in Mission Control when he described as "intuitive" the amazingly sharp thinking that first landed humans on the Moon. The hunches, the funny feelings, the experienced intuition of all involved had accomplished what reason alone could not. You, too, can use it to advantage in many ways.

1. *Intuition senses problems.* Before ordering the charge of the Light Brigade, Lieutenant General Lucan sensed a problem but ignored his doubts. Centuries later, intuition could have saved the space shuttle Challenger from catastrophe, but those in charge ignored doubts raised by workers who sensed problems. Most of us do not command armies or launch rockets, but turning a deaf ear to intuition's warnings can produce devastating results in our own lives and the lives of others.

2. *Intuition leaps across the unknown.* Modern problems and decisions often take us to the brink of the unknown, across which we must somehow leap mentally. Here, in Albert Einstein's words, "[t]here are no logical paths . . . only intuition. . . ." In some instances, only intuition can supply the inspiration to reach beyond reason and logic to find higher ground.

3. *Intuition detects unseen patterns and relationships.* Intuition allows us to detect things when we do not know exactly what we are looking for, to see hidden connections among things that at first appear unrelated. Isaac Newton discovered gravity by detecting the previously unseen relationship between a falling apple and the orbiting Moon. Albert Einstein discovered rela-

tivity in part by imagining the hidden relationship between a falling person and the dimensions of time and space.

4. *Intuition promotes creativity.* Fred Smith, founder of Federal Express, says, "If you want to innovate, you have to be capable of making intuitive judgments." Jonas Salk, who discovered a vaccine for polio and eradicated the disease from the face of the Earth, said, "We should trust our intuition. . . . Effective creative conceptualization requires that one incorporate reason and logic, as well as intuition and feeling." Intuition equals innovation.

5. *Intuition enables sound risk-taking.* As Steve Bales, Neil Armstrong, Buzz Aldrin, and Gene Kranz demonstrated in the final seconds before the first Moon landing, intuition helps us make sharp on-the-spot decisions in risky situations where conscious thought fails. The same applies even when we possess plenty of time to think.

6. *Intuition keeps us thinking when we might otherwise stop.* Hunches sometimes urge us to continue thinking even though we feel tempted to quit. The first workable solution we find may not be the best. A feeling we cannot articulate in words sometimes suggests we might develop a better solution if we will only continue thinking.

In these and many other situations, sharp thinkers let intuition accomplish what reason alone cannot. Using your intuitive skills, detect patterns that others might not discern as you examine this artwork.

Mental Aerobics

Gala Contemplating the Mediterranean Sea

Salvador Dali, the master of surrealist painting, depicted his wife looking through a window at the ocean in a work titled *Gala Contemplating the Sea*. Do you see another subject in the work? Do not move the image back from your eyes or step away from the book. Allow the pattern-seeking capacity of your intuitive mind to provide an answer.

The Group

Try another exercise. Use all your insight to answer two questions about this photograph.

What is this group?

Who is the missing person?

Practice Makes Perfect

Use Your Intuition to Its Full Advantage

List specific examples of how you have engaged your intuition in each of these ways:

- Sensing problems
- Mentally leaping across the unknown
- Detecting unseen patterns and relationships
- Thinking creatively
- Taking risks
- Continuing to think when you might otherwise stop

LEARN THE "FEEL" OF REAL INTUITION

Intuition can do what reason alone cannot, but only if we recognize its voice, sense its presence when intuition draws near and speaks in its sometimes whispered tones. Recognizing the "feel" of real intuition can make the difference between life and death, as police cadets discover during their weapons training. Many large metropolitan police departments use computers and laser simulators to train officers in the appropriate use of deadly force. Officers stand in front of film projection screens and confront computer-simulated situations requiring them to make lightning-quick intuitive decisions about whether to draw and fire their weapons.

Imagine you're a police officer standing ten feet from a floor-to-ceiling screen where life-sized people are acting out a convenience store robbery. You see the store's swinging glass doors directly in front of you about fifteen feet away. A sales clerk stands behind a checkout counter to your left. Your training officer says you're an undercover deputy carrying a concealed pistol.

On the screen you observe a teenage boy entering the store through the front doors and walking to your right. The camera, serving as your eyes, follows the boy as he proceeds toward the cold drink dispensers at the rear of the store. Quickly the camera rotates back to the front counter, where you now see a masked man pointing a revolver at the sales clerk. Since the robber has not yet noticed you, you can swiftly draw your own weapon.

Will you draw and intervene or do nothing, hoping the robber takes the money and leaves without harming anyone? If you draw and command the robber to "drop it," as I did the first time I stood in front of the training screen, the robber freezes. Then he slowly turns his back to you, still holding his weapon, but blocking your view of his revolver. If you again command the man to drop his pistol, as I did, he turns back around in your direction as his hand, with the gun, moves downward toward the floor.

What does the robber intend to do: Give up or shoot you? Will you fire or wait to see if the robber drops the gun? If you choose to wait and see, your reaction will inevitably lag behind his action.

Actions always beat reactions. He might fire the first shot and kill you before you can pull the trigger.

Only intuition supplies the answer in the split-second available. Will you shoot or wait? Seasoned police officers will sometimes shoot, but they often risk their lives and do not. What will you do? State your answer out loud now. Shoot? Wait?

The simulated robber pauses, looks directly into your eyes, moves his hand again, and drops his weapon onto the tiled floor. Did you shoot? If you fired, you killed a man doing exactly what you commanded him to do when you told him to "drop it." If you did not shoot, what will you do next? Will you command the robber to lie down face-first on the floor so you can handcuff him? Take a moment to think about it.

While you're thinking, the camera, again acting as your eyes, suddenly rotates to the right as if you have looked over your right shoulder. A shotgun blasts from the right, and the last thing you see is the young boy who earlier entered the store now holding a smoking gun aimed directly at you. Robbers generally work in pairs, something you did not consider. The projection screen fades to black.

Stunned by the turn of events, you slip your pistol back into its holster as your training officer suggests you try the simulation again. The projector restarts. This time you stand motionless, pistol tucked away, as the robber takes the cash at gunpoint and runs out of the store, followed seconds later by his youthful and armed companion.

"Should I have pulled out my weapon the first time?" you ask the training officer.

"There's no absolute right or wrong answer," he answers. "You must rely on your training and experience and do what you *sense* is right in the circumstances."

"If I drew my weapon, should I have fired when the robber turned toward me?"

"When the robber turned, he had the advantage," your trainer answers. "He could have fired first. It's a tough call, and only you can make it."

We may never face on-the-spot, life-and-death situations of the sort police officers must confront every day. Still, we must learn the *feel* of real intuition in difficult, risky situations. Police officers learn that feel in training sessions and on the beat. So, too, must we train ourselves to call up and trust intuition in the many situations we encounter where logic alone will not carry the day.

Stretch your thinking with this exercise where the solution emerges with an intuitive "aha!"

Mental Aerobics

Sense the Pattern

What pattern determines whether a number belongs inside the triangle or inside the circle? If you do not quickly find the solution, look at the shapes of the objects and numbers without thinking in verbal terms. Notice intuition's *feel* the instant it supplies the insight needed to solve the problem.

Practice Makes Perfect

Identify Your Intuitive Cues

This two-step exercise will help you identify your feelings when real intuition arrives. Recall the list of examples you compiled in the preceding Practice Makes Perfect exercise titled "Use Your Intuition to Its Full Advantage." For each example you listed there, describe as precisely as possible what you *feel* the moment you experience intuition's presence.

Now, place several small cards in your wallet or purse. Over a period of at least two weeks, write down descriptions of what you feel on each occasion when you experience intuition's presence in day-to-day situations.

Compare the results of this follow-up exercise with those of the initial one. You will likely discover that you have significantly improved your ability to sense and rely on real intuition in just two weeks. Consider how much more you can improve by *consciously* using intuition more frequently throughout your thinking.

TRUST YOUR INTUITION

Feeling the presence of intuition and relying on it are two different matters. How do you know when to trust your intuition? It's not always easy. During my stint as a lawyer, I received a call one afternoon from the owner of Central Lumber Company, a long-time client, asking for legal assistance in obtaining payment on a large plywood order sold and delivered to a local construction company. When the construction company, Upland Builders, did not respond to several letters I wrote on behalf of Central, I filed a lawsuit to collect the more than $50,000 due. I expected a fairly simple court proceeding, but Upland responded by claiming it had returned the entire order to Central's lumber yard because the material failed to meet required specifications.

I met with Central's lumber yard supervisor, Ernest Escobito, on an unusually hot summer afternoon to learn what, if anything, he knew about the returned material. Ernest protested that neither he nor any of his yard workers remembered the return. After several hours in Ernest's tiny office, with only the breeze of an old fan providing relief from the sweltering heat, we failed to locate any written record of the plywood return.

Weeks later I received a call from my client saying he had just met with Upland's owner, who handed him a copy of a warehouse receipt signed by Ernest Escobito showing Upland had indeed returned the order. Ernest soon arrived at my office in his sweaty shirt and sawdust-covered boots with the document in hand.

"I'm almost positive I didn't take back that plywood from Upland," he said.

"What about your signature on the document?" I asked.

"I don't remember signing it," Ernest replied.

"Have you ever seen it before?"

"Not that I recall."

"Look carefully at the signature," I suggested.

Ernest inspected the handwriting one last time, then said: "It looks like my signature, but I don't think it is."

Placing his strong laborer's hand on my arm as we stood to end the meeting, Ernest asked: "What's going to happen with this?"

"I don't know," I answered. "I just don't know."

The next morning I reported the details of our meeting to Central's owner.

"What really happened with the plywood?" he asked.

"I can't say for sure," I had to add, "Right now it's Ernest's word against the word of Upland's owner."

"Then, we lose!" my client growled. "Escobito doesn't have a chance against that Upland guy."

Hoping to find evidence supporting Ernest, I hired a handwriting examiner who compared samples of Ernest's real signature with the signature on the warehouse receipt. Ernest sat with me as the expert explained his results. The signature on the receipt was most likely a forgery, the expert believed, but he could not prove it with certainty. It appeared "too perfect" to be genuine, he said, but he felt the chances of convincing a jury were no better than "50/50." "People find it difficult to understand the subtleties of handwriting differences," the expert said. "Most people have never seen a forgery, they don't question signatures in their everyday lives. Upland will surely find a handwriting expert who will say the signature is genuine."

In the weeks leading up to trial I learned more and more about Ernest, not only as a lumber yard supervisor, but as a human being. Workers in the yard would do anything for him and trusted him completely to look out for their best interests. The man was the soul of honesty; everyone agreed.

I stopped billing time to the case because my client did not want to incur any more legal bills prior to trial. Still, I felt compelled to continue working for nothing, trying to find the needed proof without any specific idea what it might be. I had run out of ideas, yet I somehow sensed a solution near at hand. Reason told me to shift gears and work productively on other cases, but at the same time intuition counseled otherwise. Which should I obey? After some restless pondering, I chose intuition over logic, set aside all other work, and dove back into the case, determined to reexamine the whole matter from top to bottom.

Late one evening, out of sheer desperation, I removed dozens of documents signed by Ernest from a stuffed file folder and spread them out on a long conference-room table. Lifting a copy of the disputed warehouse receipt up to the ceiling lights directly overhead, I inspected the document as if it might be a counterfeit dollar bill, but with no clue how to distinguish it from the real McCoy. Then I grabbed another document that I knew for sure Ernest had signed, placed it on top of the disputed receipt, and held the two up to the light. The signatures did not match. Repeating the process with other papers signed by Ernest, I found to my surprise that none of the signatures matched, at least not exactly. They all varied much more than I expected.

Curious about the variations, I signed my own name on three pieces of paper and held them up to the light. They also differed significantly. Experimenting again, I tried hard to write my signature exactly the same three times in a row. Again they differed.

Not knowing what to make of this, I collected the papers from the tabletop, turned off the lights, and headed down to my car in the garage below. Sitting behind the steering wheel, I wondered, "Why can't I let this go?" Suddenly the answer struck me.

"It's a tracing!" I thought. "Two signatures cannot match exactly unless one is a forgery. If I can find a signature exactly matching the warehouse receipt, it will be *the* source of the tracing. If I can prove the document used for tracing was at some point in Upland's possession, I can make a strong case that Upland forged Ernest's signature."

Rushing back to my deserted office, I sifted through a pile of documents copied from Upland's files months before. Soon I found a copy of the loading dock release Ernest had signed and given to Upland when it first picked up its order from Central's yard. Laying the release on top of the disputed warehouse receipt, and lifting the two up to the light, I saw that the signatures matched perfectly! Drawing a deep breath and smiling ear-to-ear, I felt my tired eyes moisten as I realized that I now possessed the proof needed to exonerate Ernest. Looking back on the case, I realized that only intuition had kept me searching when reason told me to quit. I now knew, as never before, that successful lawyers must trust their intuition far more than I ever imagined.

I make this point with law students whenever I teach them how to select trial juries in the courtroom process called *voir dire*. Since the composition of a jury can greatly affect the outcome of a case, lawyers sometimes pay huge sums for behind-the-scenes advice provided by jury-selection experts. In most cases, however, lawyers must select juries without the help of such expensive consultants. I tell my students that if they will learn to trust their intuition, they can generally do the job as well as any high-priced expert. I conduct a little experiment to prove my point.

I select one student to act as the prosecutor in an imagined case and send her out into the hallway. With our prosecutor out of hearing, I pick another student to act as a potential juror, instructing him to assume a fact about himself that, if discovered by the prosecutor, will make it easy for her to decide whether to accept or excuse him from the jury. The student juror must answer all questions truthfully but treat the secret fact as if it, too, were true.

Now I call the student prosecutor back into the classroom and allow her to question our student juror. If the prosecutor asks the right questions, she discovers the secret fact and easily decides the potential juror's fate. Time and again I repeat the process with different students acting as prosecutors and jurors with different secret facts.

Would it surprise you that only about 20 percent of the student prosecutors uncover the secret fact? Still, I require all who miss the fact to announce whether they will accept or excuse their student juror. "Rely on your intuition, your gut feel," I say, "even if you don't know exactly why you feel as you do."

Those who miss the secret fact find, to their astonishment, that they still choose correctly at least 75 percent of the time. Our subconscious minds hold a vast array of information, gathered from years of experience, that enables us to make reliable intuitive judgments about people. Intuitively realizing this, sharp thinkers, including talented law students, learn to rely on their intuition in situations where others might trust only their conscious logic. My students quickly realize, as we all must, that their success hinges on using all their mental resources, conscious and subconscious, verbal and nonverbal.

Trust your intuition and reason as you solve the following crime.

Mental Aerobics

Little Boy's Mittens

You're an FBI agent who has solved so many difficult cases that local law enforcement agencies often call you for advice. One day police in Wyoming contact you in a murder case where a 2-year-old child disappeared after his mother stepped into the downstairs bathroom of her apartment complex and left him unattended in the hallway for no more than a minute at most. Thinking her child had wandered out-of-doors to play in the normally safe neighborhood, the mother ran outside, where she soon found one of her son's mittens on the blacktop of a nearby parking space. In a panic, she called 911 and frantically yelled, "Someone's kidnapped my little boy!" Police arrived within minutes and searched the neighborhood for hours without finding the boy or anyone who had seen him that day. News organizations quickly picked up the story and broadcast footage that night of the mother begging through tears for her toddler's safe return.

Three days later an anonymous package arrived at the mother's address. Inside she found her little boy's other mitten, but no ransom note. One month passed with no new leads to go on, and the Wyoming police have turned to you for help.

As an experienced investigator, you know that three types of people commit most of the child kidnappings in the U.S. not involving child custody battles: people wanting money; people who molest children; and childless people wanting kids of their own. Custody is not an issue here. The Wyoming police ask whether you feel the child is dead or alive and, if dead, who you think most likely committed the crime.

Start with your intuition, make your best predictions, and then search the facts to test whether your intuition checks out.

Practice Makes Perfect

Four Intuitive Steps

Identify an unsolved problem at work or home and apply your intuition to find the best solution using the following steps:

- Step 1: *Immersion*

  Compile facts and figures. Read materials on the subject. Talk to people. Think intensely about the problem. Develop alternatives. *Exhaust your conscious thinking without settling on a final solution.*

- Step 2: *Incubation*

  Now, *instruct your subconscious mind to solve the problem,* stepping away mentally to give your brain plenty of processing time. Consciously check in from time to time to make sure your subconscious mind knows you still want to find a solution. Add further conscious input if necessary, but allow your subconscious to continue working without interference.

- Step 3: *Insight*

  Remain sensitive to any feelings or hunches indicating your intuition has solved the problem. Capture every significant intuitive insight when it occurs, and continue the process until you believe you possess the best possible solution.

- Step 4: *Validation*

  Apply reason to test the validity and wisdom of your solution. If you're not satisfied with the result, return to either the immersion or incubation stage and begin anew.

BEWARE OF FALSE INTUITION

Intuition is indeed a powerful thinking tool, but, like all good things, it can be abused, as Lee Iacocca learned the hard way when he relied too much on intuition in his dealings with the mercurial Henry Ford II. One afternoon, Ford summoned Iacocca to his office. As President of Ford Motor Company, Iacocca had earned a reputation as one of the auto industry's most talented executives. Under his leadership, Ford had earned over $3.5 billion in the last two years, a staggering sum in those days. For nearly three years Iacocca had suspected that Henry Ford wanted to fire him, but Iacocca intuitively believed the Board of Directors would not allow Ford to squander one of the company's most valuable human assets. For once, though, Iacocca's often flawless intuition proved wrong, dead wrong.

Iacocca had become President of Ford eight years earlier, twenty-four years after he joined the company straight out of college. Responsible for running a company with over 400,000 employees and sales in the billions, he reported directly to the Chairman and CEO, Henry Ford II, grandson of the company's founder.

Under Iacocca's leadership, Ford Motor Company produced smaller, more fuel-efficient automobiles, a move that prompted the Chairman to retort: "Minicars—miniprofits." Nevertheless, Iacocca pressed on with help from Hal Sperlich, one of his best and brightest confidants. The company successfully launched the small Ford Fiesta in Europe, a product Iacocca wished to introduce into the U.S. market. Henry killed the idea. Still, Ford's revenues improved in the mid-1970s, due, in large measure, to the effectiveness of Iacocca and his management team.

Iacocca sensed trouble brewing. His growing success as President fueled his boss's fear of someday losing control of the company his grandfather had once owned outright. At some point known only to Ford himself, he decided to eliminate the perceived threat by marginalizing Iacocca and embarrassing him into quitting. Openly firing Iacocca would require the Board of Directors' consent, but, this way, Henry could rid himself of his enemy without Board approval. Iacocca stood his ground, refused to quit, and placed his confidence in the Board, feeling the Board, with its nine independent "outside" members, would protect him.

Ford, convening a special meeting of key executives behind Iacocca's back, eliminated several crucial product-development programs involving small cars and fuel efficient front-wheel-drive technology. As Iacocca later wrote in his autobiography: "Henry had waited until I was thousands of miles away to call a meeting where he usurped my power and responsibility—and where he also went against everything I believed in." Later that same year, the Chairman launched an embarrassing and wasteful $2 million investigation aimed at unearthing an excuse to fire Iacocca. While the probe failed to dig up any impropriety, it fostered a "pull the drapes and talk in whispers" atmosphere at corporate headquarters, which caused top executives to concentrate more on personal survival than on work. The company suffered tremendously as a result.

Looking back years later, Iacocca realized, "That was when I should have quit." But, he did not. Why?

Intuition. Like most high-level executives, Iacocca's corporate instincts had served him well. True, he knew Henry Ford's long history of firing perceived threats to his prestige or power, but Iacocca sensed he was an exception. "I . . . clung to the idea that I was different," he later wrote, "that somehow I was smarter or luckier than the rest. I didn't think it would ever happen to me." He sensed he could win what he called "the showdown," the decisive moment when gamblers must lay their cards face up on the table, and one player wins according to the rules of the game.

Iacocca's cards included a record of success his superior could not deny, and Iacocca enjoyed the support and confidence of people at all levels, including key members of the Board of Directors. Henry's brother Bill, who owned more stock in the company than Henry, privately told Iacocca he would not stand idly on the sidelines if Henry tried to fire him.

Looking back later, however, Iacocca admitted: "In my naivete . . . I wouldn't face reality. . . . All I had to do was review history and my autobiography was staring me in the face."

Deciding on a more direct approach, Ford met privately with the company's nine outside directors and said he intended to fire Iacocca. Because Ford effectively controlled all the company's inside directors, only the outside directors would resist him. The outside members tried to cool down the Chairman. Ostensibly responding to their urgings, Ford approached Iacocca to "bury the hatchet," although Ford had no real desire to make peace and, instead, planned to bury the hatchet in Iacocca's hide.

One month later, Henry met again with Ford's outside directors, flatly announcing that he intended to fire Iacocca immediately without further discussion. "It's him or me," Ford demanded. "You have twenty minutes to make up your minds." Push now came to shove, all resistence collapsed, and, in the end, no one dared stand on the opposite side of the line Ford had drawn in the sand.

Ford summoned Iacocca to his private office the next day. "It's been a nice association, but I think you should leave. It's best for the company," Ford said without looking Iacocca in the eye.

When Iacocca pressed for a reason, Ford snapped, "It's personal, and I can't tell you any more. It's just one of those things."

Bill Ford, the only other person present, accompanied the fired executive out of Ford's office.

"This shouldn't have happened, he's ruthless," Bill Ford said.

"Thanks, Bill," Iacocca replied, "but I'm dead, and you and he are still alive!"

Lee Iacocca soon discovered just how dead he really was. His company friends, whom he had confidently thought would stand with him, melted into the corporate woodwork, fearing Ford might fire them as part of an Iacocca purge. "It was the greatest shock of my life," Iacocca later said. Ford had easily intimidated and defeated any and all opposition. Stunned, Iacocca had to ask himself, "Why didn't I sense that?" He had confused sound intuition with one of its most deceptive counterfeits, false confidence.

Real and false intuition can confuse even highly talented thinkers like Lee Iacocca. Both originate in the subconscious mind and call on information and experiences stored there. As with conscious thinking, subconscious patterns can produce both valid and invalid results. Thus, as with conscious thinking, we must test the validity of subconsciously produced thoughts. With intuition, however, we must exercise special care because, unlike conscious reasoning, we cannot objectively monitor the subconscious intuitive process.

To test the validity of a funny feeling or hunch, try asking the penetrating one-word question "Why?" Why do I sense something's wrong here? Why do I feel so certain about this? Why do I feel so strongly about this hunch? Probe further, even if the answer eludes you initially.

Unobstructed by a necessity to provide reasons, intuition generates ideas and solutions that reason alone cannot produce. The absence of conscious reasons is both intuition's greatest strength and its greatest weakness. When trusting intuition's strength, we must beware of its weakness and make sure we *consciously* apply reason to test our hunches and funny feelings. The question "Why?" insists on reasons, while standards of clarity, accuracy, comprehensiveness, sensibility, and intellectual honesty provide the benchmarks needed for testing the quality of reasons that emerge.

"*Why* do I feel these nagging doubts?" you ask. "Do sensible reasons exist for my doubts, or am I simply afraid of the unknown?"

"*Why* do I feel so sure about this?" you inquire. "Do objective reasons support my confidence, or am I only engaging in wishful thinking?"

"*Why* am I uncomfortable with this decision?" you wonder. "Have I missed something, or am I just uncomfortable because the decision requires me to step outside my comfort zone?"

"*Why* do I suddenly feel this decision to be so right?" you ask. "Am I accepting whatever first comes to mind because I'm too tired or impatient to continue thinking until I find the best answer?"

While intuition may arrive without apparent reason, sharp thinkers hold their intuition to the same high reasoning standards they apply to consciously generated thoughts. They know the *feel* of real intuition and trust it to accomplish what reason alone cannot, but they also validate their intuition whenever possible before relying on it.

False intuition tempts us to jump instantly to wrong conclusions. Resist the temptation as you solve these riddles.

--- Mental Aerobics
Intuitive Riddles

Solve both riddles before turning to the Notes for answers.

- *Small-Town Barber.* The sheriff of a tiny Old West town posts a new law intended to clean up the place and provide business for the town's poor barber. The law reads: "All men must be shaved once each week by the barber. No one can shave himself. Anyone who disobeys this law will spend a week in jail." The barber, of course, must also obey the law, as must the sheriff. Who shaves the barber?

- *Prizefighters.* Two lean, muscular, heavyweight boxers fight in Las Vegas for a $100-million purse. The bout, televised around the world, attracts the largest audience in history for a single sporting event. One boxer scores a knockout in the first few seconds of the first round, even though no man throws a punch. Explain how this happened.

Practice Makes Perfect
Detect False Intuition

List at least one example in each of the following categories where false intuition has caused you to make a serious mistake. Then, for each example, ask and answer the question: "Why did I fall victim to false intuition in this instance?"

- A mistake made in your relationship with another person
- An unsound business decision
- An unwise personal choice in your private life
- A problem you attempted to solve with an incorrect intuitive solution

PUT IT ALL TOGETHER
See the Forest, Trees, and All in Between

Intuition allows you to discover unexpected realities. Currier and Ives published *The Puzzled Fox* in 1872. Look deep within the print on the next page to see more than your mind at first comprehends. Allow your subconscious brain to put together unexpected patterns. Use intuition to make discoveries without first knowing exactly what you might find.

THINK FOR YOURSELF

Upgrade Your Intuitive Capacities

On a scale of 1–10, with 1 as least, rate the degree to which you rely on intuition as an element of thinking in *each* of the following tasks:

- Problem-solving
- Decision-making
- Creative thinking

For the task rated least, list specific steps you will take to apply what you have learned from this chapter under each of the following headings:

- Let intuition do what reason alone cannot.
- Learn the "feel" of real intuition.
- Trust your intuition.
- Beware of false intuition.

Now, repeat the second part of this exercise for the remaining two thinking tasks, beginning with the task ranked least among the remaining two.

THINK ABOUT IT

Pause for a moment to consider how you can better use your intuition to make decisions and solve problems. Ask yourself:

- What will I do to improve my awareness of when and how I use intuition?
- In what situations do I need to rely more on intuition?
- In what circumstances do I need to rely less on intuition and more on reason?
- What will I do to capture and preserve intuitive insights more effectively?

- In what specific settings will I practice using intuition to build my trust and confidence in the intuitive process?

- What will I do to make sure I do not confuse raw emotions, wishful thinking, and other forms of false intuition with the real thing?

ALWAYS CHECK TO MAKE SURE

Think intuitively as you make decisions and solve problems at work and at home.
LISTEN TO YOUR INNER VOICE:

Let Intuition Do What Reason Alone Cannot

Learn the "Feel" of Real Intuition

Trust Your Intuition

Beware of False Intuition

Notes to Chapter 6

Faster Than Any Speeding Bullet

Did you sense you would see your reflection on the inside of the spacecraft window, even if you cannot say why? Albert Einstein considered a similar problem when he imagined himself physically traveling on the tip of a light beam gazing into a mirror held in front of his face. Conventional physics said Einstein could not possibly see himself in the mirror. He strongly felt otherwise, though he could not at first explain his hunch.

Responding mostly to intuition, Albert Einstein, like you, sensed that a person traveling at light speed would see a reflection. This insight eventually led Einstein to his amazing theory of relativity. You may not understand relativity, but you, like Einstein, can allow intuition to suggest possibilities initially beyond your capacities of reason, logic, and proof.

Your ship *is* hurtling through space at light speed. Report your observations back to Earth, thank intuition for the insight, and enjoy the ride.

Gala Contemplating the Mediterranean Sea

Dali's original painting viewed from twenty meters transforms into a portrait of Abraham Lincoln modeled after his image on the U.S. $5 bill.

The Group

"The Group" is Microsoft as it existed in 1978 and the missing person is Bill Gates.

Sense the Pattern

Did you waste time trying to find a mathematical progression or formula to solve the problem? Numbers with curved shapes belong in the curved circle. Numbers made only of straight lines belong in the straight-lined triangle. If you solved the problem, your pattern-seeking, nonverbal, intuitive mind probably generated the needed insight.

Little Boy's Mittens

You're working on a case much like the one solved by FBI agent Gregg McCrary, as portrayed by the intuitive crime-solver John Douglas in his book *Mind Hunter.* McCrary surprised local police by concluding the mother likely killed her own baby. The mittens helped lead him to the insight. Finding one mitten dropped in a parking space doesn't indicate much, but what about the mitten received anonymously in the mail? The mother probably mailed the mitten to herself, McCrary thought. Only a kidnapper for cash would risk communicating with her, yet no one ever demanded a ransom. She used the word "kidnapped" when she first called police. Innocent parents initially avoid that word, hoping for the best and not wanting to face grim reality. The mother apparently tried to make it appear as though some third person kidnapped her little boy without first understanding how most kidnappers behave. When local police confronted her with McCrary's intuitive thinking, the mother quickly confessed and led police to her child's body. It later turned out the mother wanted to start a new life with her latest boyfriend without the burden of her unwanted little boy.

Intuitive Riddles

The barber and boxers are all women. If you missed this, false intuition in the form of preconception likely blocked your mind from generating correct answers.

See the Forest, Trees, and All in Between

Consider the full title of the Currier and Ives work: *The Puzzled Fox: Find the Horse, Wild Boar, Mens and Womens Faces.* Now that you know what to look for, examine the print again. Take your time. Refer to the Supplemental Solutions at the end of the book only after you have tried your best to find everything hidden within the print.

Chapter Seven

Why Didn't I Appreciate That?

Think Empathetically

Lehman Brothers, one of Wall Street's premier investment banking houses, traces its illustrious history back to Civil War days. The firm's highly respected chief executive officer of the 1970s, Pete Peterson, who served as Richard Nixon's Secretary of Commerce, focused his talents on developing new business, strategic planning, and servicing a select group of the firm's most valued clients. He delegated day-to-day operational supervision to partner Lew Glucksman, a less gregarious, nuts-and-bolts manager who secretly envied Peterson's power and prestige.

Although Peterson eventually elevated the ambitious Glucksman to "co-chief executive officer," he retained effective control of the CEO's powers. Glucksman's still-subservient role only inflamed the jealousy that lay just beneath the surface of his outward collegiality. Only eight weeks after his elevation, Glucksman privately confronted Peterson, announced his intent to take full control of Lehman, demanded Peterson's resignation, and offered to negotiate a handsome severance package as an incentive for Peterson to step aside quickly without a fight.

Peterson could easily have won any battle for control. As one insider later described the situation, "Glucksman was a guy sitting with a pair of deuces in a poker game and bumping a guy who had three aces showing." But Glucksman understood Peterson's personality better than most. He sensed that Peterson did not wish to engage in a fight that might tarnish his public image. Peterson, Glucksman calculated, would realize that one or the other must go and would himself step aside.

As Glucksman predicted, Peterson chose not to call Glucksman's bluff, folded his otherwise winning hand, dropped out of the game, and negotiated secretly with Glucksman for an immediate transfer of power in return for a $7 million "golden handshake." Notwithstanding their fiduciary duties to the firm as cochief executives, Glucksman and Peterson never sat down together to weigh the best interests of the firm. Instead, after reaching agreement secretly between themselves, the two blindsided Lehman's Board of Directors with their private deal at a meeting called without warning.

With Glucksman and Peterson out of the room, the twelve elected representatives of the firm's seventy-seven partners faced at least two key questions: whether to entrust the reigns of power to Lew Glucksman and whether Pete Peterson's huge payout made good financial sense. Unfortunately, Board members abdicated their collective duty as trustees of the firm's best interests, and, instead, each considered only his *own* personal interests rather than the well-being of the institution, its partners, and employees.

As Ken Auletta described in *Greed and Glory on Wall Street,* the Board behaved "like clerks inspecting the details of a legal document," never touching the core issues concerning the future governance and financial stability of Lehman in the wake of Peterson's hurried, involuntary, and expensive resignation. As Glucksman had shrewdly predicted, Lehman's partners, when confronted with a coup, would only wonder in relative silence: Will *my* annual bonus be cut if *I* speak frankly? Will *I* lose *my* leadership position? Why should *I* put *my* share of the profits at risk by saying anything that might upset Lew Glucksman? Will *I* be forced out of the partnership if *I* appear to take sides and lose? Not once during the fateful meeting did Board members question how Glucksman had orchestrated his coup, whether they should attempt to change Peterson's mind, and, most important, whether Glucksman possessed the temperament and sound judgment needed to succeed as the firm's sole CEO. When a single Board member, Peter Solomon, tried to raise such issues, he received only silence from his colleagues.

Once Lehman's Board passively approved the deal, Glucksman and Peterson summoned all seventy-seven partners to a conference room and announced the deal as a *fait accompli*. Glucksman then turned to Peterson and, in an ominous first exercise of his newly-seized power, insisted disdainfully, "Would *you* now leave and let me be with my partners?" From that moment forward, the Lehman partnership began tumbling downward to its ultimate demise.

With Peterson no longer around to temper his behavior, Glucksman rapidly earned a reputation for capricious, seat-of-the-pants decision-making. Predictably, he vengefully cut the annual bonus of Peter Solomon, the lone board member who had challenged him. The multimillion-dollar payout, coupled with an unanticipated business downturn, and the resignations of many valuable but disenchanted partners, siphoned off a large portion of Lehman's operating capital. Glucksman soon retreated behind a perpetual scowl and increasingly lost all capacity to control the firm's destiny.

Within a year under Glucksman's leadership, Lehman's partners sold out to Shearson/American Express to protect their equity from catastrophic loss. Incoming American Express management terminated several Lehman partners and fired a host of associates who had invested a decade or more working toward partnerships. Hundreds of Lehman employees lost their jobs, and the longest continuing investment banking partnership on Wall Street closed its doors as an independent operating entity.

Lew Glucksman had gambled his otherwise unimpressive pair of deuces and won against aces by correctly predicting how Lehman's partners would think under pressure (selfishly), understanding what primarily motivated them (greed), and sensing how they would react to a threatened coup (passively). Knowing his partners would fear retaliation if they supported Peterson and lost, Glucksman emasculated all potential opposition and leveraged Peterson out of office in short order. In the long run, however, no retaliation Glucksman could have inflicted on his partners remotely approximated the damage done by collapse of the firm. In the end, Glucksman, Peterson, and their partners surely must have asked themselves: "Why didn't I appreciate that?" The answer: They did not fully empathize with anyone other than themselves.

Empathy, taking into account the interests of others, helps fair-minded people make better decisions as they "walk a mile in someone else's shoes." Recognized as a prime virtue, empathy finds its origins in the golden rule: "Do unto others as you would have them do unto you." But this common understanding of empathy, projecting *ourselves* into the place of others, does not capture the full power of empathy.

Rather than imagining what *I* might think and feel if *I* walked in other's shoes, complete empathy concentrates on what *others*, not I, actually think and feel. Complete empathy understands others in the position where *they* find themselves, and asks how *they* think and feel, rather than how I would react if I found myself in the same position.

The common understanding of empathy confuses empathy with sympathy. Sympathy presupposes similarity between my thoughts and feelings and yours. As a sympathizer, I share your pain, your sorrow, your joy, your opinions, your goals. Empathy, on the other hand, allows me to *understand* your unique thoughts and feelings, even if they differ radically from my own. Sympathy aligns my thoughts and feelings with others and implies that I endorse them. By contrast, empathy allows me to appreciate others' differing thoughts and feelings. That's what makes it such an effective and objective thinking tool.

Sharp minds think empathetically to discover what motivates others to act as they do. Warm up your empathetic thinking as you try to read the mind of the little girl in this exercise.

Mental Warm–Up
What Is She Thinking?

You work for a piano delivery company. On arriving at the address listed on your route sheet, you see a small girl running toward you and shouting, "It's here, it's here! My new piano is here!"

"Is your mother home?" you ask.

"Oh yes, yes," she replies.

You and your delivery helper spend the next thirty minutes lugging a heavy upright piano from your truck to the front porch of the house, where you ring the doorbell. On receiving no reply, you press the button again, and again, listening to the bell ringing loudly within. Still no answer.

Seeing the thrilled little girl standing on the front lawn, you say to her, "It's our last delivery of the day. We don't want to drag this heavy piano back to the truck. I thought you said your mother is home."

"She is," answers the little girl. "I told her you're here, and she'll open the door if you ring the bell."

What is the little girl thinking?

CONSIDER WHAT OTHERS THINK AND FEEL

Complete empathy achieves insight by correctly discerning what others think and feel, as the loving King discovered when his 10-year-old daughter lay in bed ill from having eaten too many sweets. On learning that the Royal Doctor worried about his little girl's condition, the King visited Princess Lenore and tried to cheer her up by promising, "I will get you anything your heart desires."

"I want the Moon," the Princess responded. "If I can have the Moon I will be well again."

Wanting only to please his daughter, the King promised her the Moon, then returned to his throne room, summoned his sharpest advisors, and asked them how to fulfill his promise. The Lord High Chamberlain, a large man with thick glasses making him appear very smart, reminded the King of the many difficult-to-obtain things he had acquired for the royal household over the years, such as "angels' feathers and blue poodles," but he could not possibly obtain the Moon. The Moon, he observed, is 35,000 miles from Earth, much larger than the Princess's bedroom, and is made of molten copper.

The disappointed King turned to his Royal Wizard, a narrow-faced man draped in a flamboyant cloak. Reminding the King of the many magical wonders he had worked in the past, including "blood from turnips and turnips from blood," the Wizard admitted he could not conjure an object such as the Moon. After all, he said, the Moon, made of green cheese, is twice as large as the King's palace and 150,000 miles from Earth.

Displeased by the Wizard's ineptitude, the King turned to his Royal Mathematician, a balding man with a pencil behind each ear. Listing the many things he had calculated for the King, including "the distance between the horns of a dilemma" and "the price of the priceless," the Mathematician concluded he could not figure out how to obtain the Moon. After all, he reasoned, the Moon is 300,000 miles away, flat as a coin, and composed of asbestos.

Let down by all his supposedly wise advisors, and thinking no one could help him, the King summoned his Court Jester for solace. Learning the cause of the King's distress, the Jester momentarily strummed his lute, then said of the Moon: "The thing to do is find out how big the *Princess Lenore* thinks it is and how far away."

Why didn't I think of that? the King wondered, as the Jester went to the Princess's bedroom to discover what she thought about the Moon. "Oh," she giggled, "it's just a little smaller than my thumbnail, because I can hold up my thumb and cover the Moon, and it's as close as the tree branches outside my window, because sometimes it gets caught in the top branches."

Now that he understood Lenore's thinking, the Jester rushed to the Royal Goldsmith, instructing him to fashion a small gold disc strung on a golden chain. On receiving her shiny new trinket, Princess Lenore recovered almost immediately and went outside to play in the palace gardens.

Ah, but the King still faced a problem. What if little Lenore discovered she did not possess the real Moon? Again, the King summoned his three advisors who recommended various ways to prevent the Princess from seeing the Moon at night, such as cloaking her bedroom window with thick velvet curtains and covering her eyes with dark-tinted glasses. Thinking these solutions impractical, the King called for his Jester, pointed to the rising Moon, and asked, "Who can explain how the Moon can be shining in the sky when it is hanging on a golden chain around my daughter's neck?"

"Only the Princess can do it," the Jester answered, as he again set out for her bedroom.

On hearing the Jester's "silly" question, Lenore explained that the Moon is like a flower. When you pick a flower, a new one always takes its place.

"Of course!" mused the Jester, as he rubbed his chin, walked over to the open window, looked up at the Moon, and winked— and, according to James Thurber's sweet tale *Many Moons*, when the Jester winked at the Moon, he thought he saw it wink back.

The Court Jester understood that what we think and feel does not always paint a perfect picture of reality. In many situations, no matter how justified our views, we cannot know whether they will carry the day unless we fully appreciate other viewpoints, as Intel discovered when a technically insignificant defect appeared in its revolutionary new Pentium microprocessor. The Pentium, a marvel of human ingenuity, quickly became a huge worldwide success following its introduction into the digital marketplace. But nothing is perfect, of course. A curious math professor discovered a minute computational error while using a Pentium to perform billions upon billions of calculations involving prime numbers.

Alerted by the professor to the problem, Intel's talented engineers soon found a tiny design flaw that they corrected in all future production runs. Since the flaw caused errors in only the most esoteric computations, such as those conducted occasionally by math enthusiasts, Intel saw no good reason to replace the many Pentium chips already on the market, except for those used by customers making the rare complex calculations that might produce errors. From an engineering perspective, it made no sense to replace chips where they would never cause a problem.

To its chagrin, however, Intel failed to fully appreciate how ordinary consumers might react to news of the defect. When the professor published his findings on the Internet, word spread like wildfire around the world and struck alarm in the hearts of consumers. Pentium users of all kinds suddenly doubted the chip's reliability, even though Intel could prove conclusively that the Pentium remained perfectly reliable in all but the rarest circumstances. With consumer anxiety reaching fever pitch, Intel reconsidered its thinking, reversed course, and offered to replace every Pentium on the market, no matter what. The recall, which cost Intel half a billion dollars, would likely have cost less if Intel had fully appreciated possible consumer thoughts and feelings when the technically insignificant flaw first appeared. The experience left many savvy Intel executives wondering, "Why didn't I appreciate that?" A little empathy would have gone a long way toward helping the company avoid the appearance of customer insensitivity.

Complete empathy allows us to see ourselves and others from many different points of view, and often those viewpoints count more than our own. With empathy, we set aside our own thoughts of how others should think and feel, and discover what they in fact think and feel, whether we like it or not. The most creative solutions and best decisions can escape us if we do not approach situations from many different perspectives in addition to our own. Figure out what others think as you tackle this problem.

Mental Aerobics
Think on Your Seat

When three applicants report for a job interview, their prospective employer administers a test to determine who best understands how others think. Placing three chairs in a column, one behind the other, she points to five closed boxes and explains that each contains one cap, totaling three green and two white. Next she randomly removes three caps from their boxes and places one on each seated applicant so that no person sees the hat on his or her own head. The person in back sees the hats on the two applicants in front of him. The person in the middle sees only the hat on the applicant in front of her. The third person cannot see any caps. The applicants are not allowed to turn around and must look straight ahead at all times.

The employer explains she will hire the first person who correctly figures out the color of his or her own cap. All three applicants remain silent for about five minutes. Then the person in front, who cannot see any hats, says, "I'm wearing a green hat."

"Congratulations," the employer replies. "You're hired."

How did the person in the front chair solve the problem? Think empathetically as you figure out what each person was thinking.

Practice Makes Perfect

Sense Others' Real Intentions

Read the following four paragraphs one at a time, *pausing* at the end of each to write down what you believe Tom thinks and feels. Number your written answers to match each paragraph. After you complete the exercise, compare your conclusions with the Notes at the end of the chapter.

1. That afternoon, in an effort to get all her shopping done in one trip, Kelly had overestimated what she could comfortably carry home. As she climbed the few steps to the apartment building door, she saw it had been left unlatched. Next came four flights of stairs, which she wanted to do in one trip. Near the top of the third landing, one of the grocery bags gave way, tearing open and dispensing cans of cat food. The cans rolled down the stairs playfully, as if they were trying to get away from her. "Got it! I'll bring it up," the handsome young man named Tom called out as he bounded up the steps, collecting cans along the way. "Let me give you a hand."

2. "What floor are you going to?" Tom asked. "The fourth," she answered, "but I'm okay, really." He wouldn't hear a word of it, and by this point he clutched a collection of cans between his chest and one arm. "I'm going to the fourth floor, too," Tom offered, "and I'm late. Not my fault, broken watch."

3. "We better hurry," Tom said, "we've got a hungry cat up there. Did you know a cat can live for three weeks without eating? I'll tell you how I learned that tidbit: I once forgot that I'd promised to feed a cat while a friend of mine was out of town." Kelly now stood at the door to her apartment, which she'd just opened. "I'll take it from here," she said.

4. "Oh no, I didn't come this far to let you have another cat food spill," Tom insisted. When Kelly hesitated to let him in her door, he laughed understandingly. "Hey, we can leave the door open like ladies do in the movies. I'll just put this stuff down and go. I promise."

Turn to the Notes to continue the exercise.

DISCOVER WHAT MOTIVATES OTHERS TO THINK, FEEL, AND ACT AS THEY DO

Beyond merely perceiving what others outwardly say and do, complete empathy seeks to discover the underlying motivations behind words and deeds. People do not always act consistently with their true thoughts and feelings, but they rarely depart from their real motives. Underlying motives contain truth, regardless of outward words and deeds, and understanding people's motives enables us to better predict how they will behave in given situations.

Two men named Arnold and Slack took full advantage of these principles when they walked into a San Francisco bank in 1872 and handed a sack to a teller for safekeeping while they tended to other business in town. During their absence, the teller peeked into the sack and discovered $300,000 worth of uncut diamonds. Within minutes he showed the contents to the bank's wealthy owner, William Ralston, who charged outside looking for Arnold and Slack.

On finding the two, Ralston tried mightily to persuade them to tell him where they had obtained the diamonds. Knowing Ralston's notorious reputation for greed, Arnold and Slack resisted, but they eventually gave in and indicated they had mined the diamonds in Wyoming on land they did not own and did not want others to locate. Ralston convinced the two to allow his personal mining engineer to travel blindfolded to the site to evaluate the find.

After stepping off a train in a remote Wyoming town and walking miles blindfolded, Ralston's engineer inspected the site, where he found diamond dust and loose gems on the ground. The engineer returned with Arnold and Slack to San Francisco and reported his findings to Ralston, who implored the miners to let him in on the discovery. Soon Ralston persuaded Charles Tiffany, Horace Greeley, and Baron de Rothschild to invest in the venture. Following a second inspection of the secret Wyoming site, Ralston started pressuring Arnold and Slack to sell their interests, arguing that he had fronted most of the money to finance the project. When the miners demurred, Ralston threatened to sue, and eventually the two capitulated for a one-time payment of $700,000.

News of the diamond discovery leaked out and made banner headlines. Prompted by the reports, a geologist named Emmonds traveled to Wyoming, somehow discovered the site, and found gems laying exposed on the ground. A cursory inspection, however, revealed the gems had been processed with stone-polishing equipment. As it turned out, Arnold and Slack had salted the mine with diamonds purchased in England.

When news of the audacious con hit the front pages of newspapers nationwide, Ralston and his celebrity investors became instant objects of public amusement. Arnold and Slack disappeared with their ill-gotten gain, and Ralston went to his grave embarrassed that his notorious and deeply ingrained avarice had made him such an easy mark. Playing on Ralston's greed, Arnold and Slack had correctly predicted how he would react when enticed with an opportunity to make an easy fortune. Looking back on his folly, Ralston could see that Arnold and Slack were obvious con artists, and he must have wondered, "Why didn't I appreciate that?" The answer: Greed motivated his every thought and deed.

No honest person would condone the behavior of Arnold and Slack, but we can appreciate the fact that they understood a fundamental truth about the human condition. Motives matter most. By knowing what motivates a person, you can discover what he or she really thinks and feels no matter what he or she might say or do, something King Henry VIII of England understood when Sir Thomas More resisted the King with silence and passivity.

As Lord Chancellor, Thomas More became one of King Henry's most trusted and admired advisors. Yet, on July 1, 1535, More stood before a court in London's Westminster Hall accused of privately harboring "treasonous" thoughts that he had never outwardly expressed, even to his wife and closest friends. Still, Henry understood More's hidden motives and staged a rigged trial, after which More was sentenced "to be hanged till you be half dead, after that cut down yet alive, your bowels to be taken out of your body, and burned before you, your privy parts cut off, your head cut off, your body to be divided in four parts, and your head and body to be set at such places as the King shall assign."

Thomas More's career began at Oxford where he studied law. Soon thereafter he became one of England's most respected lawyers and was later elected Speaker of Parliament's House of Commons. The man's brilliance ultimately prompted King Henry to appoint him Lord Chancellor, England's highest judicial officer.

When Henry's wife, Catherine of Aragon, failed to produce a male heir, the King wanted a divorce. However, Catholic Church law, which then governed marriage in England for King and commoner alike, prohibited divorce, except in limited circumstances not applicable to Henry. The King turned to Thomas for help, hoping the marriage could be annulled because Catherine was his brother's widow. More advised the marriage could not be rescinded lawfully. Enraged, Henry tried first to persuade, then to pressure Sir Thomas into aiding his attempts to obtain the divorce. More declined, and Henry eventually gave up trying to enlist him, asking only that he not actively oppose his efforts to persuade the Pope to annul the marriage. Thomas agreed, because he assumed Henry would ultimately obey the law if he could not obtain what he wanted.

Henry dispatched a gold-embellished letter to Pope Clement, signed by many of England's most influential nobles and church officials, with one noteworthy exception—Sir Thomas More. When the letter failed to produce the desired result, Henry declared himself supreme head of the Church of England. Thoroughly disheartened by Henry's conduct, Sir Thomas obtained a private audience with the King, handed back his seal of office, bowed, and resigned as Lord Chancellor, hoping to withdraw quietly into relative obscurity.

Henry's now subservient clergy quickly nullified the King's marriage to Catherine, leaving him free to marry the already pregnant Ann Boleyn. Even though More did not say or do anything to oppose the King, Henry now understood More's underlying motives. In the beginning, Henry had thought Thomas only disagreed with him over a single law, the matter of divorce. He now realized, however, that More steadfastly opposed surrendering the *rule of law* to the rule of any King. If Henry could get away with breaking one law, More believed the King could ultimately break them all, and the winds of absolute monarchy might once again blow across England. This sobering thought motivated Sir Thomas to resist Henry, even if only with passive silence.

Determined to force More out into the open, Henry rammed an Act through Parliament requiring all English subjects to take an oath affirming the King's new status as head of the Church. Royal emissaries soon knocked on More's door, summoning him to take the oath. Appearing as required, More said he could not in good conscience swear the oath. When asked "Why?" More remained silent. Infuriated, the King threw him in the Tower of London and instructed his men to bring a case for high treason.

Sir Thomas defended himself at trial by pointing out the obvious: He had not said or done anything treasonous against the King. "For my silence," he said, "neither your law nor any law in the world is able to justly and rightly punish me." The court, however, did the King's bidding and condemned More to a traitor's death by drawing and quartering, which Henry mercifully commuted to beheading. Five days later Thomas climbed the Tower's scaffold to his death.

In the end, long after Henry's reign, history awarded Sir Thomas the victory of his convictions. Indeed, our national commitment to the rule of law stems, in part, from the ideas held by Sir Thomas More. On the other hand, to this day, Britain's monarch remains head of the Church of England. Henry VIII, for his part, enjoyed a long reign as one of England's greatest kings, whose success stemmed in large measure from his keen awareness that motives count most in human affairs.

The significance of words and deeds, even silence and passivity, is most often defined by underlying and sometimes hidden motives. If you discern a person's real motives, he or she will not easily deceive you, and you can better predict how he or she will react to anything you wish to say or do.

Think empathetically as you search for motivations explaining people's thoughts, feelings, and behaviors in response to your actions in this exercise.

Mental Aerobics
Deadly Virus

You've just discovered a vaccine against the deadly Ebola virus. While few people ever contract the disease, those who do almost invariably suffer a horrible death. If enough people will take your vaccine, Ebola, just like smallpox and polio years ago, can be eradicated from the face of the Earth.

Your vaccine comes in a "live" and "dead" form. The "live" vaccine, administered orally, effectively prevents Ebola, although one-in-a-million people who take it will catch the disease from the vaccine itself. The "dead" vaccine, administered by injection and equally effective in preventing Ebola, carries no risk of catching the disease.

You set up clinics at places around the world where Ebola outbreaks have occurred and stock them with both "live" and "dead" vaccines. Unfortunately, many people do not show up, despite your well-financed campaign promoting the vaccine and its virtues. When asked, people either say they have not heard of the vaccination program or they have not had time to visit a clinic. All agree Ebola is a deadly disease that must be eradicated if possible.

Put yourself in the place of the people you must vaccinate, and figure out what motivates them not to participate in your laudable efforts to rid the world of Ebola.

Practice Makes Perfect
Discover Hidden Human Motivations

The inventor of ATMs demonstrates an early prototype to key executives of your national bank in New York City. As President of the bank, you attend the presentation and instantly realize that ATMs could become the most important banking innovation since the introduction of credit cards. With them, banks could provide 24-hour service to customers while saving huge sums in human transaction costs. You instruct your Vice President in charge of operations to arrange a test installation of five ATMs in the open walkway leading to a local branch office. If the test proves successful, you plan to install ATMs systemwide and lead the banking industry into a new era of customer convenience and cost savings.

The Vice President begins the installation process while simultaneously taking steps to encourage customers to use the new machines at the test location. For three months running, the bank encloses a fancy brochure with customer statements announcing the coming ATMs and promoting their use. The test branch issues ATM cards to all its customers along with instructions on how to use them. On opening day, a few human tellers remain on duty to handle patrons with accounts over $5,000, but most customers are required to use the ATMs and receive live demonstrations on the simple procedures involved.

All goes well during the first few days, but the total number of customers visiting the bank begins to decline. Many do not use the ATMs and take their business to competing banks. When asked, these customers admit they find the machines easy to operate and convenient for after-hours banking, but they do not like doing business with impersonal machines. When, within two months, business dwindles to a trickle, you must either close the branch or remove the ATMs and try to lure back your former customers.

Having risen to the presidency of a national bank, you understand human motivation better than many and know people do not always openly reveal their true thoughts and feelings. Intuition tells you something more than simply not wanting to use impersonal machines motivates your customers to take their business elsewhere. Customers have long complained about standing in line waiting for service from human tellers. The average customer using an ATM can complete transactions in a fraction of the time previously required.

Develop a list of possible hidden motives behind your customers' reluctance to use ATMs. What predominant motivation explains their behavior?

LEARN HOW OTHERS VIEW AND INTERPRET YOUR WORDS AND ACTIONS

How often have you said or done something others misinterpreted? Wishing we could take back our words and actions, we later wonder, "Why didn't I appreciate that?" To better appreciate how others might view and interpret our words and deeds, we should think more empathetically, as the world discovered in 1983 when the

United States, Kuwait, and Saudi Arabia miscalculated how Iraq's volatile leader, Saddam Hussein, would interpret their words and actions.

The road to the Gulf War began in the years following the Iranian revolution, when Iran's Iatolla Khomeini publicly urged Iraq's Shi'ite majority to revolt against Saddam Hussein, and Khomeini attempted to assassinate one of Hussein's closest confidants, Tariq Aziz. Hussein retaliated with a massive military assault on Iran, starting an eight-year war that exhausted the economies of both countries and killed millions.

Iraq emerged from the war bankrupt, owing billions to Kuwait and Saudi Arabia, among others. Full recovery would take up to twenty years and cost $300 billion. Fearing a coup if he could not soon alleviate the suffering and growing discontent of his people, Hussein tried to persuade Kuwait and Saudi Arabia to forgive Iraq's debts and provide financial aid for recovery. He also attempted to convince OPEC to reduce oil production and thereby drive up prices to increase Iraq's oil revenues.

Saddam Hussein genuinely believed Iraq deserved help from its Arab neighbors because it had protected them from the growing threat of Iran-sponsored Shi'ite fundamentalism. Kuwait and Saudi Arabia reacted unsympathetically and rubbed salt in Iraq's wounds by increasing rather than cutting oil production, depressing world prices and shoving Iraq deeper into debt.

With personal and national survival very much in mind, Hussein resorted to threats. "Let the Gulf regimes know," he said, "if they do not give this money, Iraq knows how to get it." Even though Hussein controlled the world's fourth largest army, with thousands of tanks, artillery, and large stocks of chemical weapons, few diplomats thought he might actually invade his neighbors. They presumed Hussein was only bluffing. In hindsight, this apparent indifference to Iraq's post-war plight strongly affected Saddam Hussein's thinking at the time. He would, it turned out, make good on his threats.

April Glaspie, the U.S. Ambassador to Iraq, met privately with Hussein on July 25 1990—her *first* and *only* one-on-one interaction with the dictator. Having summoned Glaspie on one-hour's notice,

Hussein reiterated his often-stated belief that the United States had effectively declared "economic war" on Iraq, and he threatened: "By God, we know how to respond. We can deploy pressure and force against America, too. We cannot come all the way to the United States, but individual Arabs can, and they may reach you." What happened next in the meeting unfortunately convinced Hussein that America would not oppose him militarily if he redressed his grievances by seizing Kuwait and its rich oil fields.

Glaspie, lacking an opportunity to obtain guidance from Washington, operated on her own, as ambassadors must sometimes do. She reassured Hussein that the United States harbored no hostile intentions toward Iraq. "The USA," she added soothingly, "has no opinion on inter-Arab disputes such as your border dispute with Kuwait." By this, she meant the U.S. would remain neutral during negotiations and not pressure either side to concede or compromise. Feeling she had calmed Hussein's ire, and not suspecting Hussein might interpret her statement as a green light to invade Kuwait, Glaspie cabled Washington her opinion that, despite his threats, Hussein wanted only a peaceful settlement. Then the Ambassador booked reservations to fly out of Iraq on vacation.

Hussein quickly massed half his huge army on the Iraq–Kuwait border. When U.S. intelligence officers detected the Iraqi army deploying into attack formations, they advised President George H. Bush that an assault on Kuwait appeared imminent. Still, the Bush administration continued to rely on Ambassador Glaspie's assessment and forfeited the last opportunity short of war to send Hussein a clear message that the United States would not allow him to overrun tiny Kuwait.

Eight days after meeting with Ambassador Glaspie, Saddam Hussein launched his invasion of Kuwait. As Hussein rounded up and executed targeted Kuwaitis, the world finally realized he meant business. Many in the U.S. government and elsewhere asked themselves, "Why didn't I appreciate that?" They had failed to see the world as Hussein did.

A British intelligence officer specializing in Arab and Gulf affairs laid bare the error when he said of Hussein: "He came out of the Iran war broke, paranoic, and desperate. . . . To think that a psychotic dictator with 5,000 tanks is going to sit back alongside a defenceless neighbour, that just happens to be one of the richest countries in the world, while they stick two fingers up and tell him to push off because he's not getting any of their money, is just plain stupid. . . . It was a simple . . . matter of . . . knowing your man." The United States, Saudi Arabia, and Kuwait failed to "know" their man because they did not fully appreciate how he viewed their words and actions.

Contrary to popular misconception, wise people do not reserve empathy only for friends and allies. While empathizing with adversaries, and even enemies, can prove extremely difficult and distasteful, we must do it if we want to deal effectively with others. On these occasions, the crucial distinction between empathy and sympathy becomes more important than ever. We can empathize without sympathizing. We can, if we must, empathize with potential enemies, imagine ourselves in their position, and figure out how they interpret what we say and do, no matter how repugnant and irrational we may find their behavior.

Wise people, like talented diplomats, choose their words carefully because they appreciate how even subtle differences in expression can influence how people interpret information. The *New England Journal of Medicine* published an excellent example drawn from an experiment in which doctors were asked to recommend treatments for lung-cancer patients. Researchers created a hypothetical case and asked 167 doctors to select an appropriate treatment. Half the doctors received one description of possible treatments, half received another. As you read the first description, imagine yourself a physician who must decide whether to recommend surgery or radiation to your lung-cancer patients.

Of 100 people having surgery, 10 will die during surgery, 32 will have died by one year, and 66 will have died by five years. Of 100 people having radiation therapy, none will die during treatment, 23 will die by one year, and 78 will die by five years. Which treatment would you prefer?

Cover the first description with a piece of paper before reading further.

Doctors shown the first description split down the middle 50/50 between surgery and radiation, viewing both as equally risky. Now, without looking back at the first description, read the second and, based solely on it, select either surgery or radiation.

Of 100 people having surgery, 90 will survive the surgery, 68 will survive past one year, and 34 will survive through five years. Of 100 people having radiation therapy, all will survive the treatment, 77 will survive one year, and 22 will survive past five years. Which treatment would you prefer?

Did you select surgery or radiation? Here, 84 percent of the doctors selected surgery over radiation, an increase of 34 percent in favor of surgery. Compare the two treatment descriptions, and you will see identical risks reported in each. The only real difference lies in the choice of words. According to the second description, 34 will survive through five years with surgery while only 24 will survive past five years with radiation. Even highly skilled doctors, trained in objectivity, can be powerfully influenced by subtle differences in the words used to communicate the same thoughts.

Realizing the tremendous power of words, sharp thinkers consider how the words they use might affect others, obeying the axiom taught in all beginning speech classes: "Understand your audience." Stated differently, weigh how others will receive and interpret your words. Empathetic thinking provides a powerful tool for this purpose because it focuses attention where the rubber meets the road, at the *receiving* end of communications. Without empathy for receivers, words—however well-crafted—can fall on deaf ears or produce unexpected and unwanted reactions even if heard, as occurred with Saddam Hussein.

Think empathetically as you consider how the grown children in this exercise will react to your written words.

The Inheritance

You're the lawyer for an elderly woman worth hundreds of millions of dollars. Since her three grown children, all extraordinarily selfish and deeply engrossed in their own lives, rarely visit or call their mother, she instructs you to change her will to encourage at least occasional telephone calls. The new terms provide that any child who calls at least once a month shares her fortune equally with all other children who do the same. Any child failing to meet the minimum calling requirement receives nothing.

The plan works well at first, but the children soon tire of calling and secretly agree among themselves that none will meet the minimum requirement. Your client inherited her fortune under a will requiring her to pass the entire sum on to one or more of her children and not to anyone else. She cannot give any of the money to her children during her lifetime. The children figure as long as they remain equally self-absorbed, they will inherit equally when their mother dies, because she will not find any child more deserving than another.

Lonely and out of ideas, your elderly client asks you for advice about how she might change her will to produce a steady stream of phone calls from at least one child. What will you recommend?

See Yourself from Other Points of View

Select three people you find difficult to work with in your job or profession—perhaps a superior, a colleague at your level, and a subordinate. Take out three blank sheets of paper, draw a line down the middle of each, and use one sheet for each selected person, writing your name on the left side and the other person's name on the right.

On the right side, jot down a list of points describing how the other person sees you. Do not imagine yourself in the other person's shoes looking back at yourself; rather, figure out what that other person actually thinks and feels about you, rightly or wrongly.

Now, move to the left side of the paper and consider the role your words and actions play in causing the other person to see you as he or she does. List on the left your words and deeds that likely contribute to the other person's views described on the opposite side of the page.

Finally, sit back and consider how you might alter what you say and do to change the other person's views and improve your working relationship without compromising your integrity or job performance. Write these on the back side of the paper, etch them on your mind, put them to good use, and see if things improve. If you succeed, you will have proved an old adage: "The best way to change others is to change ourselves."

PUT IT ALL TOGETHER

Think empathetically at every turn as you solve this mystery using all you've learned from this chapter.

Catch a Thief

You're Catholic Father Brown pastoring a small church in a poor section of London. Since some of your parishioners possess criminal records, you've become somewhat of a Sherlock Holmes when it comes to understanding the criminal mind. The Bishop summons you to his chambers, where he asks you to help figure out how to transport a priceless church artifact to Rome for an upcoming convocation. Once owned by St. Augustine, the small cross dates back twelve centuries. Scotland Yard believes the infamous thief Gustav Flambeau intends to intercept the cross and install it in his collection. No one knows what Flambeau, a master of disguise, looks like. Quite possibly an aristocrat, Flambeau takes pride in outsmarting the police and steals for the sheer thrill of a good cat-and-mouse game. All efforts to catch him have failed miserably.

You set out to trick Flambeau by transporting the cross to Rome in a way he will not expect: in a brown paper parcel that you will personally carry as an ordinary traveler unaccompanied by security. You and your traveling companions, a group of priests, board a train for Rome. On the way, you make friends with a kindly priest and together you notice a stranger who appears to be following you, first on the train from London, then on the channel ferry, and finally on the train to Paris, where you must change trains for Rome. You and your new friend decide to shake the stranger in Paris, and, after some effort, lose him by sneaking into the catacombs deep beneath the city. Alone in the underground labyrinth, your companion suddenly turns on you, ties you up, and reveals himself as Flambeau. Having foiled your plan, Flambeau bids you a gracious adieu and disappears with your priceless cross.

On returning empty-handed to England, you meet with the Bishop who says the Archbishop may decide in two weeks to discipline you for losing the St. Augustine cross. With only a few days to recover the priceless artifact, you seek solace from Lady Warren, a wealthy member of your congregation. Struggling to think of a way to catch Flambeau, you wonder out loud, "What goes on inside that mind?" Knowing your past successes as an amateur detective, the beautiful Lady Warren asks how you have managed in the past to outwit criminals, and you answer, "I try to get so far inside a man that I can move his arms and legs, think his thoughts, wrestle with his passions, until in fact I become the criminal." In other words, in order to obtain the insight needed to work your snare, you empathize completely with him.

As you think about Flambeau, you realize you must somehow entice him out into the open. Lady Warren offers to allow you to use a one-of-a-kind $100,000 Cellini chess set as bait. Exercise your best empathetic thinking as you craft a plan to trap Flambeau. Ask yourself:

- What does Flambeau think and feel?
- What motivates Flambeau to think, feel, and act as he does?
- What do I want Flambeau to do?
- What can I say and do that will cause him to react as desired?

After you fully complete your plan, but not before, turn to the Notes to continue the exercise.

THINK FOR YOURSELF

Use the lessons of this chapter to achieve greater success in your dealings with people.

Persuade People More Effectively

Select a person whose thinking you want to influence. Perhaps you desire approval of an idea at work. Maybe you hope to persuade someone to trust you in some way. Perhaps you want to change another person's mind.

Empathize with this person as you figure out how to achieve your purpose:

- What does this person truly think?
- What does this person actually feel?
- What motivates this person to think and feel this way?
- What can I say to achieve my purpose?
- What can I do to achieve my purpose?
- How will this person react to my words and actions?

THINK ABOUT IT

Pause for a moment to consider how you can use empathy to sharpen your thinking. Ask yourself:

- Do I sometimes allow my own thoughts and feelings to distract me from paying adequate attention to the thoughts and feelings of others? If so, what will I do to improve my perception and appreciation of others' thoughts and feelings?
- Have I failed to discern people's true thoughts and feelings because I did not concentrate enough on discovering their underlying motives? If so, what will I do to make sure I do not overlook motives when I need to understand the minds of others?
- Am I sometimes surprised to find people misinterpreting my words or actions? If so, what will I do to anticipate how people will view and interpret what I say and do?

ALWAYS CHECK TO MAKE SURE

Make sound decisions and solve problems by fully considering the interests and views of others:
THINK EMPATHETICALLY.

> Consider What Others Think and Feel
>
> Discover What Motivates Others to Think, Feel, and Act as They Do
>
> Learn How Others View and Interpret Your Words and Actions

Notes to Chapter 7

What Is She Thinking?

The little girl doesn't understand why you're standing on a neighbor's porch. She and her mother live in the house across the street.

Think on Your Seat

If the applicant in back sees two white hats, he knows his cap is green and will say so. His silence means he must see either two green hats or one green and one white. Realizing this, the middle person figures if she sees a white hat, her cap must be green and she can speak up. If, however, she sees a green hat, she must remain silent, because her hat can be either white or green. The lingering silence of these two applicants lets the person in the front chair know his hat must be green.

Sense Others' Real Intentions

Once inside Kelly's apartment, Tom closed the door, pulled out a gun, pointed it at Kelly's head, ordered her into her bedroom, and raped her. Tom, who did not live in the apartment building, had entered through the same unlatched door Kelly used. Did you sense at some point while reading the four paragraphs that Tom could be dangerous or that he might sexually assault Kelly?

Now read the following two paragraphs and make notes as before. Turn to the Supplemental Solutions only after you finish the last numbered paragraph.

5. Tom rose from the bed, dressed himself, and closed the window. Glancing at his watch, he shook his head and grimaced. "Hey, don't look so scared. I'm not going to hurt you. Don't move or do anything. I'm going to the kitchen to get something to drink, and then I'll leave."

6. "You know I won't move," Kelly assured him. After Tom went to the kitchen, Kelly heard him opening drawers.

Turn to the Supplemental Solutions to complete the exercise.

Deadly Virus

Needle injections sting and cause muscle soreness. Many people would rather run the remote risk of contracting Ebola than experience a stinging needle injection. The oral vaccine, while painless, carries a one-in-a-million chance of catching Ebola from the vaccine itself. Why take that risk, many think, and why suffer a painful injection when the chances of contracting Ebola remain remote to begin with?

Discover Hidden Human Motivations

Citibank, in the early 1980s, did just what this story recounts. The bank did remove the machines when they proved unpopular. When an enterprising bank executive later investigated customer motivations, he discovered that the majority of customers, people with modest bank accounts, felt snubbed when Citibank provided live tellers only to patrons with large balances. As told by Michael Michalko in his book *Thinkertoys,* when Citibank eliminated bank balance distinctions, reinstalled ATMs, and made live tellers available to all customers, the new technology became an overnight success.

The Inheritance

Selfishness motivates the children's thinking. Advise the woman to change her will to give the entire fortune to only *one* child, the one who calls most between now and her death. The selfish children will inevitably cheat on their private deal and secretly call their mother, hoping to win her fortune. Mom will soon receive more phone calls than she can handle.

Catch a Thief

Father Brown, played by Alec Guiness in the classic film *The Detective*, places Lady Warren's Cellini chess set up for auction and advertises the event in newspapers throughout Europe. Flambeau takes the bait. A bidding war develops during the auction between a wealthy Indian Maharaja and a Texas tycoon. The Maharaja prevails, but the chess set he wins turns out to be a fake switched by Flambeau who, posing as an auction house employee, steals the set prior to the start of bidding.

Later that day, Father Brown and Lady Warren return to her home, where an intruder, none other than Flambeau, surprises them with the genuine Cellini chess set, which he has returned to its original place in Lady Warren's house. Having won the game of cat-and-mouse, Flambeau generously offers to give his prize back to Lady Warren.

"Why take all the trouble to steal it if only to give it back?" Lady Warren asks.

"The acts that we do for no evident reason," Flambeau answers, "are sometimes the most rational ones." Motives matter most.

"Then," Lady Warren responds, "there being no evident reason why I should accept your gift, I am delighted to do so."

The police arrive, and Flambeau flees, this time with the help of a grateful Lady Warren and Father Brown. Later, Brown discovers Flambeau's treasure trove hidden in a dilapidated chateau in the Bordeaux region of France. Impressed by Father Brown's superb sleuthing skills, Flambeau gallantly returns the St. Augustine cross. Indeed, Flambeau gives up his life of crime entirely. The Louvre in Paris exhibits his fabulous stolen art collection for all to enjoy, and Flambeau ends up worshiping at Father Brown's church, where the St. Augustine cross again hangs next to the pulpit.

How does your plot to snare Flambeau compare with the movie's story line? Did you, like Father Brown, make every effort to "think Flambeau's thoughts" and "wrestle with his passions"?

Chapter Eight

Why Didn't I
Anticipate That?

Look Before You Leap

The world came perilously close to irreversible catastrophe when Adolf Hitler's armies overran France, and only Britain stood between life as we know it and a long miserable existence dominated by Nazi Germany and its ruinous philosophy. With France doomed and the United States determined not to join the war, a Russian pact with Germany forced Britain to decide whether to negotiate for peace or face alone the full force of Hitler's rampaging war machine. Britain's choice, made against all odds, literally rescued democracy for the world.

Hitler launched Germany's invasion of Western Europe on May 10, 1940, the same day Winston Churchill became Britain's Prime Minister. Following a traditional audience with the King at Buckingham Palace, Churchill departed with his personal bodyguard who lamented, "I only wish the position had come your way in better times, for you have an enormous task." With tears in his normally steely eyes, Churchill responded, "God alone knows how great it is. I hope it is not too late. I am very much afraid it is. We can only do our best."

Within ten days the Germans had fought their way to the English Channel shores, trapping both the French and British armies against the sea. Since Hitler calculated that France and

England would jointly sue for peace within a day or two, he looked forward to placing both nations under his iron fist. The commanding general of Britain's armed forces called the situation "the greatest military disaster in history." No one understood the nation's peril better than its newly appointed Prime Minister. With its army at the edge of annihilation along the French coast at Dunkirk, and France all but lost, Britain would soon face Germany without allies. The chances of evacuating any effective portion of the army from Dunkirk seemed impossible, and neither Britain's air force nor its navy appeared capable of turning back an invasion.

France tried to draw Britain into negotiations, reasoning the two countries could obtain more favorable terms by surrendering jointly, saving Hitler the trouble of a cross-channel invasion. What person in his right mind would refuse to negotiate with Hitler in these circumstances?

Edward Halifax, a powerful member of Churchill's five-member War Cabinet, argued strenuously for negotiations and wrote a "Suggested Approach." What harm could it cause, he asserted, if Britain *at least* explored the possibilities of mediation, if it *at least* listened to any proposals Hitler might make? Why risk annihilation, when Hitler might grant concessions in return for a bloodless surrender?

Prime Minister Churchill, however, looked carefully before leaping into talks with the Führer. He worried that if Britain took even one step toward conciliation, the clamor for peace would drown out reason and inevitably lead to surrender on Germany's harsh terms. "The whole idea of this maneuver," Churchill told his War Cabinet, "is intended to get us so deeply involved in negotiations that we should be unable to turn back." Once at the conference table with Herr Hitler, Churchill later said, "All the forces of resolution which are now at our disposal would have vanished."

At the time few realized the depth of Hitler's evil intent. Still, Churchill saw in Hitler a devil with whom one must not bargain. Negotiations might avoid bloodshed in the short term, but they would condemn Britain to a long future of untold misery. Beyond Britain, Churchill saw terrible consequences for freedom and democracy worldwide. With Britain out of the way, Hitler could turn his wrath in any direction.

Looking back, we appreciate Churchill's wisdom, but at the time his thoughts did not seem so obviously correct. Britain could not win the war alone. Only the United States and Russia together could do that, and neither had shown the slightest inclination to take on Germany. On the other hand, Britain could *lose* the war. With no illusions about the consequences of his decision, Churchill proclaimed, "We shall go on, and we shall fight it out, here or elsewhere, and if at last the long story is to end, it were better it should end, not through surrender, but only when we are rolling senseless on the ground."

In making his choice, Churchill could not have suspected that Britain would miraculously manage to retrieve 338,000 troops from Dunkirk, that a few months later the nation's small air force would defeat Hitler's Luftwaffe, that one year later Hitler would turn from Britain and declare war on Russia, or that Hitler would foolishly declare war on the United States after Japan bombed Pearl Harbor. On the other hand, if Britain gave in to Hitler, Churchill reasoned "the whole world, including the United States, including all that we have known and care for, will sink into the abyss of a New Dark Age." In the end, those who favored exploring negotiations did not fully appreciate the consequences foreseen so clearly by Churchill, and later they could only look back wondering in awe, "Why didn't I anticipate that?"

Churchill's genius in May 1940 derived from his determination to fully think through the consequences of every conceivable option. None of the roads ahead appeared attractive, yet Churchill chose the least inviting of all—the one covered with blood, sweat, toil, and tears, the only pathway leading to a place where free people could live again in peace.

As Churchill demonstrated, sharp thinkers adopt a far-reaching perspective spanning the past, present, and future. Like Churchill, they possess well-developed talents for acting today with a rich appreciation of the past, a clear perception of the present, a profound concern for the future, and a keen awareness of the consequential links among all three. A common thread of consequence runs through time. Those who see the thread, who understand consequences, make the wisest judgments and find the best solutions to life's toughest problems.

In Frank Capra's *It's a Wonderful Life,* George Bailey, played by James Stewart, stood on the rail of the town bridge and, thinking he had wasted his life, prepared to commit suicide. His guardian angel, Clarence, intervened. As George thanklessly growled, "I wish I'd never been born," Clarence granted him his wish. Stumbling around town, seeing with his own eyes what life would have been like for people without him, George realized that all his contributions over the years had made a huge difference for good. "Strange, isn't it," Clarence observed. "Each man's life touches so many other lives. When he isn't around, he leaves an awful hole, doesn't he?" For the first time George saw the results of his many kindnesses and realized how seemingly small actions can have enormous consequences. He had missed the real meaning of his life by not seeing these consequences.

Chess is the quintessential game of consequences. Master players, fully aware of how the pieces came to rest in their present positions, stretch their minds to anticipate the future consequences of every possible move. Lifting a piece and holding it over a square, they ponder how a game will likely play out before committing to the next move. Just as every action produces a reaction, every choice generates consequences. Masters wisely play the game in their heads before playing it for real on the board. In the process, they anticipate all possibilities, including defeat. Calculating the likelihood and significance of every consequence, they search for the surest strategy for success. Fearlessly critiquing their own performance every step of the way, they try hard to insure that any move an opponent makes will not leave them asking, "Why didn't I anticipate that?"

Use consequences as keys to find solutions in this exercise.

Mental Warm–Up
The Big Switch

For centuries, people in Sweden drove on the left side of the road while most other Europeans drove on the right. Sweden decided to switch from left to right in 1965, a change that required a lot of thought. People cannot easily break centuries-old habits, and suddenly reversing the way people drive would pose real dangers. You're in charge of Sweden's highway system and must come up with a way to make the switch while minimizing risks to drivers and pedestrians. How will you do it? Carefully consider the consequences of every option. Lives hang in the balance. Remember to think clearly, accurately, comprehensively, sensibly, and honestly.

THINK THE UNTHINKABLE

Sound consequential thinking stretches minds beyond the expected, beyond the unexpected, to discover the otherwise unthinkable, as the CIA learned when the Soviets ferreted out and executed nearly every Russian citizen spying for the Unites States in Moscow. The first sign of serious trouble appeared in September 1985 when the KGB caught Leonid Poleschuk retrieving a hollow rock containing $20,000 in rubles hidden for him by a CIA agent in a Moscow park. For years, Poleschuk, a member of KGB counterintelligence, had provided the CIA with vital information on KGB operations against the United States.

"What the hell is going on in Moscow?" CIA director William Casey demanded when he first learned of the developing disaster. Taken completely by surprise, the CIA set out to find the causes of its losses. Ultimately, an internal CIA report concluded the misfortune probably occurred as a result of individual, isolated blunders made by the spies themselves or their CIA handlers. The idea of a Soviet mole operating high within the agency remained nearly unthinkable. After all, nothing like that had ever occurred before. Yet the unthinkable had in fact happened.

Aldrich Ames, the son of a veteran CIA officer, joined the agency in 1967. He became Chief of the CIA's Soviet counterintelligence branch by 1983, where he enjoyed access to documents identifying all U.S. spies operating in Russia. While stationed in Washington, D.C., Ames maintained person-to-person contact with Surgey Chuvakhin, a Soviet Embassy employee whom he had been assigned to recruit as a CIA spy. Short of money and needing a fast buck, Ames decided to use his contact with Chuvakhin to swindle the Soviets out of $50,000 in what Ames thought would be a one-time scam. He had learned through a Russian source that the KGB planned to dangle three double agents in front of the CIA. Ames's plan: secretly offer to name three KGB turncoats in return for $50,000. The KGB would surely pay up, Ames reasoned, because they knew he worked for the CIA, and the KGB did not want the agency to think the three were double agents.

Ames penned a note to the KGB chief resident in Washington, D.C., saying, "I am Aldrich H. Ames and my job is branch chief of Soviet counterintelligence at the CIA." With note in hand he walked openly through the front door of the Russian embassy, knowing FBI surveillance would spot his entry. Once inside, he handed his note to a Soviet security guard and walked out. When questioned the next day by his CIA superiors about the unscheduled embassy visit, Ames convincingly replied that he had made a spur-of-the-moment decision to try and persuade Chuvakhin to join him for lunch.

One week later, Ames again entered the Soviet embassy, this time informing his CIA superiors of the trip. There a Soviet agent secretly handed Ames a note: "We accept your offer and are very pleased to do so." Chuvakhin then accompanied Ames to a local restaurant, where they lunched openly while Chuvakhin slipped him $50,000 in cash.

The next day Ames reflected on the consequences of his misdeed. "My God," he worried, "I had talked to the KGB! I had sold out! I was suddenly a man with no one to help me. . . . Now I had to worry about security, survival, protecting myself." Looking for ways to avoid the consequences of his treachery, Ames remembered studying CIA records showing that Americans caught spying for the Russians were almost always exposed using tips supplied by Russian traitors. Could he safeguard himself by giving the KGB the names of Russians spying for the CIA? Without giving it a second thought, he quickly contacted Chuvakhin, set up another luncheon, and there passed the stunned Soviet a list of Russians spying on Moscow for the U.S.

Fully expecting the information to condemn at least ten Russians to certain death, Ames later remarked, "Let's be frank. The men I betrayed knew what they were doing. They knew the risks. So their deaths, while sad to me, are not really my responsibility. They have no one to blame but themselves for putting their lives in danger. It wasn't personal. It was simply how the game was played."

With the deaths behind him, Ames began a career of supplying Russia with a goldmine of U.S. counterintelligence secrets. The Russians, for their part, paid him more than $2 million and used every trick of the trade to insulate their prized asset from discovery.

One elaborate KGB ruse involved Vladimir Smetanin, a spy recruited by the CIA who supplied the U.S. with reams of top-secret KGB documents, some of which detailed how the Soviets had identified the spies captured and executed in 1985. In each case, the documents listed errors made by the spies, together with dates and locations of contacts with their CIA handlers. While much of the information matched the CIA's own contact records, the KGB had fabricated the materials at key points to hide the existence of a high-level mole inside the CIA, Aldrich Ames. The KGB ruses might have succeeded if Ames himself had not supplied the CIA with a crucial clue that investigators did not immediately explore: Ames and his wife lived beyond their means.

To catch Ames, people at the CIA needed to begin thinking the unthinkable, and eventually CIA investigators Jeanne Vertefeuille and Sandy Grimes, along with a few others, did just that. Obtaining a court authorization to examine Ames's banking records, they found charges of up to $30,000 a month on a $70,000 annual income. Matching large deposits with known Chuvakhin luncheons finally exposed the espionage connection. On February 21, 1994, a full *nine* years after Ames began spying, FBI agents pulled him over driving to CIA headquarters on a Saturday morning.

"You're under arrest!" agent Mike Donner said as he yanked a cigarette from Ames's lips and made him stand with hands on the roof of his car.

"For what?" Ames demanded.

"For espionage," Donner answered.

"This is unbelievable. *Unbelievable!*" Ames retorted as Donner slipped cuffs on his hands.

If for years the CIA had difficulty thinking the unthinkable, so did Aldrich Ames. "My biggest regret," he said, "is that I was too blind to see what was coming during 1993." He could easily have escaped to Moscow and lived the remainder of his life in a government-furnished dacha. As it turned out, the one who first thought and acted on the unthinkable won the game. Now Aldrich Ames languishes in federal prison, serving a life sentence without possibility of parole.

As the Ames affair underscores, history's catastrophes often occur when people do not or will not think the unthinkable. "God himself could not sink this ship," boasted the White Star Line as the *Titanic* loaded passengers for its maiden voyage across the icy Atlantic. The "impossible" often lurks on the horizon, and, while the odds may be one-in-a-million, it only takes one "impossible" occurrence to break them. Who, for example, would think a few hundred votes out of millions, or one vote on the U.S. Supreme Court, would elect a President of the United States? Before 2000, Hollywood would have rejected as unmarketable any movie project based on such an incredible idea. No serious author would write the script. No legitimate director would make the movie. No sane investor would put up the money. Yet, after the 2000 election, the media clamored to tell the story of the unthinkable that became reality before our very eyes.

Historian David Halberstam reported that when the United States first began escalating its military involvement in Vietnam, a senior official from a prior administration asked President Lynden Johnson's Special Assistant for National Security Affairs, McGeorge Bundy, what might happen if the North Vietnamese responded by escalating its troop infiltrations into South Vietnam. "We simply are not as pessimistic as you are," Bundy answered. Pressed further, Bundy responded, "We just don't think that's going to happen." But "just suppose that it did occur," the senior official proposed. Bundy refused to continue the discussion, ending it with, "We can't assume what we don't believe." In other words, we will not waste time thinking the unthinkable. If Bundy and others had not so blythly ignored consequential thinking, they might have spared America one of its worst national nightmares.

Those who stop thinking when they reach the limits of possibilities miss seeing the dangers presented by so-called "impossibilities." On the other hand, those who beat the odds, avoid catastrophe, achieve unimaginable success, often do so by thinking what others find unthinkable. In the end, the prize belongs to the latter.

Stretch your thinking beyond first impressions as you solve this problem.

—————————————————————————— Mental Aerobics
Capital Marriages

In the 1950s and 1960s a prominent man in Washington, D.C. married at least ten women. Leaders of the nation, including Senators, Congressmen, and even Presidents, attended some of the weddings and joined in the celebrations afterward. The man never obtained a divorce, and no one considered divorce necessary in his case. The possibility he might be a polygamist remained utterly unthinkable. Why?

—————————————————————————— Practice Makes Perfect
Deal with Deadly Consequences

Imagine you're President Jimmy Carter's closest advisor, National Security Advisor Zbigniew Brzezinski. Computer failures in the United States' early warning system have recently prompted emergency alerts by American strategic nuclear forces. Thankfully, the errors did not result in launches of nuclear missiles or bombers.

In one incident, you receive a middle-of-the-night call from your chief military contact indicating that early warning radars have detected 220 Soviet missiles on their way to the United States. Realizing the President has less than seven minutes to order a full retaliatory strike, you wait breathlessly for confirmation of the Soviet launch. Within a minute or two, your contact comes back on the line with news the Soviets have launched an all-out attack with 2,200 missiles. While reaching for your Presidential hot line, you learn at the last possible second that certain backup warning systems have not detected Soviet missiles in the air. As it turns out, a military training tape had been erroneously inserted into the active computer system, generating a very real-looking but false warning. You take a long, deep breath and return to bed without waking your wife.

Now suppose you receive information from an absolutely reliable source deep inside Soviet leadership that Russian strategists refuse to attribute the U.S. alerts to computer glitches. To the contrary, they think the U.S. deliberately feigned the mistaken alerts to create a false impression of reassuring "computer errors." The Soviets genuinely believe the U.S. hopes the experience will cause Russian leaders to drop their guard if and when America launches a preemptive first strike.

Think the unthinkable as you construct at least three potentially catastrophic scenarios that can occur as a consequence of the Soviet's misunderstanding of U.S. intentions.

EXPECT THE UNEXPECTED

Admiral Raymond Spruance flew to Wellington, New Zealand in mid-1943 with top-secret orders to launch an offensive that would ultimately lead to the defeat of Japan. Meeting in a tightly guarded room with Marine Corps battlefield commanders, he revealed his plan to attack Japan through the Central Pacific, beginning with an assault on the tiny island atoll of Tarawa. While no one in the room other than Spruance had ever heard of Tarawa, the operation soon developed into the bloodiest three-day fight in Marine Corps history.

Tarawa atoll consisted of several small islands arranged in a circle with a lagoon at the center, something like a punch bowl. Principal among the islands was Betio, a narrow, mile-long strip about the size of the Pentagon's parking lots, on which the Japanese had built a strategically important airstrip. The tiny island, surrounded by a shallow, flat coral reef spreading 1,000 yards outward from the shoreline, had been heavily fortified with over 500 gun emplacements, reinforced bunkers, and pill boxes. Betio, manned by over 4,000 battle-hardened Japanese marines, held the heaviest concentration of Japanese weaponry anywhere in the Pacific.

The daunting task of figuring out how to take the island fell primarily on the shoulders of a staff officer, Lieutenant Colonel David Shoup. He believed the operation could only succeed by landing at the weakest point in the Japanese defenses. Otherwise, the Japanese defenders would slaughter the force at water's edge. The least-defended beaches faced the inner lagoon at the center of the atoll. Because the lagoon had only a small opening, and this would not permit entry of large troop ships, Japanese defenders believed any attack must come from the side facing out to sea, where they had planted thousands of mines and steel obstacles to halt any assault dead in the water.

Shoup did indeed plan a surprise lagoon approach, but he also knew that landing from the lagoon presented huge risks, principally from the flat coral reef stretching up to half a mile out from the shoreline. Marines traditionally used small flat-bottomed, propeller-driven Higgins boats to land on hostile beaches. The small wooden craft needed at least four feet of water to operate.

"How deep is the water over the reef?" Shoup asked.

No one knew for sure. The latest hydrographic chart bore a date of 1848. Intelligence reports indicated that normal tides would likely provide enough water, but a fisherman told Shoup that tides in the Tarawa area sometimes behaved unpredictably.

Shoup next asked, "What might happen if the unexpected occurs, and the tide fails?" The answer: a potential disaster, with Marines forced to abandon their boats and wade a thousand yards in belly-deep water over a flat reef straight into deadly Japanese machine-gun fire. While the chances of a failed tide seemed remote, Shoup anticipated the unexpected and searched for an innovative way to transport troops across a reef in shallow water. He found what he needed in the LVT-1 Alligator, a small, tracked amphibious vehicle originally designed as a resupply ferry. Alligators could navigate in deep water and crawl up over coral reefs.

Possessing only enough Alligators for the first three troop waves going ashore, Shoup knew the bulk of his force would need to follow in traditional Higgins boats. If the unexpected occurred, and water levels somehow proved inadequate for Higgins boats to cross the reef, he planned for Alligators to return from the beach to the reef's outer edge, take on more troops from stalled Higgins boats, and head back to shore.

Shoup completed his plans, and the 2nd Marine Division boarded transport ships bound for Tarawa. On the way, the full colonel leading the assault suffered a nervous breakdown, and the commanding general promoted David Shoup to full colonel on the spot, placing him in command of the landing Marines. Shoup would now go ashore and personally implement his plan for taking Betio.

When the fleet arrived off Tarawa early on the morning of November 23, 1943, it initially caught the Japanese by surprise as they watched little tracked vehicles crawling up onto the lagoon-side coral reef and heading to shore with combat troops aboard. The Japanese defenders immediately redeployed to oppose the attack and opened fire on the lightly armored Alligators, destroying many as they approached.

Marines first arriving on shore found themselves pinned down by intense Japanese fire behind a three-foot-high coconut log seawall at water's edge. The main body of troops, urgently needed to reinforce the first three waves trapped on the beach, plowed through deep water in their Higgins boats heading toward the reef.

Suddenly the Higgins boats ground to a halt at the reef's outer edge. As the fisherman had warned, the tide had unexpectedly dropped, leaving startled Marines exposed to withering gunfire as they tried to wade the half mile to shore. Dave Shoup, among those caught on the reef, began wading shoreward and, although twice wounded on the way, somehow managed to reach the beach. Many who started the long walk with him did not survive the trek.

From his position on shore, Shoup watched helplessly as his contingency plan to shuttle troops over the reef using Alligators collapsed. Too few Alligators had survived the initial assault to conduct effective shuttle operations. Reinforcements spent the night bobbing in the ocean in Higgins boats. Next morning these seasick and dog-tired Marines suffered horrendous casualties trying to wade across the coral reef in the face of incessant Japanese fire. The Marines on shore, desperately hoping for relief, watched the demoralizing slaughter from behind the low seawall. Seeing the carnage, Shoup managed to radio a message to his commanding general at sea: "The situation does not look good ashore. . . . Situation still uncertain," a brave Marine's way of saying "unless something happens soon to turn this around, we may all die."

As has often occurred at moments like these in Marine Corps history, something did happen to turn things around, and that something came in the form of conspicuous gallantry in the face of near-certain death. Through acts of bravery too numerous to describe, Marines crawled over the seawall, gradually pushed across Betio, and eventually secured the island. Many taking part in the push had initially landed in Shoup's Alligators. Not one Japanese soldier surrendered; all fought to the death.

Following the battle, President Franklin Roosevelt bestowed the Congressional Medal of Honor on David Shoup who won the award as much with his mind as with his gallant heart. Without Shoup's Alligators, the Marines, however brave, would not have taken Tarawa. If Shoup had not anticipated and creatively planned to overcome the unexpected—a freakish low tide—America might have lost the first crucial battle in the long and perilous offensive leading to Japan's defeat.

Looking back at the failed tide, Shoup did not need to ask himself, "Why didn't I anticipate that?" At the time, however, he did not suspect just how freakish the failed tide had truly been. Forty years after the battle, a physics professor in Texas discovered a tidal condition, unknown in 1943, that produced freakishly low tides in the Tarawa vicinity on two, and only two, occasions in 1943. One occurred the very morning Marines first landed at Betio, just as the first waves of Higgins boats crashed against the outer edge of Betio's deadly reef.

The battle for Tarawa holds a dear place in my heart, not only because I'm a former Marine, but because my father commanded one of the Marine battalions that landed on Betio that first day. He was among those forced to wade ashore. Only God knows how he survived the terrifying and deadly trek. The Silver Star that Admiral Nimitz personally pinned on his chest after the battle hangs on a wall of my den at home, a continuing reminder of the fight that nearly cost him his life.

Unlike Shoup and my father, many do not deal well with uncertainty. Rather than expecting the unexpected and thinking of ways to prepare for it in advance, people tend to ignore uncertainty. While the future always contains unknowns, most people plan for known or expected events and let the unknown and unexpected take its own course. Sharp thinkers, on the other hand, take into account the possibility that events will not unfold as planned, accidents will happen, problems will materialize, opportunities will appear, and lightning may strike at any moment.

Knowing this, sharp thinkers deal with future uncertainties by building flexibility into their thinking, creating fall-back positions, holding precious resources in reserve, and taking precautions that may later prove unnecessary. Anticipating the unexpected, they ask in advance: "What might I do if things go unexpectedly wrong, and how will I exploit the situation if things turn out better than I expected? How will I guard against wondering later: 'Why didn't I anticipate that?'"

Expect the unexpected as you confront this situation.

_____ Mental Aerobics

Murder in Manhattan

Bob and Carole and Ted and Alice move into a fabulous luxury apartment on Manhattan's Upper East Side. One evening Bob and Carole go out for dinner at their favorite bistro. Midway through the meal Carole senses that something's wrong at home. Bob dismisses her worries, and they finish their dinner without further interruption. On returning home, however, the two find Alice lying dead on the floor in a pool of blood, with Ted sitting calmly on the sofa as if nothing has happened. Carole screams and sobs uncontrollably while Bob holds her secure in his arms until help arrives. Many neighbors say they heard Alice calling out "Help! Help!" during the brutal attack. Everyone in the building knows Ted killed Alice, but no one reports the incident to the police, and the District Attorney never prosecutes Ted for the killing.

Expect the unexpected as you solve the puzzle.

_____ Practice Makes Perfect

Learn from History

Recall a situation where your words or actions produced unexpected consequences that ruined or significantly harmed your plans or goals. You may have pursued a career that proved unsatisfying or unrewarding. Perhaps you said something to a friend that caused unintended, adverse consequences for you or other people. Maybe you made a decision that seemed right at the time but proved wrong later.

Write the unexpected consequences at the bottom of a blank sheet of paper. Next, beginning at the top, list each step you took leading to the consequences. Place the steps in sequence from first to last, with the first at the top of the paper.

Now imagine you can return to the first step, without ever having taken subsequent ones, weighing the adverse consequences that you might reasonably have anticipated at that point. Continue the process, step by step, until you reach the step where you should have fully anticipated the unexpected consequences listed at the bottom of your page.

Ask yourself why you did not fully appreciate the consequences at that crucial step. Based on what you've learned from this bit of history, what will you do in the future to improve your ability to anticipate and deal with adverse consequences before they ruin your chances of success?

CONSIDER BOTH THE SIGNIFICANCE AND LIKELIHOOD OF CONSEQUENCES

Anticipating consequences, especially the unthinkable and unexpected, sets the stage for the next crucial component of consequential thinking. You must evaluate the significance and likelihood of each particular consequence, something Exxon failed to do when it began shipping crude oil in supertankers out of Alaska's Port Valdez.

Late on the evening of March 22, 1989, the supertanker *Exxon Valdez* docked at the Port Valdez oil terminal located at the end of the 800-mile-long pipeline pumping crude oil from Alaska's North Slope. The crew worked through the night and the next day loading 1,286,738 barrels of heavy crude into their huge ship stretching more than three football fields from bow to stern. At 8:00 P.M. on the second night, the ship, with its tired crew, headed through the Valdez narrows on its way out to sea.

With a calm sea, light winds, and clear visibility for eight miles, Captain Joseph Hazlewood ordered his helmsman to steer out of the charted shipping lanes to avoid icebergs sighted ahead. Hazlewood, who had consumed alcohol before leaving port, then retired to his cabin leaving Third Mate Gregory Cousins with instructions to return to the lanes at a predetermined point. Once clear of the ice, Cousins ordered ten degrees right rudder to bring the ship back into the lanes. When the massive *Exxon Valdez* did not turn so quickly as desired, and with Bligh Reef dead ahead, Cousins ordered twenty degrees right rudder. Realizing the ship still was not turning fast enough to avoid the underwater reef, Cousins commanded "hard right rudder." Then he called the captain, saying he feared the ship might run aground.

"Where's the rudder?" the captain demanded.

"It's hard right," Cousins answered. Seconds later the giant ship, moving low in the water, its tanks brimming with heavy crude oil, plowed headlong into Bligh Reef, grinding the tanker to a dead stop.

As Hazlewood rushed to the bridge, Cousins threw on the ship's external floodlights and spotted oil bubbling from beneath the hull. To stabilize the ship and prevent it from sinking, Hazlewood ran the engines ahead and rammed the *Exxon Valdez* farther up onto the reef.

"Hard aground," Hazlewood radioed the Coast Guard Station on shore. "Evidently, we're leaking some oil."

Within half an hour 100,000 barrels of sticky oil had escaped, forming a one-and-one-half foot deep layer on the water surrounding the ship. Soon the spill would reach 11 million gallons.

Alyeska, a consortium of oil companies, operated the terminal and had prepared a required oil-spill Contingency Plan. The Plan envisioned a response with oil skimmers and water barriers beginning a couple of hours after a spill. Alyeska claimed it could contain any spill within fifty miles of Port Valdez in twelve hours. While the *Exxon Valdez* spill occurred inside the 50-mile radius, Alyeska did not arrive on scene for about fifteen hours and, even then, with inadequate equipment to handle the job. Even though the sea remained calm, providing ideal conditions for oil recovery, the massive spill completely overwhelmed the effort.

Following three days of ineffective operations that resulted in only 3,000 barrels of recovered oil, a hurricane-force storm blew in with 75-mile-an-hour winds and 25-foot waves. The churning sea mixed oil and water into a bubbly emulsion, spreading oil hundreds of miles from the original spill and making it extremely difficult to remove from the ocean's surface. Black oil spread along 1,000 miles of originally pristine shoreline, killing hundreds of thousands of seabirds, sea mammals, and fish. Even to this day, unsightly oil remains at locations along the Alaskan shoreline.

Despite the Contingency Plan, the *Exxon Valdez* grounding caught Exxon and Alyeska completely off guard. The few skimmers available to suck oil off the water operated too slowly and, even if they could have pumped faster, the recovery effort lacked places to dump recovered oil. A barge designed for the purpose sat out of service and unavailable. Stockpiles of chemical dispersants intended for recovery operations proved wholly inadequate, and the number of water barriers on hand to surround and contain the slick far too few. One week after the spill, only about 2 percent of the spilled oil had been recovered.

While experts had calculated the chances of an oil spill the size of the *Exxon Valdez* at 1 in every 240 years, the possibility did exist. In economic terms alone, the monetary cost to Exxon proved staggering. The initial cleanup cost $2.1 billion. Settlement of civil lawsuits added up to $9 billion, and the company suffered a punitive damages award of $5 billion. The total bill exceeded $16 billion.

The incident highlights the fact that most people do not pay sufficient attention to the possible future consequences of their present decisions. Consequential thinking does not come naturally. Children must be taught to do it, even forced into it. Think about it. As a child you seldom foresaw many consequences of your choices on your own. You must touch that hot stove, despite your parent's warnings, before you realize it will burn you. Then, once burned, you become twice shy. As adults, however, we need not burn our fingers to appreciate the danger of hot stoves.

Not only must we try to see consequences, we must also learn to gauge their significance and assess their likelihood, and we must always give special consideration to those with enormous significance, even if their likelihood appears relatively small, as a young Army officer learned when he allowed Japanese Zeroes to slip through America's last line of defense on their way to attack the U.S. fleet at Pearl Harbor.

About one hour before bombs began dropping at Pearl, two privates operating an army radar on the opposite side of the island observed on their screen a flight of aircraft headed in Pearl Harbor's direction. On learning of the observation, the officer on duty faced a crucial choice. Should he sound the alarm? If he did, he would cause turmoil at the base on an otherwise peaceful Sunday morning. He knew the sighting might be Japanese aircraft, but the

United States and Japan were not at war. On the other hand, war with Japan remained a real possibility. Considering the chances of attack remote, the officer told his radar operators to disregard the sighting, saying a flight of American B-17 bombers were expected to arrive soon in Hawaiian airspace from the mainland. Unfortunately, even though the chances of a Japanese attack appeared remote, the catastrophic consequences associated with disregarding the sighting argued that the officer should not have ignored it.

Japanese planes arrived unopposed over Pearl Harbor in part because one man failed to correctly weigh both the significance and likelihood of the consequences of his decision in circumstances where an attack without warning could result in disaster. Later, he could only look upon the nightmarish scene of a burning fleet and ask himself, "Why didn't I anticipate that?"

The explosion of Chernobyl's nuclear power plant created a nightmare, the consequences of which will last for thousands of years. With power surging out of control, expanding gas literally blew the lid off the huge reactor and spewed pulverized graphite from the reactor's inner core onto the surrounding grounds like black snow. Chernobyl's engineers, peering outside, wondered what had happened. Unable to accept a reactor failure, they simply could not believe their eyes, even with obvious evidence falling from the sky. Within hours they would be dead, having suffered exposure to massive radiation doses.

The incident began with the best of intentions, as seasoned engineers ran a test to improve system safety in the rare event of an electrical power outage. While commercial nuclear reactors produce vast quantities of electricity for consumers, they also use it to run cooling pumps and other safety devices. Should a reactor fail, these devices must rely on other power plants and backup diesel generators for essential electricity. If outside sources fail to kick in quickly during a turbine shutdown, a Chernobyl-type reactor can rapidly overheat. Even the short delay in starting and running up diesels can create an opportunity for an explosion.

Searching for a fail-safe against this last remote possibility, Chernobyl's engineers realized that the plant's electricity-generating turbines continue spinning for a time following any unforeseen shutdown. Could this energy provide sufficient stop-gap electricity during the moments required to start up diesel generators? To test the hypothesis, Chernobyl's engineers set up their experiment by first turning off the reactor's automatic safety systems to prevent them from sensing a test-induced anomaly and interfering with their experiment. When power output dipped unexpectedly below minimum requirements, the engineers chose to speed up the reactor by removing all but 6 of the reactor's 211 reactivity-inhibiting control rods. Safety regulations required a minimum of 30, but the highly experienced operators felt confident 6 would work fine.

The engineers, thinking they had restabilized the reactor, commenced their actual test run at 1:23 A.M. by closing valves feeding steam from the reactor into the turbines. As the huge turbines began winding down, they continued supplying electricity but at rapidly decreasing levels that, in turn, slowed down water pumps supplying coolant to the hot reactor core. Within 30 seconds, highly pressurized steam accumulated inside the core, producing a condition that rapidly accelerated heat-producing nuclear reactivity. Sensing an emergency, an engineer punched the red panic button to drop control rods back into the reactor to slow it down, but sudden intense heat bent the tubes receiving the rods and blocked insertion. With cooling and other safety equipment turned off for the test, the reactor instantly raced in a runaway fission reaction up to 100 times peak design power.

A steam explosion occurred at 1:24 A.M., followed rapidly by a fuel vapor explosion, lifting the heavy steel lid off the reactor's housing and ejecting into the atmosphere tons of highly radioactive particles and debris equivalent to the fallout produced by ten Hiroshima-type detonations. Over 100,000 people were evacuated from the surrounding area, many died from radiation exposure, and many more will die from lingering effects. Today, the destroyed reactor lies encased in a massive cement sarcophagus with an estimated life of 30 years, which means it must be replaced again and again over the thousands of years it will take for the enclosed radioactive material to decay to safe levels.

Chernobyl's operators made horrendous mistakes, but not because of sheer stupidity. Far from stupid, they never thought for an instant that their well-intended actions would lead to catastrophe. While they understood the significance of a reactor meltdown, they grossly miscalculated its likelihood. Like the *Titanic*'s Captain Smith, they knew they were taking chances, but experience in living with nuclear risk caused them to underestimate the possibility of disaster as they proceeded with their experiment despite unexpected difficulties.

Most people do not court disaster and will shun even a small possibility of catastrophe, unless the rewards of success appear great. Unfortunately, people sometimes mistakenly confuse "small" with "nil," as Chernobyl's engineers did when they saw no possibility of a reactor explosion despite the signs of growing danger. Even after an explosion occurred, the engineers found it hard to believe. Hindsight argues that, given the possibility of catastrophic consequences, they should have stopped the experiment at the first sign of trouble. Contemplation of such possibilities might also have prevented the *Exxon Valdez* and Pearl Harbor disasters.

On the other hand, our willingness to take risks tends to increase as the rewards of success grow, a principle every Las Vegas gambler and Wall Street trader understands. Still, the likelihood of consequences, even good ones, remains crucial. Calculate the likelihood and significance of success as you solve this problem.

Mental Aerobics
High-Flying Proposition

You're traveling first class with thirty companions on a 13-hour flight from Los Angeles to Hong Kong. After several hours in the air, a wealthy passenger poses a challenge to the thirty people sitting in first class. "This will make time fly," the passenger proposes. "I'm interested in people's birthdays. Let's each put $,1000 into a pool. Write the month and day of your birthday on a slip of paper. No one will write down the year, so don't worry about anyone learning your age. Then we'll go around the cabin and reveal the month and day of our birthdays. I'll pay $30,000 to every first-class passenger if it turns out any two people were born on the same month and day. Otherwise, I'll keep the $30,000 pool; no great sum, considering the risk I'm taking. We will, of course, verify birthdates if any two match."

The wealthy passenger strolls into the cockpit for a tour, leaving you and your traveling companions to discuss the proposition. Each can easily afford to participate, but who wants to throw good money down the drain on a losing proposition. All eyes turn to you as the group seeks your thoughts. "Should we take him up on the deal?" they ask. Yes or no, and why?

Practice Makes Perfect

Calculate Consequences

Identify a choice you need to make involving at least two alternatives, where each option can produce both good and bad consequences. Perhaps you must choose between accepting a new position at work and staying in your present assignment. Maybe you're thinking about a career shift or a major investment.

Write the choice you must make at the top of a sheet of paper. Divide the page into a number of blocks equaling the number of alternative courses of action you can choose. Moving from block to block, list inside every possible consequence, both good and bad, that can flow from that alternative. Think at your creative best as you come up with possible consequences. Leave no stone unturned.

Once you have listed all possible consequences, consider the likelihood and desirability of each consequence in every block. Assign numbers using percentages for likelihoods (e.g., .25 = a 25 percent chance the consequence will occur) and a scale of 1–10 for significance (1 = least desirable and 10 = most). Determine the utility of each consequence by multiplying likelihood times significance, and sum your numbers to calculate the total utility of each alternative. The calculation looks like this:

Choice Involved

Alternative 1

    Consequence $.25 \times 5 = 1.25$

    Consequence $.75 \times 8 = 6.00$ Utility total $= 7.25$

Alternative 2

    Consequence $.50 \times 9 = 4.50$

    Consequence $.20 \times 3 = 0.60$ Utility total $= 5.10$

Now use the utility totals to assist you in evaluating alternatives, with the highest total tending to indicate the best choice. Before making a final decision, you may decide to take a second pass through the blocks, adding additional consequences and refining numbers to produce more accurate estimates.

With all blocks completed, make your final choice. You do not necessarily need to select the alternative with the highest utility estimate, but the process will help you more fully develop and weigh all the consequences of your options.

INVITE AND VALUE BLISTERING CRITICISM

Since we all lack a certain amount of objectivity about ourselves and the consequences of our decisions, we sometimes need a healthy dose of blunt criticism to expose flaws we do not see on our own. Shunning such criticism can lead to calamity, as President Lyndon Johnson learned when he escalated the war in Vietnam.

Fearing opposition might undermine his foreign policy, Johnson greatly expanded U.S. involvement in the war without first placing the issue squarely before Congress and the people. As a result, he misperceived the political risks involved, miscalculated the consequences of his decisions, wounded the nation deeply, and lost the confidence of the American people. Years later, having learned from Johnson's error, President George H. Bush wisely asked Congress for a Declaration of War before committing hundreds of thousands of American troops to combat in the Gulf War. That Declaration passed in the Senate by a narrow 52/47 margin, a risk President Johnson unfortunately refused to take.

When Lyndon Johnson took office following the assassination of John F. Kennedy, the United States had only placed a few advisors on the ground in Vietnam. The fighting involved only North Vietnamese insurgents and South Vietnamese military units. With the South Vietnamese becoming increasingly ineffective, Johnson feared a North Vietnamese victory would set off a domino reaction, with other countries in the region quickly falling behind the iron curtain.

When the North Vietnamese attacked two U.S. destroyers in the Gulf of Tonkin, Johnson sought and obtained a resolution from Congress authorizing a response. Acting on the resolution, not a declaration of war, he introduced limited U.S. air, naval, and ground forces into Vietnam. In the beginning, American forces suffered few casualties, and public opinion supported the effort. Then, in January 1965, Johnson met behind closed doors with his National Security Advisor and Secretary of Defense and secretly decided to escalate America's military presence in Southeast Asia.

Johnson initially launched a secret aerial bombing campaign against the North. Next, he introduced a small contingent of Marines to guard U.S. air bases in the South. When the CIA reported the North Vietnamese had infiltrated regular army battalions southward in response, Johnson authorized offensive operations beyond mere air base security. Little by little, month by month, the public watched the escalation continue, while Johnson avoided debating the matter publicly.

Defense Secretary Robert McNamara, realizing that escalation would inevitably lead to higher casualties, urged the President to tell Congress he had changed the U.S. military mission from defense to offense, with massive reinforcements on the way; but Johnson declined, writing in a secret cable: "It is not [my] intention to announce the whole program now but rather to announce individual deployments at appropriate times." Secretary McNamara later said, "We chose to sweep the debate under the Oval Office carpet. . . . The fact that the nation had embarked on a course carrying it into a major war was hidden."

The President never fully appreciated the grave implications of his decisions, in part because he did not expose them in advance to potentially blistering criticism from those who might oppose his policies. Instead, he allowed Americans to discover reality gradually, after he had made commitments from which he could not withdraw without damaging U.S. credibility abroad. Consequently, when full-blown opposition to his Vietnam policies came, it erupted with volcanic fury, starting with a young father of three pouring gasoline on his body in front of Robert McNamara's Pentagon window and burning himself alive.

Time after time General Westmoreland, the U.S. commander in Vietnam, requested more and more troops, first 82,000, then 175,000, up and up to 540,000. Again and again the President approved the requests without first offering his choices for real public debate. With the U.S. military fully engaged, Secretary of State Dean Rusk and Robert McNamara urged the President to explain candidly the military situation to the American public, but Johnson, not wanting to incite what he considered demoralizing dissent, still refused to go public with his escalation decisions, even though he found them privately agonizing. At the same time, he quietly admitted to his Secretary of Defense, "We know, ourselves, in our own conscience, that when we asked for this Tonkin Gulf Resolution, we had no intention of committing this many troops."

Johnson even discouraged criticism within the small group of key advisors helping him make the crucial decisions leading to escalation. Those who questioned the policy became objects of a favorite Johnson phrase: "I'm afraid he's losing his effectiveness." Johnson repeatedly said of one close advisor, "Well, here comes Mr. Stop-the-Bombing." When McNamara expressed second thoughts, Johnson told a U.S. Senator, "That military genius, McNamara, has gone dovish on me." Johnson felt critics were playing into the hands of the enemy "like a man trying to sell his house with a family member telling the buyer the house had leaks in the basement."

With North Vietnam continuing to fight and refusing to negotiate, Johnson learned from the Joint Chiefs that he could only win militarily by mobilizing the reserves at home, invading North Vietnam, possibly using nuclear weapons, and risking military engagement with China and Russia. Shocked that his escalation had come to this, and understandably unwilling to risk war with China and Russia, President Johnson found himself suddenly trapped in a war of attrition in which he could only hope to wear down his opponent to some sort of negotiated conclusion. He had gotten himself into this predicament by not fully exposing his thinking to the kind of criticism that would reveal its flaws. Looking back thirty years later, Secretary of Defense McNamara admitted regretfully, "We never carefully debated what U.S. force would ultimately be required, what

our chances of success would be, or what the political, military, financial, and human costs would be if we provided it. Indeed, these basic
questions went unexamined."

McNamara finally wrote Johnson a memorandum expressing
serious reservations that proved more than the President could tol-
erate, so Johnson gave his close advisor, turned critic, the boot. With
criticism now surfacing from deep within his inner circle, Johnson
submitted the Vietnam question to a distinguished panel of military
and foreign policy experts he dubbed the "Wise Men." "Should we
get out of Vietnam?" he asked. Unfortunately, Johnson withheld
crucial information from this group, including a key report rating
the chances of military victory in Vietnam very low and a CIA analysis concluding, contrary to conventional wisdom, that an American
withdrawal from Vietnam would *not* severely damage U.S. efforts to
halt the spread of communism worldwide. By holding back this
information, Johnson again insulated himself from criticism that
might have helped him anticipate the terrible consequences of his
continuing escalation.

Looking back years later, after the war had been lost and
America had moved on to other challenges, Secretary McNamara
criticized the flawed thinking of President Johnson and his closest
advisors this way: "We failed to draw Congress and the American
people into a full and frank discussion and debate of the pros and
cons of a large-scale U.S. military involvement in Southeast Asia
before we initiated the action." Had it occurred, the debate might
well have opened the President's eyes to the potentially devastating
consequences ahead. In the end, however, events originally within
Lyndon Johnson's control forced him to face the nation and regretfully announce his decision not to run for reelection. Looking back,
he must have asked himself many times, "Why didn't I anticipate
that?"

President Johnson said he thought criticism encouraged the
enemy. But I suspect he held deeper, unexpressed reasons for
actively avoiding criticism. Criticism, by its nature, implies failure:
failure to come up with the best idea, failure to see a potential problem, failure to please others. People naturally fear failure—and

proud, domineering, manipulative people like LBJ, accustomed to getting their way, often fear it most.

To obtain the benefits criticism offers, we must willingly accept the failure that criticism implies and see it as an opportunity to learn, grow, refine, start over, and even cut our losses and quit. Making friends with criticism, inviting it into our lives, while not always easy, creates huge benefits. As a judge, I enjoy the companionship of criticism every day of my working life. While on the bench, I expose my thinking to possible objections from all sides. In deciding cases, I can write tentative opinions, which all parties criticize before I settle on a final ruling. In chambers, away from litigants and their lawyers, I invite criticism from staff attorneys and even my judicial colleagues, whom I trust to tell me the brutal truth. Ultimately, every decision I make is subject to review by courts of appeal, and I am comforted to know appellate court justices never hesitate to criticize my thinking where appropriate.

Criticism makes me a better judge both mentally and emotionally. It sharpens my daily thinking and it keeps me humble. Arrogant thinkers avoid criticism to their peril. Sharp thinkers entertain and benefit from it. Sometimes the critical process gets a little heated, even blistering, but it's better to end up with unpleasant blisters than deadly burns. It's better to let criticism expose consequences than to avoid criticism and later face consequences that leave us asking, "Why didn't I anticipate that?"

This book began years ago as an idea in my mind quite different from what you have been kind enough to read. I hope the end result makes a big difference in your thinking. What you've experienced became possible only as I embraced and learned from tough criticisms from family, friends, agents, and editors that helped me turn an idea into a tangible work. Without those many criticisms, and my openness to them, the original idea would never have matured into anything worth reading, and I would have ended up browsing through other interesting titles on my local bookstore's shelves asking myself, "Why didn't I think of that?" Indeed, the thought of that unpleasant consequence inspired the title you now see on the cover of this book.

Criticize your own thinking as you come up with better ideas to solve this problem.

Mental Aerobics
Dangerous Designs

You're the chief designer of a multimillion-dollar sewer system to be installed in a new high-technology community under construction in Arizona. A seemingly small detail involves the shape of manhole covers. Ever the creative problem-solver, you design square covers made out of a new, lighter, super-strong material able to withstand ten times the weight of any car or truck. The lighter material allows sewer maintenance workers to remove covers easily without risking back injuries. Moreover, the material costs less than half the price of heavy steel covers, saving huge sums in construction costs.

Years ago you created what you call "The Murder Board," a group of senior engineers assigned to critique all designs before you sign off on them. Over the years, The Murder Board has spotted many errors that, if undetected, would have exposed your company to ruinous liability. The Board just issued a blistering report on your manhole-cover design. The lighter covers, while cheaper and stronger than heavy steel, make it easy for vandals to remove, leaving open holes into which people can accidentally fall.

Seeing the consequences of your flawed design, you rewrite the specification to require heavy steel material that discourages vandals from attempting to remove them. As you lift your pen to sign off on the new design, you think, "Is there anything else about this design that creates adverse consequences I can easily correct now?"

Expose your revised design to the kind of serious criticism you received from The Murder Board. What design changes, if any, will you make?

Practice Makes Perfect
Use Negatives to Create Positives

Sometimes negative criticism provides the springboard for positive results. Test this truth by exposing one of your best ideas to the harshest possible criticism, and use the criticism to make changes that improve your idea and make it even better than before.

First, write your good idea on a sheet of paper. Describe the concept in detail, using graphics and illustrations if necessary. State your goals, what you want to do with your idea, and how you think you can transform it into a practical success. Admit known weaknesses and describe how you plan to overcome them. Make your write-up easy to read, applying standards of clarity, accuracy, comprehensiveness, sensibility, and honesty so that it correctly and fully describes your concept.

Now show your write-up to a person who possesses relevant experience and expertise. Ask for a no-holds-barred critique. Let the person know you *welcome* tough criticism because you want to improve your idea in every possible way.

Arrange a time to meet face-to-face to receive the critique. Do not become defensive when it occurs. Rather, use the opportunity to make sure you fully understand the criticisms offered. Later, try hard to use what you've learned as a springboard to refine or drastically change your idea to achieve your ultimate goal.

PUT IT ALL TOGETHER

Apply everything you've learned about consequential thinking to this practical problem.

Maximize Profits, Minimize Costs

You're the CEO of a major American car manufacturer. Your research and development people have developed a process called "E-Coating" for applying paint in a way that greatly improves the rust resistance of metal surfaces. By running an electrical charge through metal parts while dunking them in large paint vats, the process forms a strong paint-to-metal bond and pulls paint into the tiniest indentations and crevices. E-Coating will cost about $10 million to install in each of your manufacturing plants.

Market research reveals E-Coating will not likely increase car sales, even if you advertise rust resistance to consumers. On the other hand, warranty return and repair expenses from prematurely rusting car bodies have increased in the past few years, and research shows consumers are beginning to associate your cars with rusting problems. Last year Japanese, German, and one major American competitor began painting cars with a process similar to E-Coating.

However, research does not indicate you've lost sales to competitors who use the new painting practice.

Think consequentially as you decide whether to invest in E-Coating. Remember to:

- Think the unthinkable.
- Expect the unexpected.
- Consider both the significance and likelihood of consequences.
- Invite and value blistering criticism.

THINK FOR YOURSELF

Now use your consequential thinking skills to improve your quality of life.

See the Consequences of Your Current Situation

Divide your life situation into categories such as home, work, health, finances, and so forth. Select one category and write it at the top of a blank sheet of paper. List key facts describing your circumstances down the left side of the paper. As an example: If you select health, the list might include certain habits (good and bad), behaviors, emotional conditions, weight, and so on.

Next, divide the right side into two columns, writing "5 Years from Now" at the top of one column and "15 Years from Now" above the second. Further divide each column into two subcolumns labeled "good" and "bad" consequences. Starting with the first fact on your list, consider and write down the good and bad consequences likely to flow from that fact in 5 and then 15 years.

When finished, review your complete list to decide whether you want to make changes in your present lifestyle that will enhance the future good consequences and diminish or eliminate the bad. If so, what changes would you make?

Consider whether you want to apply this form of consequential analysis to other categories of your life. If so, take out a fresh sheet of paper and begin anew.

THINK ABOUT IT

Pause for a moment to consider how you can better anticipate the consequences of your choices, both good and bad. Ask yourself:

- When do I most need to stretch my mind beyond possibilities to "impossibilities," to think the unthinkable? What will I do to expand my thinking in these circumstances?
- When I make decisions and solve problems, do I always anticipate how I will deal with the unexpected when it occurs? If not, how will I make sure I treat the unexpected as a necessary element of every sound decision and solution?
- Do I sometimes fail to balance both the significance and likelihood of possible consequences? What will I do to make sure I take both fully into account?
- Do I sometimes shy away from potentially useful criticism or ignore it? If so, when am I most likely to do so, and why? What changes do I need to make in my approach to criticism to insure I obtain and use it to my full advantage?

ALWAYS CHECK TO MAKE SURE

Think consequentially as you make decisions and solve problems at work and at home.
LOOK BEFORE YOU LEAP:

> Think the Unthinkable
>
> Expect the Unexpected
>
> Consider Both the Significance and Likelihood of Consequences
>
> Invite and Value Blistering Criticism

Notes to Chapter 8

The Big Switch

  The Swedish Government made the change at 5 P.M. on a selected day. They considered the possible consequences of switching at an early-morning hour and decided people on the road at that hour might be less alert and more likely to forget it was *the* time and day to change. Such groggy-minded errors could easily lead to deadly head-on collisions.

Capitol Marriages

The man was the U.S. Senate Chaplain, who married many couples during his tenure, including members of Congress. The humor of this exercise makes a point. The punch line of a joke, sometimes nearly unthinkable, catches us by surprise and produces laughter. In real-life situations, however, when the unthinkable surprises us, the consequences are not always humorous.

Deal with Deadly Consequences

As one possible consequence, the Soviets could decide to initiate their own "false alarms," placing Russian nuclear forces on full alert and then quietly informing the U.S. through diplomatic channels that a "computer glitch" has occurred. While this might confuse U.S. strategists, it would run the potentially catastrophic risk of prompting a responsive U.S. alert, taking both countries to the brink of nuclear war.

As reported by former CIA Director Robert M. Gates in his book *From the Shadows*, the KGB in fact transmitted a highly classified warning to its agencies around the world in June 1980, stating that recently observed U.S. nuclear alarms were emphatically *not* caused by computer failures as claimed. Soviet leaders assumed the U.S. false alarms were part of a plan to cover an eventual preemptive first strike on the Soviet Union. When Zbigniew Brzezinski received his middle-of-the-night emergency phone call, he did not wake his wife, because he believed both he and she would die in less than half an hour.

Murder in Manhattan

Again, humor makes a point. To successfully anticipate the unexpected, we sometimes must consider possibilities others may dismiss as laughable. Alice is Carole's parrot and Ted is Bob's cat.

High-Flying Proposition

The odds are 435 in 366, a near certainty, that two people in any random group of 30 will share the same birthdate. You should expect it rather than be surprised by it. Here's how to figure the odds. With only two people, the chances are 1 in 366 that your birthday will match the other individual (assuming the longest possible year). Adding another person, the odds rise to 2 in 366 that the third individual will match either your birthday or that of the second person. Each time you add another person, the new individual's odds of a match increase in the following pattern: 3 in 366, 4 in 366 and so forth up to 29 in 366. Totaling the odds enjoyed by all (1/366 + 2/366 +3/366 and so on to 29/366), the likelihood of at least one match becomes 435 in 366. If you need convincing, try it with any random group of 30 people. The wealthy passenger's high-flying proposition gives you a near certain chance of instantly increasing your $1,000 stake by 3000 percent. Of course, you must convince all your traveling companions to join in the fun, and, to do that, you must explain both the significance and likelihood of the consequences involved.

Dangerous Designs

Manhole covers are round for a reason. Round covers, if removed, cannot easily be inserted into open holes and dropped into sewers. A square or rectangular cover, on the other hand, can be turned sideways and quickly dropped through its hole. Experience shows that vandals generally do not toy with round manhole covers.

Maximize Profits, Minimize Costs

Ford Motor Company invented E-Coating in 1958, but did not generally apply the process to U.S. car production for more than 15 years. Manufacturing could not convince Ford's finance division that the company could recover the cost of installing E-Coating through added car sales generated by the new feature. In the meantime, Ford experienced a rash of quality-control problems, including vastly increased warranty and repair expenses from rusting cars. With Ford's market share and reputation for quality taking a nose dive, the company eventually implemented many manufacturing improvements, including E-Coating, in all Ford plants. The E-Coating experience, among others, proved once again that long-term consequences sometimes swallow short-term profits. Today at Ford, "quality is job one."

Epilogue

I'm Glad I
Thought of That!

We've studied many cases and examples, but none stands out in my
own mind as vividly as the classic clash between Intel and Motorola
over dominance of the microprocessor industry. Let's conclude our
exploration of creative problem-solving and decision-making by seeing how that competition illustrates virtually every point I've tried to
make in the preceding pages. First, review this summary of those
points:

1. **THINK PERCEPTIVELY:**

   Obtain a clear view of reality.

   Double-check perceptions.

   Concentrate on crucial facts.

   Ask penetrating questions.

   Study both the forest and the trees.

   Lead with your mind, follow with your heart.

2. **THINK DELIBERATELY:**

   Deliberate.

   Accept responsibility for your thinking and its results.

   Understand before judging.

   Focus on diagnosis before attempting to cure.

3. CONTROL THE QUALITY OF YOUR THINKING:

Is it clear?

Is it accurate?

Is it comprehensive?

Does it make sense?

Is it intellectually honest?

4. THINK SYSTEMATICALLY:

Start with what you know is true.

Connect it up.

Weigh pros and cons.

Consider the odds.

Pursue the critical path.

5. USE YOUR IMAGINATION:

Exercise a vivid imagination.

Imagine courageously.

Imagine your way through adversity, frustration, and failure.

Think beyond the bounds of conventional wisdom.

Imagine the very best solutions.

6. LISTEN TO YOUR INNER VOICE:

Let intuition do what reason alone cannot.

Learn the "feel" of real intuition.

Trust your intuition.

Beware of false intuition.

7. THINK EMPATHETICALLY:

Consider what others think and feel.

Discover what motivates others to think, feel, and act as they do.

Learn how others view and interpret your words and actions.

8. LOOK BEFORE YOU LEAP:

Think the unthinkable.

Expect the unexpected.

Consider both the significance and likelihood of consequences.

Invite and value blistering criticism.

Now, let's look closely at the battle for market supremacy between Intel and Motorola. Robert Noyce, one of Intel's founders, created the integrated circuit *[use your imagination]*, the key innovation leading to development of today's incredibly sophisticated microprocessors such as the Pentium and its progeny. Intel at first dominated its industry, partly because larger technology companies, Motorola for instance, had missed important opportunities. When Intel introduced the first 8-bit microprocessor, however, Motorola followed with its own 8-bit chip and began developing a much more capable and faster 16-bit processor.

Racing to beat Motorola, Intel launched a crash program to bring to market its own 16-bit processor, the 8086, one full year ahead of Motorola. The more deliberate path taken by Motorola *[think deliberately]* ultimately produced the 68000, a 16-bit processor technically superior to Intel's 8086.

Resting on past laurels, Intel did not at first react to Motorola's competitive entry. Even as Motorola made inroads with Intel's established customers, Intel's management blamed the company's own sales engineers for the deteriorating situation rather than crediting Motorola with a superior product. Ultimately one of Intel's field engineers, Don Buchout, broke through the self-delusion *[lead with your mind, follow with your heart]* with a blistering memorandum honestly describing stark reality in clear, accurate terms *[clarity, accuracy, comprehensiveness, sensibility, intellectual honesty]*. An aggressive competitor, Motorola, with a superior product, the 68000, would likely defeat the 8086 if Intel did not come up with an effective counter-strategy in a hurry *[imagine your way through adversity, frustration and failure]*.

To his credit, division manager Bill Davidow opened his mind *[invite and value blistering criticism]* and faced Intel's dangerous predicament. In Davidow's words: "If Intel tried to fight the battle only by claiming our microprocessor was better than theirs, we were going to lose." Intel had to confront one inescapable reality *[concentrate on crucial facts]:* the company lacked sufficient time to develop a new, more competitive microprocessor.

Caught between a concrete wall and a bulldozer, Intel searched for a way out. As Davidow later wrote in his book *Marketing High Technology,* the 8086 was "the lynchpin of the entire corporation." Defeat could produce catastrophe *[consider both the significance and likelihood of consequences].* Every lost 8086 sale caused Intel to forfeit sales of associated peripheral devices and chips worth up to ten times the value of an 8086. Worse yet, when high tech companies lose a competition for one generation of capital-intensive technology, they often do not survive to compete in the next product evolution *[think consequentially].*

Alerted to the problem *[obtain a clear view of reality],* Intel's legendary CEO Andy Grove assigned Davidow the responsibility to find solutions. With the clock ticking loudly, Davidow did not rush to judgment *[understand before judging].* Deliberating continuously for three long days with a group of Intel's finest minds *[think deliberately],* and not delegating the task to others *[accept full responsibility for your thinking and its results],* Davidow defined the problem as precisely as possible before searching for remedies *[focus on diagnosis before attempting to cure].*

Motorola's 68000 indeed posed a problem *[obtain a clear view of reality],* a tree Intel would like to cut down, but the forest of similar problems Motorola could eventually create for Intel presented a far greater threat. Considering the big picture *[study both the forest and the trees],* Davidow reasoned *[think systematically]* that more than beating the 68000, Intel must defeat Motorola itself or risk getting shoved into the dark reaches of a competitive wilderness from which it might never emerge *[think consequentially].* While this consequence might appear unimaginable for the Intel we know today *[think the unthinkable],* it looked like a real possibility in 1978 with Intel a relative fledgling company compared to Motorola.

Davidow had to admit *[intellectual honesty]* that many customers felt his company had grown arrogant in the absence of effective challengers *[consider what others think and feel],* and these customers openly savored the chance to force Intel to its knees *[discover what motivates others]*. The company's demoralized sales engineers needed a credible pitch they could embrace enthusiastically *[is it sensible?]* one that would convince customers to stick with Intel rather than switch to Motorola *[discover what motivates others]*, even if the 8086 did not outperform Motorola's alternative.

To develop the message *[imagine the very best solutions]*, Davidow and his team stepped into the shoes of Intel's customers *[think empathetically]*, analyzing *[think systematically]* the competition from their viewpoints *[consider what others think and feel]*. In the end, Davidow's team discovered that Intel most often lost out in situations where customers did not fully understand the intangible, long-term advantages associated with purchasing microprocessors from the company *[learn how others view and interpret your words and actions]*.

Could Intel do a better job of helping customers appreciate the benefits of purchasing Intel microprocessors compatible with the broad range of innovations the company would offer in the future *[ask penetrating questions]*? Intel boasted the most complete product line *[start with what you know is true]*. Its sales engineers ranked number one in the business. Customers who designed Intel processors into their products knew they could depend on the company's talented engineers to insure those devices worked in their systems. By contrast, Motorola lacked Intel's proven track record in microprocessor technology, something customers would surely consider when making final design decisions. Taken together *[connect it up]*, Intel's pros outweighed Motorola's, and the cons tipped against Motorola, as long as customers' purchasing decisions did not rely strictly on a narrow technical comparison of the 8086 and 68000 *[weigh pros and cons]*.

With Intel's strengths and Motorola's weaknesses comprehensively and sensibly stated *[control the quality of your thinking]*, Davidow fashioned a pitch redefining the "product" to include the bundle of services and expectations where Intel enjoyed real advantages *[pursue the critical path]*. The company would fight to persuade customers that the best product included these intangibles.

Sensing *[listen to your inner voice]* Motorola would rush to answer all of Intel's intangible claims, Davidow calculated *[consider the odds]* that his strategy would distract his rival from exploiting its own competitive advantage. But he could not rely on hunches alone, however likely, to assure success *[beware of false intuition]*. He needed to catch Motorola by surprise with a bold move *[imagine courageously]* that might prompt an ill-considered reaction.

Intel had always refused to tout new products not yet in production. "Intel delivers," a longstanding and favorite slogan, meant that the company never risked promoting "paper tigers," ideas in development that might not make it to market. Other companies had lost all credibility advertising what the industry derisively labeled "vaporware." Breaking with Intel's deeply held conventional wisdom *[think beyond the bounds of conventional wisdom]*, Davidow produced a comprehensive 100-page Futures Catalog listing numerous planned innovations *[is it comprehensive?]*, many of which amounted to little more than ideas on paper. If Motorola responded in kind, Davidow believed it would inevitably expose the comparative weakness of Motorola's product development plans and capabilities.

When Intel launched its competitive offensive, code-named "Operation Crush" after the Denver Bronco's unbeatable "Orange Crush" defensive unit, Motorola jumped instantly into the fray with its own far less impressive catalog, and, sure enough, Motorola's publication revealed the very weaknesses Intel sought to exploit, a consequence Motorola did not anticipate *[look before you leap]*. As Davidow later described it: "Ultimately the Motorola catalog became an Intel sales tool, possibly the best one we had."

As the competition progressed beyond catalogs, Motorola lost focus trying to match Intel's every intangible claim and strayed from the ground on which it possessed a clear advantage, the technical superiority of its 68000 *[pursue the critical path]*. "We had lured our principal competitor into fighting us on our own turf," Davidow observed *[imagine the very best solutions]*. "Had Motorola chosen to remain aloof from our challenge, I think Intel would have been in deep trouble."

As often happens in high-stakes contests, an unforeseen turn of events offered Intel an opportunity to score beyond all expectations *[expect the unexpected]*. IBM introduced the Personal Computer. Pressed for time by growing competition, IBM abandoned its traditional insistence on making its own proprietary components and, responding to Intel's well-thought-out pitch, selected the 8086 for its new PC line. As business consumers worldwide flocked to purchase PCs and competing clones based on IBM's architecture, Intel's 8086 became the industry standard, and the company's profits soared. Operation Crush soon squeezed Motorola's market share to a comparatively insignificant 15 percent.

Today, Intel tops the industry with its Pentium chips, and Motorola no longer makes microprocessors, an outcome unthinkable when the giant Motorola introduced its technically superior 68000 *[think the unthinkable]*. Crushed by the weight Intel's success and its own mistakes, Motorola's executives could only look back at Intel's winning strategy and wonder: *"Why didn't I think of that?"* On the other hand, Davidow and his colleagues could take pride in their sharp thinking, justifiably congratulating themselves with a hearty: "I'm glad I thought of that!"

As you grapple with problems and decisions, both large and small, at work and at home, try keeping all the lessons you have learned here in mind. It's not really all that complicated, once you develop the knack. Then, you too, can look back on a solution or a decision and say: "I'm glad *I* thought of that!"

Supplemental Solutions

Chapter 2

Chickens and Foxes

Chapter 5

Find Hidden Treasures by Learning from Failures

Imagine dividing the grid into two equal parts, such as an upper and lower half. Ask the genie if you'll find the treasure in the upper half. Her answer will tell you which half to eliminate. Again divide the correct half into two parts, and proceed with the strategy of elimination until you locate the correct square in eight or fewer tries. Now, go dig up your treasure and use the lessons learned in this chapter to help figure out how to enjoy your fortune in the most imaginative way.

Chapter 6

See the Forest, Trees, and All in Between

A horse stands at the center, facing to the right, with its haunches next to the large tree trunk on the left side of the print. A boar approaches head first beneath the horse. A lamb rests in the lower left corner. A profile of a woman's face with a man behind her appears in the tree trunk above the lamb. You can find more faces in the leaves and branches of the trees. Another face looking left appears above the fox's right front paw. Keep looking in this general area to see a number of other faces.

Chapter 7

Sense Other's Real Intentions

When Tom closed the window after raping the real-life Kelly, she sensed that he intended to kill her. Did you sense it too at that point, or even before? Kelly somehow knew Tom worried about noise, quite probably the noise of a victim fighting and screaming for her life. When Tom walked out of the bedroom, Kelly followed unobserved behind. As she escaped out the front door of her apartment, Kelly heard Tom opening and closing kitchen drawers searching for a butcher knife. Kelly slipped through a neighbor's unlocked door across the hall, held up a finger signaling the surprised inhabitants to remain quiet, and locked the door behind.

Figuring out Tom's thinking under extreme pressure saved Kelly's life. Unfortunately, unlike this example adapted from Gavin de Becker's national bestseller *The Gift of Fear*, many victims in similar circumstances would have remained in the bedroom, not wanting to risk escalating the situation, and hoping Tom would honor his word.

Appendix

Sharp–Thinking
Checklist

THINK PERCEPTIVELY:

❑ Obtain a clear view of reality.

❑ Double-check perceptions.

❑ Concentrate on crucial facts.

❑ Ask penetrating questions.

❑ Study both the forest and the trees.

❑ Lead with your mind, follow with your heart.

THINK DELIBERATELY:

❑ Deliberate.

❑ Accept responsibility for your thinking and its results.

❑ Understand before judging.

❑ Focus on diagnosis before attempting to cure.

CONTROL THE QUALITY OF YOUR THINKING:

❏   Is it clear?

❏   Is it accurate?

❏   Is it comprehensive?

❏   Does it make sense?

❏   Is it intellectually honest?

THINK SYSTEMATICALLY:

❏   Start with what you know is true.

❏   Connect it up.

❏   Weigh pros and cons.

❏   Consider the odds.

❏   Pursue the critical path.

USE YOUR IMAGINATION:

❏   Exercise a vivid imagination.

❏   Imagine courageously.

❏   Imagine your way through adversity, frustration, and failure.

❏   Think beyond the bounds of conventional wisdom.

❏   Imagine the very best solutions.

LISTEN TO YOUR INNER VOICE:

❏   Let intuition do what reason alone cannot.

❏   Learn the "feel" of real intuition.

❏   Trust your intuition.

❏   Beware of false intuition.

THINK EMPATHETICALLY:

❏   Consider what others think and feel.

❏   Discover what motivates others to think, feel, and act as they do.

❏   Learn how others view and interpret your words and actions.

LOOK BEFORE YOU LEAP:

❏   Think the unthinkable.

❏   Expect the unexpected.

❏   Consider both the significance and likelihood of consequences.

❏   Invite and value blistering criticism.

References

Ackroyd, R., *The Life of Thomas More* (New York: Doubleday, 1998) [Chapter 7, Sir Thomas More]

Alexander, J. H., *Utmost Savagery* (Annapolis: Naval Institute Press, 1995) [Chapter 8, Tarawa]

Auletta, K., *Greed and Glory on Wall Street* (New York: Random House, 1986) [Chapter 7, Lehman Brothers]

Bennett, L., *What Manner of Man Martin Luther King, Jr.* (Chicago: Johnson Publishing Co., 1964) [Chapter 5, Martin Luther King, Jr.]

Block, S. S., *Benjamin Franklin* (New York: Hastings House, 1975) [Chapter 4, Benjamin Franklin]

Brian, D., *Einstein, A Life* (New York: John Wiley & Sons, 1996) [Chapter 4, Marie Curie]

Brown, J. M., *Gandhi, Prisoner of Hope* (New Haven: Yale University Press, 1989) [Chapter 2, Mahatma Gandhi]

Davidow, W. H., *Marketing High Technology* (New York: The Free Press, 1986) [Introduction and Epilogue, Intel's 8086]

Douglas, J., *Mind Hunter* (New York: Pocket Star Books, 1995) [Chapter 6, Mental Aerobics Exercise "Little Boy's Mittens," adapted from true story presented by Douglas]

Earley, P., *Confessions of a Spy* (New York: Berkley Books, 1998) [Chapter 8, Aldrich Ames]

Easwaran, E., *Gandhi the Man* (Petaluma: Nilgiri Press, 1978) [Chapter 2, Mahatma Gandhi]

Emery, F., *Watergate* (New York: Simon & Schuster, 1994) [Chapter 3, Gordon Liddy's plans]

Flesch, R., *The Art of Clear Thinking* (New York: Harper & Brothers, 1951) [Chapter 3, van Gogh painting]

Gilbert, M., *Churchill, A Life* (New York: Henry Holt and Company, 1991) [Chapter 2, Clementine's letter to Winston Chruchill)]

Gross, D., *Forbes Greatest Business Stories of All Time* (New York: John Wiley & Sons, 1996) [Introduction and Epilogue, Intel's 8086]

Gunther, G., *Learned Hand* (New York: A. A. Knopf, 1994) [Chapter 3, Learned Hand and *Masses* v. *Patten*]

Halberstam, D., *The Best and the Brightest* (New York: Random House, 1972) [Chapter 3 "McNamara's statistics and calculations . . ."]

Halberstam, D., *The Reckoning* (New York: William Morrow, 1986) [Chapter 1, George Vincent and the labor unions; Chapter 2, Henry Ford and the Model A]

Henderson, M. A., *How Con Games Work* (Secaucus: Carol Publishing, 1997) [Chapter 7, Arnold and Slack]

Hughes-Wilson, J., *Military Intelligence Blunders* (New York: Carroll & Graf, 1999) [Chapter 7, Saddam Hussein attacks Kuwait]

Iacocca, L., *Iacocca, An Autobiography* (New York: Bantam Books, 1984) [Chapter 6, Lee Iacocca]

Iyer, R., *The Moral and Political Writings of Mahatma Gandhi* (Oxford: Clarendon Press, 1986) [Chapter 2, Mahatma Gandhi]

Jackson, T., *Intel Inside* (New York: Dutton, 1997) [Introduction and Epilogue, Intel's 8086]

Keeble, J., *Out of the Channel* (Cheney: Eastern Washington University Press, 1999) [Chapter 8, *Exxon Valdez*]

King, C. S., *My Life with Martin Luther King* (New York: Holt, Rinehart & Winston, 1969) [Chapter 5, Martin Luther King, Jr.]

Lovell, J. and Kluger, J., *Apollo 13* (New York: Pocket Books, a Division of Simon & Schuster, 1994) [Chapter 2, Apollo 13]

Lukacs, J., *Five Days in London* (New Haven: Yale University Press, 1999) [Chapter 8, Churchill's decision to fight on alone]

Maas, P., *Killer Spy* (New York: Warner Books, 1995) [Chapter 8, Aldrich Ames]

McCullough, D., *Truman* (New York: Simon & Schuster, 1992) [Chapter 2, Harry Truman and the atomic bomb]

McNamara, R., *In Retrospect, the Tragedy and Lessons of Vietnam* (New York: Random House, 1995) [Chapter 8, Lyndon Johnson's decision to escalate Vietnam]

Medvev, Z., *The Legacy of Chernobyl* (New York: W. W. Norton, 1990) [Chapter 8, Chernobyl]

Mitroff, I., *Smart Thinking for Crazy Times* (San Francisco: Berrett-Koehler, 1998) [Chapter 7, Pentium defect]

Morison, E., "Gunfire at Sea: A Case Study," *Men, Machines and Modern Times* (Cambridge: M.I.T. Press, 1966) [Chapter 5, Lieutenant William Sims]

Oates, S. B., *Let The Trumpet Sound, The Life of Martin Luther King, Jr.* (New York: Harper & Row, 1982) [Chapter 5, Martin Luther King, Jr.]

Pflaum, R., *Grand Obsession, Madame Curie* (New York: Doubleday, 1989) [Chapter 4, Marie Curie]

Quinn, S., *Marie Curie, A Life* (New York: Simon & Schuster, 1995) [Chapter 4, Marie Curie]

Russo, J. and Schoemaker, P. J. H., *Decision Traps* (New York: Simon & Schuster, 1990) [Chapter 7, Cancer surgery decision example]

Sculley, J., *Odyssey* (New York: Harper & Row, 1987) [Chapter 5, Repackaging Pepsi-Cola]

Severance, J. B., *Gandhi, Great Soul* (New York: Clarion Books, 1997) [Chapter 2, Mahatma Gandhi]

Shepard, A. and Slayton, D., *Moon Shot* (Atlanta: Turner Publishing, 1994) [Chapter 2, Apollo 13; Chapter 3, Apollo 1; Chapter 6, Apollo 11]

Sherrod, R., *Tarawa* (New York: Duell, Sloan & Pearce, 1944) [Chapter 8, Tarawa]

Thurber, J., *Many Moons* (New York: Voyager Books, Harcourt Brace, 1943) [Chapter 7, Princess Lenore]

Van Doren, C., *Benjamin Franklin* (New York: Penguin Books, 1991) [Chapter 4, "If a proportional representation . . ." and "there are several parts . . ."]

Woodham-Smith, C., *The Reason Why* (New York: Penguin Books, 1958) [Chapter 6, Charge of the Light Brigade]

Younger, I., "The Art of Cross-Examination," *American Bar Association Section of Litigation* (Chicago: American Bar Association, 1975, pp. 26–28) [Chapter 1, Max Steuer defending the Triangle Shirt Waist Company]

Several stories in this book are fictionalizations not intended to depict real persons or events, but rather to serve only as fictional accounts to illustrate teaching points made by the author. The fictional stories are: Chapter 1, Tucker's story and Massey Business Systems story; Chapter 4, Medical malpractice case story; and Chapter 6, Central Lumber story.

List of Exercises

Index